In Search of Lake Monsters

IN SEARCH OF LAKE MONSTERS

Peter Costello

Coward, McCann & Geoghegan   New York

For my Parents and their patience

"long looked for, comes at last"

First American Edition 1974

Copyright © 1974 by Peter Costello

SBN: 698-10613-X

Library of Congress Catalog Card Number: 74-77595

Printed in the United States of America

Grateful acknowledgements for permission to reproduce material are due to Edwin Morgan and the Castlelaw Press for *"The Loch Ness Monster's Song"* from *Twelve Songs* by Edwin Morgan; Ted Hughes and Faber and Faber for twelve lines from *Nessie the Unmannerly Monster* by Ted Hughes; and the Controller of Her Majesty's Stationery Office for the JARIC report (Crown Copyright reserved)

Contents

Acknowledgments

The writing of a book of this length involves debts to many people, some of whom may not even realise they have contributed. So thanks firstly to those who have lived with Nessie, an ungrateful mistress, for the past few years.

And to Reamonn Costello who did some of the photography; Marie and John Hunt for other photographic work; Brian Costello who read an earlier version of this book while driving me around Scotland; Hubert Mahony who drove me on the second trip and took more photographs; and to my father, who doesn't believe Nessie exists, for his scepticism.

The helpful staffs of the National Library of Ireland, the Irish Folklore Commission, Trinity College Library Dublin, the University of Michigan Library, the Atlanta Public Library, the British Museum Library, the British Museum (Natural History), the Newspaper Library Colindale, and the Guildhall Library London, must be thanked for their patient assistance.

Thanks also to Tim Dinsdale, Elizabeth Montgomery Campbell, P. A. MacNab, David James, Maurice Burton, Anne Kinsella, Alphonsus Mullaney, and an anonymous Kerry correspondent. Gordan To gave unstinted help with the Swedish material. The Mountain Expedition photographs were provided by Eagle Star Insurance. Mr Cecil Gould gave some of his valuable time in searching the basement of the National Gallery (without success) for his father's papers on Loch Ness.

Special tributes are due to my predecessors: to the pioneering investigations of Dr Peter Olsson and Dr Clementi Onelli; to Rupert Gould for his careful curiosity; to Mrs Constance Whyte for providing rare photographs, information and perceptive comments on the evidence; and especially to Bernard Heuvelmans for encouraging this effort and providing material, references and a prodigous example of scholarship and industry. The mistakes, of course, are still all my own work. And finally, thanks to Nessie and her relatives around the world, for all the fun its been.

Peter Costello

Sssnnnwhufffll?
Hnwhuffl hhnnwfl hnfl hfl?
Gdrobloblhobngbl gbl gl g g g g glbgl.
Drublhaflablhaflubhafgabhaflhafl fl fl-
gm grawwwww grf grawf awfgm graw gin.
Hovoplodok-doplodovok- plovodokot-doplodokosh?
Splgraw fok fok splgrafhatchgabrlgabrl fok splfok?
Zgra kra gka fok!
Grof grawff gahf?
Gombl mbl bl-
blm plm,
blm plm,
blm plm,
blp.

The Loch Ness Monster's Song
Edwin Morgan

1

The Start of the Search—
An Introduction

"Oh, that's the best explanation you can give, is it?"
"Well, sir, what is yours?"
"The obvious one that the creature exists."

Arthur Conan Doyle: *The Lost World*

THERE ARE FEW people who have never heard of the Loch Ness
Monster. One of the more intriguing mysteries of our time, it
is at once exciting and yet slightly absurd. For though it may
well turn out to be one of the most interesting zoological
discoveries of the century, its odd history displays in full all
the fantasies and follies man is heir to.

First reported in the early summer of 1933 as a mysterious
animal haunting a large Scottish loch, by the autumn the
Monster had become a major sensation, a lighter topic between
the international crises and domestic disasters.

Reporters were dispatched by most large newspapers to
cover this dream of a story. Soon the little town of Inverness to
the north of the loch was crowded with the correspondents of
such far-flung journals as the *New York Herald Tribune*, *Le
Matin* and the Tokyo *Nichinichi*. These were the careless,
ruthless years of Evelyn Waugh's newspaper novel *Scoop*: one
can well imagine Boot of *The Beast* blissfully tracking the
Monster through the lush places of darkest Scotland.

The reports of the monster as they appeared in the papers
were often vague, and the witnesses oddly contradictory. From
person to person the dimensions of the creature altered alarm-
ingly, from a small black hump in a patch of foam to a great
prehistoric reptile over 60 feet long. Was all this merely a joke?
A publicity gimmick to attract tourists? Or was the Great Glen

of Scotland really some sort of Lost World, and Loch Ness infested by a Sea-Serpent?

In Inverness rumours flew around with wild abandon. The monster was said to have bounded across the road in broad daylight with a sheep in its mouth. An old woman disappeared, and was said to have been carried away by the rapacious creature. An enthusiastic reader of the *Glasgow News* offered to swim across the loch "as a challenge to the monster", while a skin diver said he was daring enough to tackle the animal with only a knife and his bare hands. A party of English Boy Scouts kept a "monster-watch" on the loch for a week, and another hopeful expedition came all the way from Monte Carlo. And of course there was the inevitable hoax. A Big Game Hunter sponsored by the *Daily Mail* found the "spoor" of the monster on a beach; but later the tracks were proved to have been made by a mounted hippopotamus foot.

Everyone had different ideas about what the monster was. Someone claimed it was a crocodile brought back from South Africa as a pet which had escaped and grown up in the loch. Others said it was merely a large grey seal. Or a rare white whale. Or a string of mines laid down by the Navy. Or the half-submerged fabric of a zeppelin shot down in World War One.

While it lasted, the story was an entertaining stunt. But as always with mysteries boosted by newspapers, editors lost interest before the truth of the matter could be discovered. Having had many more than its statutory nine days, the Loch Ness monster had to give way to newer sensations: the Saragossa Ghost, the talking Mongoose of Cashen's Gap, the German Occupation of the Rhineland.

Zoologists at the time were contemptuous of the idea that there might be an unknown animal in Loch Ness, but they made no attempt to discover what was actually behind the reports. Those who were interested enough to investigate the mystery on the spot came away convinced that there really was some strange animal in the loch. Sightings of that strange something – whatever it might be – have continued down the years, and recently interest in solving the mystery has revived.

Much of the credit for this belongs to Mrs Constance Whyte, who collected over a hundred reports for her book on the monster, published in 1957, which she called appropriately *More Than a Legend*. Some of her readers, impressed with the large amount of solid evidence from eye-witnesses and photographers, agreed with her that it was high time that something was done to explain the mystery: either there was an unknown animal in the loch, or some very curious happenings were giving people the vivid impression that there was.

In 1962, soon after a sensational film had been taken of the monster, the Loch Ness Phenomena Investigation Bureau was set up. This group not only mounts expeditions to the loch, but is also trying to collect whatever evidence it can in permanent form. The Loch Ness Investigation with other groups and individuals, has spent many months surveying the loch, sounding its depths and searching its restless surface.

Yet despite all this hectic activity, most people, if asked their opinion of the reports from Loch Ness, would say they were only clever publicity to attract tourists to the Scottish Highlands. As an American scientist remarked in 1934, "who ever heard of Loch Ness before the monster appeared there?" Very few indeed, and fewer still had visited it.

But the monster was there long before Thomas Cook created the modern tourist, or Henry Ford made him mobile. There were rumours of a strange beast in the loch during the last century, and according to local folk tradition the water around Foyers was the haunt of the "Water Horse". Moreover, in a ninth century biography of an Irish saint we are told that the holy man saved a swimmer from "an aquatic monster" in the River Ness. Even if one is sceptical of such far-fetched stories, there is the more than ample evidence of over 3,000 witnesses who claim to have seen the monster's long neck and humped back since 1933. Much of this evidence gets lost in the ephemeral pages of the daily press, but a large part has been collected by Mrs Whyte and other writers.

The first book about the monster was published while it was still a sensation back in 1934. *The Loch Ness Monster* by Rupert Thomas Gould – a retired naval officer known for his interest in the unusual, who had earlier written a fascinating book about the Sea Serpent – is a collection of some 47 sightings complete with drawings and photographs, together with a critique of the various theories about what the monster was,

some of which were very odd indeed. Gould undoubtedly gave
credence to the idea that there was an unknown animal in the
loch, even though the reports he quotes gave some readers a
very confused impression of it. Certain scientists at the time
thought the monster was merely a large grey seal, the commonest variety around Britain's coasts, which had somehow or
other got into the loch from the sea. Popularly it was thought
to be some kind of prehistoric reptile, some sort of dinosaur.
Gould had the original idea that the Monster was a hitherto
unknown animal along the lines of a vastly enlarged newt with
a long neck. No one seems to have believed him, except the
producer of a horror movie.

Mrs Whyte's was the second book. Though she attempts to
be impartial, she is clearly convinced not only that the monster
does exist, but that it *is* a prehistoric animal, probably a plesiosaur, a reptile thought to have been extinct for 60 million years.

This is the theory which Tim Dinsdale, an aeronautical
engineer who gave up his career to hunt the monster full time
after he had been lucky enough to film it in 1960, supports in
his three enthusiastically partisan books about his adventures.

A naval officer, a housewife, an engineer: these are hardly
qualified authorities on natural history, nor would they claim
to be. The only book on the monster to date written by a
professional zoologist was published in 1961 by Maurice
Burton, formerly on the staff of the British Museum, Natural
History Department, now the nature correspondent of the
Daily Telegraph. Dr Burton is not unprejudiced, but his
scepticism and expertise are most refreshing. Having disposed
with swift determination of much of the evidence as reports of
masses of floating, rotten, gas-filled vegetation—hence the
humps most often seen – he decided that perhaps a slender case
could be made out for the existence of a long-necked otter-like
animal in Loch Ness. But in an article written two years later,
he concluded that there was not even enough evidence for that
notion. What witnesses for over 30 years had consistently
imagined to be a large long-necked animal, was actually quite
an ordinary otter!

Opinion on the sea serpent, with which the Loch Ness
monster is often compared, also divides into two groups. One
side supports the existence of large long-necked serpent-like

animals in the oceans. The other side explains the now in-numerable reports of strange sea monsters as glimpses of known animals such as dolphins, or even sea-weed and standing waves. I have included here a supplement of sea-serpent sightings for comparison with the lake monster reports (see ch 17) but the interested reader will find fuller details of the cases (and some 600 other ones) in Dr Bernard Heuvelmans exhaustive book *In the Wake of the Sea Serpents*, to which the present writer owes an immense debt. Not only have I adapted some of Dr Heuvelmans theories as my own, but he has kindly provided information and reports for this book.

Heuvelmans distinguishes nine different types of sea-serpents. Two of these appear to be so rare or vaguely known that we can leave them aside. The other seven types are as follows:

(1) *Marine saurian*: a primitive sea-going crocodile
(2) *Super-eel*: limbless serpent-like animal, probably a fish
(3) *Super-Otter*: a long-tailed mammal resembling a giant otter
(4) *Many-finned*: a long jointed mammal with rows of triangular fins
(5) *Many-humped*: a long mammal with a blunt head, short neck, one pair of flippers, with a series of humps along the back which moves with an undulating movement
(6) *Long-necked*: a tail-less seal-like animal with a very long neck and fatty humps on the back
(7) *Mer-horse*: an animal similar to that above, except that it has large eyes, whiskers and a mane; it may have a tail.

These last two animals are so similar that I am inclined to think that they are actually the same animal, and that the variations are due to sexual differences. Heuvelmans believes, quite rightly as we shall see, that the lake monsters reported from Loch Ness and elsewhere are such long-necked mammals.

After all these books, and especially after the work of Bernard Heuvelmans, is there any need for another book by an amateur? An honest answer would be the usual one: I wanted to write it because the topic interests me. But in fairness to myself, I believe I can claim that this book "fills a long felt need".

Like most people, I first knew of the monster as a public joke along with the Martians, the Missing Link and Whistler's Mother. I saw Tim Dinsdale's film when it was shown on television, but I was not very impressed with the distant sight of a single small hump swimming down the far side of the loch nearly two miles away. Later, however, I happened to pick his first book off the shelf in a Dublin Public Library. My absorbed reading of how he came to take the film coincided with the first expeditions of the Bureau to Loch Ness, and with a series of reports from some Irish lakes with which I was familiar.

From then on I was caught by the enthusiasm of the others: I too became a Monster hunter. Soon I was reading Gould and Mrs Whyte, delving into dusty newspapers and writing off for information to complete strangers. It has not been possible for me to visit Loch Ness more than a couple of times, but my researches in three countries on two continents have brought to light evidence of Monsters in other parts of the world besides Scotland, and even in Scotland Loch Ness is not unique.

This is not just "another book about the Loch Ness monster", but rather a detailed survey of the evidence for similar animals around the world. I have tried to give an account of the events and investigations at Loch Ness since the 1930's. Here we have the basic evidence for the existence of these animals, but it only begins to make complete sense in the light of the reports from other parts of the world. So after the chapters on Loch Ness and other Scottish lakes, there follows a kind of safari round the world in search of monsters.

Our search will take us from Loch Ness and the Highlands of Scotland to the deserts of Utah and the mountains of British Columbia, from the pine forests of Sweden to the jungles of Africa, from Iceland to New Zealand, from Italy to Japan. We shall discover that these animals have been known for far longer than is commonly realised, are more widespread and less remarkable than is often imagined.

I hope that in the end some of the mystery surrounding them will be dispelled. But yet they remain mysterious to me, and will remain so until a living specimen is captured for scientific study.

There is no end in sight to the information on these animals: we are now only at the beginning, and every year more is added. I have included in this book only those reports which struck me as being in some way interesting or exceptional. I would be most interested to hear from anyone who has anything to add to my dossiers. For example, the undiscovered article by Lord Ellesmere, mentioned in Chapter Five, is one of the smaller problems that remains unsolved and to which some reader may know the answer. A larger one is what became of the baby monster captured alive at Fish Haven, Utah, in 1871?

Wherever possible I have concentrated on such arresting evidence: special eye-witnesses, photographs, unusual drawings. Many run-of-the-mill reports have had to go down the stream, but then I do not believe in completeness merely for completeness' sake. The selected evidence in this book, I think, has greater impact than an immense mass of trivial anecdotes.

I have tried to document this book as completely as possible, and have provided a bibliography which should help those interested in reading further towards the main sources, both for and against. While some of the evidence in this book will be well known to those already familiar with the mystery, there is much that even they will find new and surprising. For it is amazing what lies neglected in such an obvious source as the *Inverness Courier*, or even the London *Times*. Other writers have left many stones unturned: no doubt I also have.

Though Loch Ness is, as Master Frazer said in 1699, one of the wonders of Scotland, yet no one has really given an adequate account of what has happened there. Nor, to my mind, have any of the previous writers given adequate attention to the traditions about these monsters, though Bernard Heuvelmans would be the first to agree about the value of these to the zoologist. The most recent book about the monster, by F. W. Holiday, has some curious (if extremely unlikely) speculations along the lines I mean, about the dragons of folklore.

Nor has the psychological appeal of these traditions been considered in any reasonable way. Why, after all, should people get so excited about the Loch Ness monster? Why do they continue, against all the evidence to the contrary, to think of it as a prehistoric reptile? Unless such matters are considered, the real truth about the Monster will never be known, for the zoologist cannot discover the whole truth alone. If in the end he should show that there is no Monster – a most improbable eventuality, as we shall see – an account of what people have chosen to believe about it should still be of value.

For these reasons some of this book is taken up with what may seem to be extra-zoological speculations, with fantasies and follies. But in this investigation even what the poet says is evidence, for as Robert Graves warns us:

> Be assured the Dragon is not dead
> But once more from the pools of peace
> Shall rear his fabulous green head.

2

The Loch Ness Enigma—
A Real Monster?

The lake Ness, though oft mentioned by our
historians as one of the wonders of Scotland,
yet they give but ill account of it.
Master Frazer of Kirkhill in 1699

THE STORY OF the Loch Ness monster is best begun in 1933. The creature was first seen – so far as the media were concerned – from the new road along the north shore of the loch on April 14 1933. The well respected local paper, the *Inverness Courier*, published on May 2 an account of the sighting written by its Fort Augustus correspondent, Alex Campbell.

When the editor of the paper, Dr Barron, read the report, he is said to have remarked, "We can't go on calling this thing a creature. If it's as big as people say it is, then it must be a real *monster*". So in the Press the mysterious animal became the Loch Ness Monster. It was however a rival paper, the *Northern Chronicle*, which first used the name in a headline on May 8.

In his report Campbell noted that for generations Loch Ness had been credited with being the haunt of "a fearsome-looking monster", though until then this animal had been thought entirely legendary.

Now, however, comes the news that the beast has been seen once more, for on Friday of last week, a well-known business-man, who lives near Inverness, and his wife . . . when motoring along the northern side of the loch were startled to see a tremendous upheaval on the loch . . . The creature disported itself for fully a minute, its body resembling that of a whale, and the water cascading and churning like a simmering cauldron . . . Both on-lookers confessed that there was something uncanny about the whole thing, for they realised this was no ordinary denizen of the deep.

No indeed: for a few years before a party of Inverness anglers had "encountered an unknown creature, whose bulk, movements and the amount of water it displaced suggested that it was either a very large seal, a porpoise, or, indeed, the monster itself!"

Fig. 1. The Mackay's monster.

Campbell's anonymous witnesses were John Mackay and his wife, who owned the hotel at Drumnadrochit and had no desire to seem to be courting publicity.* His suggestion that the pair might well have seen a seal seemed plausible to many people at the time. Sir Compton Mackenzie, for example, claimed that he himself had seen "the monster" days before the Mackays had, and he had no doubt that it was a wounded Grey Seal. As late as 1957, Richard Carrington, discussing the mystery of Loch Ness, claimed the seal had come and gone in a few months. But the still-continuing reports show that the monster, whatever it is, remains in the loch and is nothing so commonplace as a Grey Seal.

The strange geography of Loch Ness should be made clear from the beginning, as much of the mystery of the place revolves around its curious features.

Until 1933 the only road around the loch was General Wade's Road along the southern shore from Inverness to Fort Augustus, which had been built after the Jacobite Rising in 1715 to open up the rebellious western Highlands. For much of the way this road ran through the hills, and where it touched the shore the view was often obscured by trees and bushes. Then in 1932 work began on a new main road along the northern shore. This scheme involved clearing away the undergrowth and also a great deal of rock-blasting – later it was

* Though this did not prevent some newspapers, among them the *New York Herald Tribune*, from claiming this was their motive.

even suggested that the noise of this had disturbed the monster, bringing it to the surface more often.

Drivers along this new road were soon given an almost completely unobstructed view of Loch Ness, as we can see from contemporary photographs. The great lake which they saw stretched out before them is the largest body of freshwater in these islands. Long and narrow, 24 miles by one mile and some 50 feet above sea-level, Loch Ness lies in the Great Glen, the major geological fault slanting across Scotland. The chain of lochs in the Great Glen – Lochs Ness, Oich, and Lochy – are now part of the Caledonian Canal, connecting Inverness with Fort William. The shores of Loch Ness plunge steeply into the water, in some places 750 feet to the flat bottom.† The bed of the lake is covered in sediment; samples tested in 1962 were found to be free from gas-forming bacteria. Peat carried down by the mountain streams and rivers stains the water a dark, rusty colour – even a few feet under the surface divers find their vision restricted and photography almost impossible. Though I myself found the water chillingly cold, in fact it is nearly constant in temperature at 42 degrees centigrade all the year round, making the loch a heat trap that never freezes over. For Dr Samuel Johnson, who passed this way to the Hebrides in 1773, this was the only mystery about Loch Ness: the scientists of his day could not explain why it should be so.

From Inverness, the old road (along which Johnson and Boswell rode) goes down the southern shore through Dores and Foyers, passing Whitefield and Inverfarigaig. The road runs close to the shore here, which is fairly level, with many small beaches. At Inverfarigaig the river Farigaig enters the loch in a small bay. At Foyers, after dropping over the celebrated Falls of Foyers, another river enters a somewhat larger bay. These beaches and river mouths are significant because of the great number of sightings made in these areas.

Beyond Foyers, where the hotel provides a magnificent view over the loch, the road turns off into the hills for several miles before dropping down into Fort Augustus, where the famous Abbey is situated on the loch shore. Here, Borlum Bay and Inchnacardoch Point are two important sites. At Inchnacardoch

---

† More recent research has found that a depth of 970 feet is reached at one point south of Urquhart Castle.

the shallow marsh and overgrown peninsula are very little visited; in the bay is the wreck of the little steamer that used to ply the length of the loch at the turn of the century. From here the new road goes right along the edge of the shore through Invermoriston, where there is a deep pool at the mouth of teh river, Drumnadrochit and Abriachan, and back to Inverness again. In Urquhart Bay, below the picturesque ruins of the medieval castle, where two rivers flow into the lake, there is an extensive area of swampy marsh and rough bushes, yet another little-visited place. Altogether there is quite a bit of wilderness around the shores of Loch Ness.

From the map it appears that large areas of the loch should be visible from the roads. But this is not so. On Wade's Road trees screen all but a few miles of the shore, and along much of its length trees and bushes have grown up along the new road since 1933. The best vantage places are at Foyers, Fort Augustus and Castle Urquhart, though if we really want to find the monster it must be sought in more inaccessible places.

Only after the Mackays' story was published and the monster became of interest to the press, were earlier rumours of a strange animal in Loch Ness taken notice of. The party of anglers, which Campbell mentioned, had seen their strange creature back in July 1930. Mr Ian Milne and two friends had been out shooting on the loch early one evening when they saw an object surface in Dores Bay with a splash of spray and move in a wide semi-circle before sinking out of sight. About 22 feet

Fig. 2. Ian Milne's "strange sight".

long, it seemed to be propelled from the tail end. Milne glimpsed two or three shallow humps which moved in undulations. An account of this incident appeared in the *Northern Chronicle* as "A Strange Experience on Loch Ness": but even this does not seem to be the first press account of the monster ever published.

Mr Milne's report drew a letter from a local reader signing

himself "Camper". Three years before, he related, he had been camping beside the River Ness at the home farm of Ness Castle. Early one morning he heard a tremendous splashing and snorting in the river. Looking out of the tent, he saw what he took to be a very large seal playing on the surface with a fish in its mouth. The animal had a flat head and was of great size. He went to pull his boots on but when he came out "the monster had disappeared". For some reason interest in this mysterious animal stopped there in 1930: 1933 was to be quite different.

It was not long before someone pointed out that the earliest reference to a monster in the loch was in the 8th century biography of Saint Columba, the Irish poet who converted the Picts, written a century after his death by his compatriot, Adamnan. One of the chapters is entitled: *Of the Driving Away of a Certain Water Monster by Virtue of the Prayer of the Holy Man*. The incident took place about 565 A.D., perhaps at Bonar Narrows at the head of the loch.

At another time, again when the holy man was staying for some days in the Province of the Picts, he found it necessary to cross the river Ness. When he came to the bank, he sees some of the local people burying an unfortunate fellow, whom – so those burying him claimed – some aquatic monster had shortly before snatched while he was swimming and viciously bitten. The corpse had been rescued by some boatmen armed with grappling hooks. The holy man orders one of his companions to swim out and bring over a coble moored on the other side. Hearing and obeying the command, Lugne Mocumin without delay takes off his clothes except his loin cloth and casts himself into the water. But the monster perceiving the surface of the water disturbed by the swimmer suddenly comes up and moves towards him as he was crossing in the middle of the stream, and rushed up with a great roar and open mouth.

The holy man seeing it ... commanded the ferocious monster saying "Go thou no further nor touch the man – Go back at once". Then on hearing this word of the saint the monster was terrified and fled away again more quickly than if it had been dragged on by ropes, though it approached

Lugne as he swam so closely that between man and monster there was no more than the length of one punt pole.

This strange story has naturally enough presented recent writers with a problem. Mrs Whyte tucks it away in a back chapter of her book along with other odds and ends of folklore. Rupert Gould, ever sceptical, declined even to comment on it. I personally feel it is a true story, and only slightly over-drawn. As we shall see later, this is by no means the only story of a monster from an earlier period, and though this is the most convincing account, Irish saints and poets have been seeing such animals for a very long time. It all depends on how much credence you put in Irish saints and poets. True this is the only time we ever hear of the Loch Ness animal attacking anyone, but with any large wild animals such an event is never impossible. The details in the story, the animal's sudden appearance, size, speed and equally swift disappearance, all are confirmed by more recent reports. The one detail we might boggle at, the loud roar the animal lets out, is actually a point in favour of the story's truth. For though the Loch Ness animal has been heard to utter a sound on only one other occasion (when it was nearly run down by a motor car in 1923), a sharp staccato cry has been reported from other parts of the world. So on its own the story seems strange, in context it does not.

We should, of course, be critical in accepting evidence such as this, but on the whole I feel Adamnan passes muster. Others do not. The theory of a 19th century writer, that Loch Ness is named for a suppositious Celtic water nymph named Nessa, which nearly every modern writer seems to have taken up, is quite without evidence. The origin of the name is unknown but is probably Norse. Oddly enough though, the Roman historian Dio Cassius reports that the Caledones, the tribe which lived around Loch Ness in Roman times, had a taboo against eating fish from the lake.

A little nearer our own times, the first references come from three centuries ago. Richard Frank's *Northern Memoirs* (1658) mentions "a floating island" in Loch Ness, which could be a reference to the monster's single hump showing above the surface. The seventh edition of Daniel Defoe's *Tour Through the Whole Island of Great Britain* is said to contain in volume four an account of "the leviathans" which frequently disturbed the soldiers building Wade's Road in 1716. Unfortunately none of the editions I have examined at the British Museum have such an exciting episode. The *Tour* was a much revised book and some editions may well contain such an interesting tit-bit. I suspect however that "the leviathans" are as fabulous as the goddess Nessa.

Traditions of a "water horse" were current around Loch Ness for many centuries. The folklorist Campbell of Islay, writing in 1860, said he had been told that the loch was full of "water bulls" but "they never go up to the Falls of Foyers". Several old people have recalled being warned as children of playing too near the banks because of a great beast that lived in the loch. And rumours abounded of earlier sightings.

The earliest witness whose name we know is a Jimmy Hossack, who saw the monster about 1862; he was a friend of E. H. Bright, who had his own curious story about the monster which we will come to in due course.

A Mr Mackenzie of Dalnairn told Rupert Gould that he had seen the monster in October 1871 or '72, near Abriachan, coming across the loch from Aldourie. At first he thought it was a log drifting on the surface of the water, but when it reached the middle of the loch it assumed the shape of an upturned boat and went off at great speed, churning up the water.

About 1878, according to an anecdote William Mackenzie of Cannich used to tell, a labourer washing his feet in the loch after his day's work was surprised out of his life when the monster's head appeared out of the water 20 yards away.

In the summer of 1885, according to David Murray Rose, "stories were circulated about a strange beast being seen by many people about Loch Ness" though it only appeared on the surface for a few minutes so that no-one could properly describe it. Mr Murray Rose, a local historian, seems to have been a mine of eccentric information, with which he regularly filled the correspondence columns of the Inverness press. The monster found him in his element, He claimed that according to some chronicle the monster "was lately seen" in 1520. And that one Patrick Rose, an ancestor of his, had been told of an appearance in 1771 of a monster which was a cross between a horse and a camel with its mouth in its throat. I have not been able to track down the sources of these tit-bits, either.

About 1880 an Abriachan mason named Alexander Mac-Donald often used to see the strange animal playing on the loch in the early morning. He travelled daily by steamer between Abriachan Pier and Inverness, and was known to arrive at the pier in subdued excitement after seeing what he called "the salamander". The crew and skipper of the steamer also saw the animal on occasion, though they said it was a furry animal with legs and not an amphibian. Mr Roderick Matheson was the owner of the schooner *Bessie* which often made trips through the Caledonian Canal. On one of these trips, Mr Matheson, then a mate, saw what he described as "the biggest eel I ever saw in my life". The animal had "a neck like a horse, and a mane somewhat similar". So it seems that even in the last century no-one could quite make up their minds about what the monster really was, a fish, a lizard or a furry mammal.

The animal was something of a local secret. In 1889 H. J. Craig and his brother were fishing near Urquhart Castle on a still, calm loch. Suddenly a "huge form" reared out of the water nearby and sped off towards Inverness. They rowed quickly ashore in a near-hysterical state. After listening to their story – "it was like a huge serpent" they claimed – their father impressed upon them that they must never again refer to the animal or tell anyone else about it. This perhaps understandable reticence explains why it took so long for the monster to be heard of outside Inverness.

Their father need not have been bothered, as some people *were* beginning to talk about the monster. When he rented the salmon fishing on Loch Oich and the River Garry in 1895, the Duke of Portland often heard the forester, the hotel keeper and his ghillies talking about a "horrible great beastie" as they called it that was to be seen in Loch Ness. When an odd animal turned up dead in the bottom of Corpach lock at Fort William it was thought to have come down the Caledonian Canal from Loch Ness. The animals in Loch Ness were even well known enough to be mentioned in the *Glasgow Evening News* in 1896. More surprising still, in November 1896 an article about the loch, complete with a realistic woodcut of the monster itself, appeared in the Atlanta (Georgia) *Constitution*. But what was news in Atlanta was never heard of in London.†

After the turn of the century the reports became even more frequent. Some time between 1903 and 1907, John MacLeod of Invermoriston, in the company of a writer from Inverness, was fishing in the pool at the mouth of the river Moriston. Preparing his gear, he noticed a large creature lying motionless along the surface of the water on the far side of the pool. After a while he tossed his line in its direction and it made off. The animal was 30 to 40 feet long with a head like an eel and what appeared to be a long tapering tail. MacLeod used to entertain visitors with this story. J. MacRobertson heard it in 1908 and C. W. Broun in 1910. Mr Broun was rather sceptical about this "fisherman's story", and jokingly asked why they had not tried to catch the creature with a net. The pool was too wide, came the serious reply!

MacLeod was one of the witnesses that Rupert Gould talked to on his travels but, as Gould discovered, he was not the only one who claimed to have seen the monster before 1933.

One day in December 1903, Mr Frazer of Knockie and two other men were rowing over to Invermoriston to catch the steamer when they saw an object like "an upturned boat". They rowed after it but had to give up the chase as it was too fast for them. Local rowing boats, by the way, are about 15 feet overall, a reasonable length even for a monster.

Rupert Gould was told by Kenneth Mackay, the brother of the man whose report had begun it all, of an incident that he recalled from during the First World War. One evening the head keeper at Balmacaan Estate, James Cameron, came into the bar of the Drumnadrochit Hotel and asked for a large brandy. Later he told Mackay, who had insisted on walking part of the way home with him, what had so affected him. While he had been out fishing on the loch an "enormous animal" had surfaced beside his boat. The shock made him dizzy and he fell to the bottom of the boat. He would not say more and swore Mackay to secrecy, so it was not until the

---

† The American writer John Keel claims in a recent book to have seen this article, but a search of the paper for November 1896 failed to turn it up. Still, it may be there, so I have let the reference stand.

hectic days of 1933 that Mackay recalled the story and saw its significance.

Gould was also told of sightings in Dores Bay in July 1914, and near the shore at Abriachan Pier in May 1923, by William Miller and his wife; again the animal suggested "an upturned boat". Mr Miller had heard "tales" about a monster – which is hardly surprising – but had never really believed them. In August 1929, a Mrs Cumming saw a hump also near Abriachan; and James Cameron, a postman, saw "an upturned boat" in February 1932 off Shrone Point.

Despite these persistent rumours from the past of some strange animal in Loch Ness, the initial reaction to the MacKay's story was sceptical. Yet the matter was not allowed to drop. For well over a year both local papers carried weekly reports and theories about the monster. Due to Dr Barron's sharpwittedness the monster was brought to wider fame, to the eager attention of newspaper readers the world over. Since that April day in 1933 there has been a steady stream of reports, which now number over 3,000 by some estimates.

Some of the earliest are typical of the sort of things that have been seen repeatedly since. On May 11, Mr Alexander Shaw and his son were standing on the lawn of Whitefield House (where they were nearly 150 feet above the water) when they saw a wake on the surface about 500 yards out. The back of an animal then emerged near Urquhart Bay opposite them. They

Fig. 3. Alexander Shaw's monster.

had the impression of something long and undulating stretched out in front; behind, the water was thrown up, as if by an outboard motor.

Other early witnesses were the MacLennan family of Temple Pier near Drumnadrochit, who saw the monster on several occasions in 1933. Mr Thomas MacLennan said it was an animal about 30 feet long, and he had the impression that it had four flippers. Mrs MacLennan caught glimpses of the animal's head, neck and tail-end. The head was three feet above the water on a tapering neck, the head being little wider than the neck below it. The humps were less prominent when the animal was moving. On the back of the neck was what appeared to be hair or wool. The tail "resembled that of a fish", by which I take her to mean that it appeared to be bilobate, divided in two parts like a fish's.

Another typical appearance was on May 27 at Alltsaigh, where Miss Nora Simpson saw the monster at a distance of

Fig. 4. Nora Simpson's monster.

45 yards, lying motionless on the surface, showing two humps, overall about 30 feet in length. The front hump seemed to be smaller than the rear one. After ten minutes the animal sank, and a few moments later she saw a V-shaped wake moving off into the centre of the lake. There it sank with a sudden splash, and ripples from this soon broke on the shore.

Such reports certainly seemed to confirm the legends that there was a large animal in the loch. Mistakes, of course, were made. The *Courier* reported, on June 25, that a squad of workmen, engaged on blasting operations near Abriachan,† had been startled the day before to see the monster going up the centre of the loch in the wake of a passing drifter. They said the beast "had an enormous head and a large heavy body". This report should have fooled no-one. The workmen had in fact mistaken the long rolling wake of the drifter for the large humps of the monster. Excitement was letting people see things on Loch Ness.

I have no intention of repeating at any length reports of mere humps and wakes. So only the more revealing or curious reports will be included here, such as one which appeared in the *Chronicle* on June 7. An airman reported that while flying over the loch in late May, in the vicinity of Castle Urquhart, he beheld in the depths "a shape resembling an alligator, the

† They were finishing off the new road, which was officially opened that autumn.

size of which would be about 25 feet long by 4 feet wide".†
He suggested that an airplane should be used to depth-charge
the animal. Thankfully no-one took up this idea.‡

If an alligator seems strange enough, there were stranger
things to come.

On the afternoon of July 22, Mr George Spicer, a London
company director, and his wife were driving south from John
O'Groats. After Inverness they took the road along the shore
of Loch Ness to Foyers. Shortly after passing Whitefield, they
were approaching a rise in the road.

Suddenly, from the bracken on the hillside to their left, there
emerged an extraordinary animal. A long neck and then a large
body jerked itself across the road in seconds and disappeared
into the bushes by the lochside. Accelerating (the car was still
200 yards away), they arrived on the spot too late to see anything more. Whatever it was, it had got away into the water.

Fig. 5. The Spicer's version of the animal ashore.

Later they recalled other details of the animal. The long
neck had moved up and down "in the manner of a scenic
railway", according to Mr Spicer. They noticed no head as
the animal was across the road too quickly. The body was
fairly large, with a high back. If there were any feet, Mr Spicer
thought they must be of "the webbed kind". The rise of the
road had prevented them from seeing the lower part of the
animal clearly. Nor did they see any tail, but on consideration
decided that an object they had seen flapping over the back of
the neck was the tip of a tail curved around to the animal's side.
This would be a very odd way for an animal to move. Their

† There is a local story of a South African releasing a couple of baby crocodiles
into the loch, which someone has tried to authenticate with a "monster's foot"
found on the shore which was actually a crocodile foot.

‡ A BBC man flying over the loch in 1939 saw a seal-like head and two humps
for a brief moment.

first impression seems sounder to me, as the object was very probably the appendage Mrs MacLennan had described earlier as "hair or wool" about the back of the animal's neck. (Mrs Spicer was quoted in the papers as saying she thought the object was a deer or small animal's neck, as if the monster had slung a carcase over its shoulder before fleeing back to the loch. A great deal of fun was made of the monster "with a lamb in its mouth", which bore little relation to the real facts.) The animal was a "terrible, dark elephant grey, of a loathsome texture, reminiscent of a snail". Mr Spicer estimated that the animal stood four feet high. His first estimate of its length was six feet, but when he learnt that the road at that point was 12 feet wide, he changed his mind and said the true length was 25 feet; three years later this had become 30 feet. Again I think the first impression is likely to be more accurate.

Mr Spicer wrote to the *Inverness Courier* (August 4, 1933) describing their odd encounter, and asking what the animal was, and was it well known. This was a little disingenuous of him, for the couple had been told all about the rumoured monster by the first person they met after the sighting, a road-mender on a bicycle.

Mr Spicer's letter caused a small sensation in Inverness. Just *what* was this animal that caused such a commotion on the water and which it now seemed came on the shore as well? "Is It a Variant of the Plesiosaurus?" the *Chronicle* asked on August 9. The idea that the Monster might be prehistoric was very pleasing to the public. The ghost of the great dinosaurs had returned, and was going to be a long time in the laying.

Actually, this was not the first time that the monster had been seen on the shore. Here it will be convenient to group together some earlier encounters, as well as two more from 1933. We shall come to other land sightings later on.

William MacGruer, who lived all his life in Fort Augustus, had a strange story to tell in the columns of the *Inverness Courier* in October. Over 20 years before, around about 1912, a party of five or six children between 10 and 12, set out to hunt for birds, nests in the scrublands of Inchnacardoch Bay. They had not got far from the road when they saw a queer-looking creature emerge from some bushes and make for the loch, only a few yards away, and disappear into the water.

Mr MacGruer recalled that the animal reminded them of nothing so much as a camel. It had a long neck, a humped-back and fairly long legs. It was, however, considerably smaller than a camel, but the coat was almost the same colour, a sort of sandy pale yellow.

The children ran quickly home, where their excitement showed that this was no fairy story. Mr MacGruer's parents remembered the incident perfectly, and though they had scoffed at the time, were now inclined to believe in the monster.

We should remember that this story, so unlike the Spicer's in many details, yet similar in the long neck and lack of tail, was published in October 1933. This was just before the monster became a national sensation, and so this account – unlike the Spicer's – was forgotten.

This was not the only time the monster had been seen ashore in Inchnacardoch Bay. In 1936 Lieutenant-Colonel Guy Liddell recalled in a letter to the *Times* that on a visit to the youth hostel in Inchnacardoch House, he had been told by the warden there, a Mrs Peter Cameron, that she had seen the monster ashore in 1919.

She was then a girl of fifteen and, with her two young brothers, was playing one sunny September afternoon on the beach close to the boat house of Inchnacardoch House. The loch is very shallow here around the edge of the scrublands. As the children were larking about, they saw an animal on the shore of the marshland opposite them lurching down into the water, "humping its shoulders and twisting its head from side to side". It seemed somewhat heavy in its movements, rather like an elephant. It had a long neck and a small head, which reminded her of a camel, as also did the light colour. There were four limbs, and as no mention is made of a tail, we may assume there was none to be seen.

These children also fled swiftly home. Their parents realised that something untoward had happened, but this being Scotland, solemnly warned them that the Devil would have them for gathering nuts on the Sabbath.†

If the monster had preferred Inchnacardoch Bay for its

---

† Mrs Cameron saw the monster in the water in July 1934, two months before she spoke to Liddell.

excursions then, by 1933 it had settled on the Dores Road, where the Spicers saw it. In December a Mrs Reid, the wife of the postmaster at Inverfarigaig, was motoring into Inverness, when she saw a strange animal lying in a glade on the wooded slope away from the loch shore. The animal was about 100 yards distant and partly obscured by the bracken. She was not very definite about the details, but thought she saw a thick hairy mane on the neck, and the beast generally seemed hairy. From what little she saw, it was six or seven feet in length, shaped like a hippopotamus. It seemed a slow moving type of animal with a large rounded head, short thick legs, and very dark in colour.

This curious report, like William MacGruer's, has not been noticed by other writers. Whereas his is straightforward enough, I am afraid there is not much we can make of this "very strange animal". Another strange animal was seen in this same area in August by Mrs MacLennan, whose earlier sightings have already been mentioned.

Mrs MacLennan saw her animal ashore near Whitefield on the first Sunday of August. She and her family had crossed the loch to attend church. On the way back, she took off her shoes, which were hurting her, and so came upon the animal unawares. It was resting on a ledge above a beach just below the level of the road, about six feet above the water: she thought it must have "climbed like a monkey" to have got where it was. (This spot was identified to Gould as having Urquhart Castle in line with Temple Pier.) On seeing the animal, she yelled "Daddy", and with that the animal lurched itself up and slithered over the edge of the cliff. When her family ran up, there was nothing to see.

She told Gould that the animal was lying "hunched-up", end on to her, facing the water, but with its head thrown back. The back was ridged "something like an elephants" and was grey in colour like an elephant as well. There were humps on the back, but these did not seem quite so prominent as when she had seen the animal in the water. She estimated it was about 25 feet long.

In November 1959 Mrs MacLennan supplied Maurice Burton, who was then preparing his book on the monster, with some further details, especially about the animal's limbs.

It had short, thick, clumsy legs, but most decidedly legs, with a kind of hoof very like a pig's, but much larger . . . It doesn't seem to have any ears, but believe me it can hear. It lurched itself up on the two forelegs (it had four legs), then slithered hoofs forward over the cliff . . . It did not stand up like, say, a cow. It kept the hind-legs on the ground seal-wise. It seemed to be too heavy in the body for its own legs. It went down quietly with a great splash. The rings were all my boys saw, thanks to my yell.

Here we have very important testimony about the animal's limbs and way of moving. The Spicers saw nothing of the legs because of the rise in the road, and though MacGruer and Mrs Cameron mention them, they give no details. Clearly we seem to have here some large seal-like animal. The fanned-out rear limbs, clearly flippers, and the way of rearing up on the front ones to move, point to that. But just as clearly this is no ordinary seal known to science, for none of them have long necks. And what are we to make of the hooves?

These puzzled Burton as well, but shortly afterwards Mrs MacLennan wrote to him again, clarifying what she meant. In the meantime he had noticed that the feet of a terrapin, adapted for use on land as well as in water, sometimes could be disposed so as to resemble a hoof. Then she sent him a cutting showing a restored dinosaur, pointing out that "hoof" which she had seen. Actually in the picture the dinosaur's foot was obscured, so that only two claws could be seen, which did indeed look like a cleft hoof. So we can guess that in some way the animal's feet have the appearance of being cloven, perhaps because they are claws joined by a webb, as with terrapins, otters and the seals.

On the evidence I have quoted so far, it might seem that the existence of some large animal in the loch was well established, something of its appearance revealed, and a clue to its identity found. But that was not how it seemed at the time.

Mrs MacLennan's encounter was not much publicised. There were too many other reports of sightings of humps and wakes for a clear picture to be seen. Rumour, ever-active, turned the Spicer's flapping object into a lamb in the monster's mouth: this was the subject of a topical postcard quickly produced for the nine days wonder. Other equally fantastic stories were also in circulation. Reports from the loch (despite their seeming contradictions) were eagerly received by the press in Scotland and England. As the affair developed during the summer, so did national interest. By the autumn the *Scotsman* and the *Daily Mail* had sent special correspondents, Philip Stalker and Percy Cater, up to Loch Ness to investigate what was really going on. Reporters made much of the loch's gloomy appearance and sinister depths. Were people really seeing the things that the newspapers reported with avidity?

That they were not was the firm opinion of the Director of the Aquarium at the London Zoo, E. G. Boulenger. He wrote in the *Observer* (October 29, 1933) that:

The case of the Loch Ness Monster is worthy of our consideration if only because it presents a striking example of mass hallucination ... For countless centuries a wealth of weird and eerie legend has centered round this great inland waterway ... Any person with the slightest knowledge of human nature should therefore find no difficulty in understanding how an animal, once said to have been seen by a few persons should shortly after have revealed itself to many more.

Another scientist, W. R. Pycraft, the science correspondent of the *Illustrated London News*, dismissed the monster in an article on November 11. He found the fact that Loch Ness was in possession of a "sea-serpent" of great interest: this would be an opportunity to knock the last nail in the coffin of an old legend. Twenty-eight years earlier, however, he had sung to a different tune. When two English naturalists saw a sea-serpent in 1906 he had declared sententiously:

Seriously, we can no longer regard the "sea-serpent" as a myth. There can be no question but that the ocean harbours some secret that we have not yet penetrated.

Now following the lead of his colleagues, he would have no secrets in Loch Ness. The monster, showing itself only to laymen who knew no better, could only be a seal. These strictures would have been more reasonable if there had been verbal reports only of something strange in Loch Ness. Soon theories of mass hallucination and wandering seals had to be reconsidered when the first photograph alleged to be of the monster was published.

On Sunday, November 12, 1933, Mr Hugh Gray was walking near his house on the loch shore at Foyers. He was carrying his camera, in case he might by chance see something in the loch. He reached a cliff about 30 feet high, which overlooked the loch half a mile below Foyers. Suddenly the calm water below him burst into commotion. A large body reared up, stretched out before which was what appeared to be a long neck. Mr Gray took five photographs during the few moments the animal remained on the surface. He was not able to distinguish it very well, because of all the spray it was throwing up.

The film was left in a drawer, and it was three weeks before his brother took it into Inverness to be developed. Four of the five negatives were blank. On the fifth appeared the image of the body which he had seen, shrouded in spray as he described. The photograph was published in the Scottish *Daily Record*, along with a statement by Mr Gray about his experience.

"An object of considerable dimensions," was how he described the monster. It rose two or three feet above the water. He did not see the head, for what he assumed to be the front end was under the water, "but there was considerable movement from what seemed to be the tail," which was the part furthest from him. He added that he could make no estimate of size, other than "it was very large". Dark greyish in colour, the skin had appeared smooth and glistening.

The negative was examined by technicians at Kodak's, who certified that it had not been tampered with to produce a 'monster'. Prints were shown to several zoologists for their expert opinions. Professor Graham Kerr of Glasgow University thought the photograph "was unconvincing as a representation of a living creature". Mr J. R. Norman, of the British Museum, said "the possibilities levelled down to the object being a bottlenosed whale, one of the larger species of shark, or just mere wreckage". Another scientist suggested that the object was a rotting tree trunk, raised to the surface by the gases of its decomposition, which sank when these escaped.

These various suggestions are still revived from time to time. Yet reading their opinions, one cannot help wondering if these scientists had actually examined the photograph and considered Gray's story.† Judging by some of the ill-considered remarks attributed at the time to eminent zoologists, I imagine that a reporter must have arrived at an inconvenient moment, asking silly questions like "What is the Loch Ness Monster really?" The scientist, unfamiliar with the loch or with the detail of the reports, hastily assumes that there is nothing to them, or that some large sea animal has somehow or other got into the loch. Thus all this talk about belugas, bottle-nosed whales and seals. None of these, even if they could get into the loch, would explain the one prime feature of the monster: its long neck.

When the matter of an investigation was raised by the local M.P. in the House of Commons on November 12, the Government spokesman felt that such activities were "more properly a matter for the private enterprise of scientists aided by the zeal of the press and photographers". The Press were certainly zealous enough, but the lack of any real scientific interest is odd. Weren't they even interested in a land-locked whale? But, of course, scientists are only human, and jealous of their *amour propre*, of appearing foolish. Losing face would never do!

Though taken in November, Hugh Gray's photograph was not published until December 6, by which time people had become worried about the monster's fate. The protection of the creature, whatever it was, had been raised at the Annual General Meeting of the Loch Ness Fishery Board on November 11. Rewards were raised for the capture of the Monster – alive, fortunately. Bertram Mills Circus had offered £20,000 for the animal, the New York Zoo had countered with $5,000, and a private person with £1000. The local people grew concerned about all this. The Chief Constable of Inverness issued an order to prevent the capture or molesting of the monster. Contrary to popular belief, Parliament passed no measures to protect the monster.

† A highly retouched version emphasing the black shadow at the water line rather than the larger but vaguer shape of the body was published in the *Daily Telegraph* (December 6 1933): several scientists seem to have based their opinions on this version of the photograph. An Oslo paper even managed to print this version upside down!

However, by this time the first thorough investigation was under way. Commander Rupert Gould, a writer known for his interest in the unusual and the unexplained, and the author of the latest book on the sea serpent, had been invited by a wealthy Scottish friend† to undertake a private inquiry. Buying himself a second-hand motorcycle, he travelled around the loch between November 9 and 23, gathering evidence from eye-witnesses. Altogether he interviewed 51 persons. When he had completed his on the spot investigation, he drafted a short communiqué to give to the Press Association. When he rang the Association's office in Glasgow to check on its publication, the bored voice of a young secretary at the other end informed him, on hearing the fatal words "Loch Ness":

"Oh, we don't want that. We don't believe in it".

As a result his statement appeared only in the *Inverness Courier* and the *Scotsman*. This would seem to suggest that interest in the mystery was waning: it was soon revived.

To begin with, three days after Hugh Gray's photograph was published, a long article by Commander Gould, surveying in a masterly fashion the evidence for the monster, appeared in the *Times* on December 9. From what he had learned, he wrote, it was clear that there was indeed some strange animal in Loch Ness. He thought it was a stray sea-serpent, of a type long familiar, and that its appearance suggested nothing so much as a vastly enlarged newt. This was a new theory of his, which he left to be evaluated by qualified scientists with open minds on the subject.

But the scientists were still unconvinced. W. T. Calman, of the British Museum, said he would not believe in the monster till he examined a specimen. Scientists, he claimed, deal only with specimens. (This was not really true, for there were even then several sorts of whale listed in the zoological records which had only been sighted, but not captured.) Those with more impartial minds were reassured by Gould's article that there was something worth looking into up at Loch Ness. The *Times*, which had ignored the vulgar sensation till then, backed Gould's article with a leader, opened its columns to letters on the subject, and even began to publish reports from

† Alexander Keiller, the well-known archaeologist and businessman.

its local correspondent about new sightings. The *Illustrated London News*, despite the agnostic attitude of its science writer, sent its special artist S. H. Davies up to the loch, who collected an impressive number of accounts illustrated with supervised drawings which appeared in an early issue of the new year.

Some of these new reports added a little to the details of the monster's appearance. Engineer-Commander Richard Meicklem had had an excellent sighting on August 5. The monster was showing a single hump, motionless off Cherry Island. He was able to examine the hump for three minutes

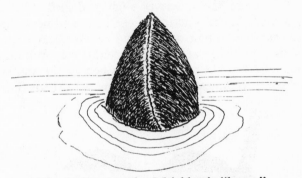

Fig. 6. Commander Meicklem's "hump".

through his binoculars. It was facing him end on. Bluish-grey in colour, it had a ridge along the back, which seemed to taper down to the water. The body seemed to be slightly curved as well. The skin appeared to be "knobbly and warted", certainly granulated. The ridge, which was part of the body, was blacker than the rest of the hump. The sides sloped almost perpendicularly to the water line.

On August 11, another engineer, Mr A. H. Palmer, had an odd sighting while camping near Achnahannet. Early in the morning his attention was attracted by a noise "as though a gale of wind had struck the loch". He hurried down to the shore to find the surface of the water was a seething mass of foam for two hundred yards either way. He returned an hour later to find the water calm, but out in the loch was what he took to be the head of an animal. It was rather like an inverted plate, with two small "horns". The mouth was wide, and opened

Fig. 7. Head seen by A. H. Palmer.

and closed, showing a red interior, as if the animal were breathing heavily.

On September 22, 1933, four women saw the animal from the Half-Way House Tea Room at Alltsaigh. It was about 1,000 yards away, nearly halfway across the loch. Miss Frazer concentrated on the head and neck. It reminded her of "a mythical creature", though the face was slightly dished, like a more homely terrier. At the junction of the head and neck there was a sort of frill like "a pair of kippered herrings". A large bright eye was visible, though at that distance this may well have been an optical effect of the sun which was behind the animal. Miss Howden saw two humps with a splashing at the rear. (Doubtless

Fig. 8. Miss Howden's sketch.

due to those seal-like flippers seen by Mrs MacLennan.) Mrs H. Frazer also saw these humps, followed by a silver streak and then the splashing. The animal moved off towards Invermoriston and sank out of sight.

That "pair of kippered herrings" are odd appendages, unless we assume that they are the same things that the Spicers saw flapping on the neck of their animal, and what others have described as "a mane". A. D. W. Morrison, who saw the monster the same day, observed that the head was nearly the same bore as the neck and only visible when raised. He also saw that the animal undulated up and down, and not with the lateral motion which might have been expected from "a giant eel". This is an important point, by the way, indicating that the animal is almost certainly a mammal.

A master at the Fort Augustus Abbey School, B. A. Russell, saw the head and neck on October 1, about 800 yards out in the loch. Occasionally it turned from side to side, but as one

Fig. 9. Neck seen by B. A. Russell.

piece, rather as a ship's davitt moves. He also observed that the head was not much larger than the neck, but at that distance could make out no other details. The colour was dark. Mr Russell, like many others, had assumed that a seal had got into the loch, but he now realised that this was something much more remarkable. Also in October, Mrs J. Simpson saw the monster for the fifth time, with its head and neck raised two feet over the water. Where the neck entered the water, she glimpsed two flippers "moving like those of a sea-lion", an animal she had seen for herself at a circus some years before.

If these clear and fairly consistent reports were not enough, the first film of the monster was taken by a newsreel crew in December. The film was made by Mr Malcolm Irvine, of Scottish Film Productions, with the aid of two colleagues, Stanley Clinton and Scott Hay, on December 12. The party had arrived in Inverness and surveyed the loch, collecting whatever local information they could about the monster on December 4 and 5. Having decided on their strategy, they returned to Inverness to wait for good weather. This came on December 12. That day, the first day they had visited the loch since their survey, they got in position by 11 in the morning. Three hours later, and just about where they expected it, the monster appeared.

When one remembers the many futile efforts of others since to photograph the monster, one is amazed at Irvine's luck. Yet his plan was simplicity itself. His theory was that the monster was probably feeding on the salmon and trout in the loch, and must therefore visit the known feeding banks of those fish. To approach and leave the banks, he thought it would be likely to pass through the shallow water just off Inverfarigaig. That was where he set up the film cameras. Mr Irvine stationed himself on a slope, the other two on the shore about 150 yards from each other, and 400 yards below him.

When the monster appeared, it swam past them about 100 yards from the nearest camera. They estimated its length at 16 feet, and its speed at not more than 20 miles an hour. Their coup was kept secret till the films were developed and edited for distribution as newsreels. On January 3, 1934, the film was shown to a private audience in London.

The present whereabouts of this film is uncertain, but a description of what it showed appeared in The *Times* (January 4, 1934). The part of the film showing the monster is only two minutes long. It could be seen moving towards the right, getting further away as it passed, and seemingly to dive as it left the camera's view. The cameramen claimed to have seen seven or eight humps, and some of these were visible in the film. The main mass is preceded by a smaller object which, like the rest of the object, is mostly under the water.

> The most clearly evident movements [according to the *Times* reporter] are those of the tail or flukes. This appendage is naturally darker than the body. The photographers describe the general colour of the creature as grey, that of the tail as black. Indeterminate movements of the water beside the monster as it swims suggests the action of something in the nature of fins or paddles.

All of which seems to confirm what we already know about the tail fins and front flippers. Irvine also filmed a log floating on the loch, and the contrast was plain. All that survives of this film now are some stills. These do show some large dark object, but deprived of movement are nearly useless.

Unfortunately, just as the monster was beginning to receive some serious attention, a rather ludicrous hoax was perpetrated. Early in December an expedition sponsored by the *Daily Mail* arrived at Loch Ness with great to-do. The leaders were a self-styled game-hunter and film maker named Weatheral and his friend Mr Pauli. This pair scoured the lake in a hired boat, and were soon able to discover signs of the monster on the shore, similar to hippopotami spoor which they had seen in Africa. Local gamekeepers were sceptical about this discovery, as they themselves had been on the look-out for months for just such traces. On December 20, Weatheral and his friend were lucky enough actually to find tracks made by the monster.

It is a four-fingered beast with pads or feet about 8 inches across. I should judge it to be a very powerful soft-footed animal about 20 feet long. The spoor clearly shows the undulations of the pads and outlines of the claws or nails.

On January 1, 1934, a cast of the spoor was delivered to the British Museum, Natural History Department for examination by Dr Calman. A few days later he and his colleague Martin Hinton announced:

We are unable to find any significant difference between these impressions and those made by the foot of a hippopotamus. The closest agreement is with the right hind foot of a mounted specimen not quite fully grown.

Later it was rumoured that a hippo foot mounted as an ash tray had been used. Its great discovery now discredited, the *Daily Mail* attempted to discredit the monster as well. For them it became, and stayed for a time, a grey seal.

The report on the "Monster's Spoor" was published on January 4. By an unlucky coincidence, the next night the monster was seen ashore. On Friday, January 5, Mr Arthur Grant, a young medical student, was returning from Inverness to his parent's home at Drumnadrochit, riding his motorcycle. It was nearly one o'clock, and the sky was over-cast. About three miles from Lochend, coming down into Abriachan, the sky cleared and the road was flooded with bright moonlight. A little way ahead, he saw a dark object in the shadow of the bushes on the right-hand side of the road. As he approached, something bounded out in front of his cycle, crossed the road in two bounds, diagonally away from him, and vanished into the bushes on the loch shore.

I had a splendid view of the object. In fact, I almost struck it with my motorcycle. It had a long neck and large oval-shaped eyes on the top of a small head. The tail would be from 5 to 6 feet long and very powerful; the curious thing about it was that the end was rounded off; it did not come to a point. The total length of the animal would be 15 to 20 feet. Knowing something of natural history I can say that I have never seen anything in my life like the animal I saw. It looked like a hybrid – a cross between a plesiosaur and a member of the seal family.

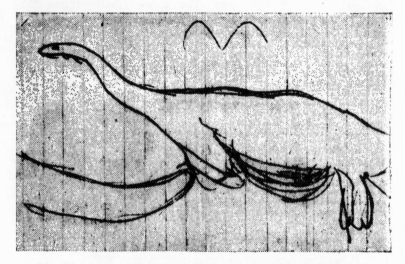

Fig. 10. Arthur Grant's midnight monster, the first version.

Grant leapt off his motorcycle and chased after the animal. But when he reached the shore it had made off into the loch with a great splash. He marked the spot, and went home where he woke his younger brothers and told them what had happened. Sitting in the garage he drew, by the light of a storm lantern, a crude sketch of what he had seen.

Later he recalled these details of the animal's appearance:

A head rather like a snake or an eel, flat on top, the large oval eye, longish neck and somewhat longer tail. The body was much thicker towards the tail than the front portion. In colour it was black or dark brown and had a skin rather like a whale. The head must have been about 6 feet from the ground as it crossed the road, the neck 3½ to 4 feet long and the tail 5 or 6 feet long. Height from belly to the back would be about 4½ feet and overall length 18 to 20 feet.

This description is more or less confirmed by the drawing he made the same evening. It can be seen that this sketch is in two parts. The front and top of the animal are drawn clearly and with confidence. But there is a wavering uncertainty about the underparts and the tail. I guess that Grant saw the neck and back clearly enough in the beam of his light, but could not completely make out the rest. These uncertainties were cleared up in a version of the drawing published in the Aberdeen *Press and Journal* (January 8, 1934) where the tail is tacked on at the end and the outline of the belly and legs firmly drawn. The outline becomes even more definite in a version Grant drew for the Dutch zoologist Dr Oudemans, where he also shows three digits on the rear flipper. Second or third thoughts are not always best. The midnight sketch is to be preferred.

Fig. 11. Final version drawn for Dr Oudemans.

The next morning Grant returned to the scene of his adventure. News of the incident had got around, and soon the game hunter Weatheral turned up. Grant was photographed with Weatheral examining with interest a mass of sheep's wool which was found on the shore. The beach there was littered with bones and also the fresh carcase of a goat. Inevitably much was made by the press of the carniverous monster. A footprint with three digits was also found, but the earlier hoax had quite discredited any kind of "tracks" and no-one gave it much attention.

Luckily, more sober minded investigators were also on the spot. A party of students from Edinburgh College of Art were spending a week of their Christmas vacation around Loch Ness looking for the monster. They gained two glimpses of the monster's humps, but their most important work was to investigate the scene of Arthur Grant's encounter. They spent two days in his company going over the ground carefully. His description gave them a clear idea of how the animal had moved: it had "loped" across the road using all four flippers, first putting down both front ones, then arching its back and heaving foreward the hind ones in the manner of a sea-lion, the stomach raised clear of the ground.

Mr H. F. Hay, the leader of the group, who was a Fellow of the Zoological Society of Scotland, described their investigation:

> We checked the tracks at the point where the creature had gone down the steep bank into the loch, and confirmed the fact that there was no "body drag", though without doubt something large had gone down there. The marks of the feet or flippers – as they were scrapes or "skids" in the soft earth, there was no telling the nature of them – were about five feet apart.
>
> This fact gave some indication of the width of the animal. It also does away with the seal theory, as it impossible for a seal to use his hind flippers on land. It follows that his stomach and whole body is dragged along the ground . . .
>
> Some seventy yards further up the beach from this point (near Abriachan) we discovered what appeared to be a set of foot or flipper prints in the shingle, measuring 24 inches long from toe to heel, 38 inches across from right to left, and 30 inches from heel to heel. Nearby was a large crushed down area in the bracken as if an over-sized cow had lain there, though no farm beast could have reached that spot.

Sensibly, they attached no importance to the bones or to the dead goat: these had obviously been washed up on the beach by the current, as they proved by experiment.

On returning to Edinburgh, they examined the animals in

the collection of the Royal Scottish Museum, and found that their measurements and deductions fitted the dimensions of a fully grown bull-walrus, even down to the width across the belly. They admitted that the walrus theory would not explain the long neck seen by Grant. But it was possible that in the weak beam of his headlamp he had seen only the highlight along the head and back. "The thick upturned tail he mentions may well be explained by the habit of the walrus throwing up the hind flippers when going down a sudden declivity." A photograph they found in the *Scottish Naturalist* showed a walrus doing just that.

I agree with them about the hind flippers being mistaken for a long tail, as this has happened on other occasions. But that the monster really is a *walrus* seems most unlikely. Certainly they are fast moving animals, for all their bulk, but as another member of the party, Alastair Erskine-Murray, pointed out at the time, the long neck still had to be explained.

It was a pity that these conclusions got mixed up with the earlier hoax. They shed important light on the identity of the animals in Loch Ness, but were discredited by association.†

Indeed, reports of the monster ashore seem in general to have been discredited by the hoax. As we shall see the monster was seen ashore twice in 1934, but both incidents got little or no publicity. Indeed one of them has been completely forgotten. The following account of the monster ashore has escaped the notice of other writers, even though it was reported in the *Glasgow Herald* (March 3, 1934). According to the paper's local correspondent, who interviewed the witnesses, the incident happened at the beginning of February.

The animal was seen less than a mile from Fort Augustus, at a spot where the Inchnacardoch burn runs underneath the then newly reconstructed road into the loch. One evening two young girls from Fort Augustus, Jean MacDonald and Patricia Harvey, were walking along the road when they were startled by the appearance of an animal which crossed the burn on the shore below them and disappeared in the direction of the loch. The moon was full, and as the animal was only about 20 feet

† Burton mentions these tracks in his book, but has the date wrong and so fails to connect them with the Grant incident.

from them, they had no difficulty in seeing it was something out of the ordinary.

> In a statement [the *Herald* reporter continues] the girls said the creature appeared to be from eight to ten feet long, and had four feet. From the fore feet to the top of the head was a height of about six feet, and the thickest part of the body appeared to be at the shoulder: The body tapered considerably towards the tail. The creature was of a distinctly dark colour, and the under part of the neck was perfectly white. The legs were short, but the creature moved with great rapidity, and the girls were astonished at the speed with which it made towards the loch. When in motion the creature made no sound, a fact which surprised them because of its bulk.

They fled back to Fort Augustus, deciding on the way to say nothing about what they had seen – hence the delay in reporting it. Incidentally, besides confirming the general appearance of the monster, this report also suggests that the monster may well be much smaller than the incredible lengths sometimes suggested, and its tail, despite Arthur Grant, quite unnoticeable.

But this is with the benefit of hindsight. In January 1934 the monster was still a mysterious creature with eccentric habits. Inverness, as can be imagined, was crowded with reporters, who were writing a lot of pleasant nonsense to entertain their readers. A group of Boy Scouts searched for the creature in a rowing boat. At the Windmill Theatre a stand-up comic had built a complete routine around the monster's asthma. Post cards appeared showing the monster gallivanting about the loch shore with a sheep in its mouth. The monster, in the most astonishing varied costumes, was a frequent guest at New Year parties and village carnivals.

Sir Arthur Keith, then well-known for his reconstruction of the Piltdown skull, which later turned out to be a hoax, writing in the *Daily Mail* early in January, thought that the very large number of people claiming to have seen the Loch Ness monster proved that it was imaginary. People were seeing what they wanted to see. The problem was not one for zoologists but for psychologists. If the animal had been around for as long as was claimed "then concrete and unmistakable evidence of its

existence would have been in our hands long before now". The
Piltdown skull, on which Sir Keith worked so lovingly, might
well be taken as a warning that other kinds of evidence must
also be taken into account besides solid bits of bone.

But few were ready to consider in detail the evidence from
the loch, such as we have just been through. This is clear from
the varied opinions expressed at the time. An article in *Nature*
stated authoritatively that the monster was an eel which had
strayed into the Loch from Beauly Firth. But in New York,
William Beebe, the naturalist, thought the monster was a squid.
R. L. Ditmars, the herpetologist, scoffed at the whole idea of a
"sea-serpent" in Loch Ness; there were no sea reptiles that size,
he said. A reader of the *New York Times* reminded the editor
that a monster seen in Silver Lake in Upper New York State
had turned out to be a hoax: could the Loch Ness Monster
also be a publicity stunt. *Punch* had a sharp cartoon showing
the monster trying out "a new advertising medium", sign-
writing on the water an incomplete "Daily M...". Nearer the
point, Dr Calman's associate, Martin Hinton, attempted
finally to dispose of the monster in an article in *The Field* on
January 27; he also thought it was a seal.

But the monster would not be disposed of: it had become a
legend. There it was, during all those months, between the
Fascists and the financial crises. Any normal person, faced with
obscure events in remote countries of which he knew little, and
with problems beyond his understanding, would have turned
with relief to the latest news from Loch Ness. A prehistoric
monster – as everyone now took it to be – was quite as probable
as Mussolini, Mosley or General O'Duffy. Anyhow, it was more
endearing.

The Duke of York (later George VI), as the Earl of Inverness,
was guest of honour at the annual dinner of the London
Inverness Association in April and, naturally, he spoke of the
county's most famous resident, the Loch Ness monster.

It's fame has reached every part of the earth. It has entered
the nurseries of this country. The other day, I was in the
nursery, and my younger daughter, Margaret Rose, aged
three, was looking at a fairy-story picture-book. She came
across a picture of a dragon, and described it to her mother:

"Oh, look Mummy, what a darling little Loch Ness Monster".

Her Royal Highness was not the only distinguished admirer of the monster. The Abbot of the Monastery at Fort Augustus was surprised that such a locally accepted animal should cause all this fuss. The Right Rev. Sir David Hunter-Blair wrote that four of his monks had seen the monster while fishing in the Loch. (He himself was to watch it with two of his pupils on a later date, "gambolling" in Borlum Bay.) He expressed himself forthrightly:

I do not intend for a moment to imply that I entertain the slightest doubt as to the real and objective existence of a strange and unknown beast in the profundity of the great loch I have known for half a century.

Oddly enough, we learn from other sources that the Abbey School had its own traditions about a monster in the loch long before 1933. A Fr Francis McElmail of Stroud, one of the original 20 boys taken to found the school at Fort Augustus by Prior Jerome Vaughan in 1878, recalled that the monster was well known to exist at that time. His lair was supposed to be in Corrie's Cave, which was forbidden to the boys but well explored by them. The local people had stories of some queer beast living there. This was confirmed by another priest, Fr Wilfred Gettins of Argyll, who also remembered the monster traditions among the school-boys.

The Abbot confirmed this belief.

Let me record my own belief that the monster is a true amphibian, capable of living either on land or in the water, with four rudimentary legs or paddles, an extraordinarily flexible neck, broad shoulders and a strong, broad, flat tail, capable of violently churning the waters round it.

As a summary of the evidence this was fair enough, agreeing with the reports gathered by Gould, those published in the press, and with the descriptions from the Spicers and Grant, except that the "tail" is really the hind pair of flippers.

But if the monstei did exist, what could it be? Was it, as Sir David suggested, an amphibian? Rupert Gould had mentioned in his *Times* article that it resembled "nothing so much as a vastly enlarged newt". This theory was elaborated by Dr Malcolm Burr in an interesting article in *The Nineteenth Century* for February.

> I see no real reason [he wrote] why our sea-serpent should not be a hitherto unrecognised relative of the newts, adapted to life in the sea, developed to a relatively large size, timid and nocturnal in habit, and consequently little seen.

Dr Burr's treatment was elaborate, ingenious, and well-informed about the actual evidence. But he seems to have been the only scientist with an open mind to have taken Gould's work seriously, and the only influence his theory had was to provide the shape of the monster in a thriller filmed at Loch Ness called *The Secret of the Loch*. (A full critique of this theory can be found in Heuvelman's book on the sea-serpent.)

Then in April 1934, the best known photograph of the monster was taken. A London Surgeon, Mr Kenneth Wilson, was returning from his holidays in northern Scotland. He had brought with him a friend's camera to photograph trains. Three miles outside Ivermoriston, on the road to Inverness, at a point where the road is 200 feet above the loch, he stopped the car. The time was about 7.30 a.m. He got out and climbed down the slope a short distance to relieve himself.

He noticed a commotion in the loch, about 200 to 300 yards out. As he watched something broke surface "and I saw the head of some strange animal rising out of the water". He fetched the camera from the car: it was a three-quarter plate camera fitted with a telephoto lens. Finding a vantage point 50 yards further down the slope, he exposed four plates before the object disappeared.

As soon as he reached Inverness, Mr Wilson had the plates developed by a chemist named Morrison. Two of the plates were blank failures. The third showed the long neck arched over the water from the thick body, now so familiar from eye-witness accounts. The last plate showed a smaller object, apparently the head, about to submerge.

The better photograph was sold to the *Daily Mail*; the original negative has been destroyed.† A copy of the other photograph was kept by Mr Morrison, to whom its preservation is due.

It has been suggested that the photograph shows either a log brought to the surface by its own gases, or the tip of the tail of a diving otter. This second suggestion (made by Maurice Burton) is quite ingenious: but what, then, is the object in the second picture? Seeing how closely the photograph resembles the long-necked aspect of the monster so often drawn and described – even to those little horns which a few witnesses have mentioned – can there be any reasonable doubt that this is a photograph of the Loch Ness animal? But if so, what is it?

In London, Dr Calman "could not hazard a guess" as to what it was. A few days after the photograph was published, Roy Chapman Andrews of the American Museum of Natural History in New York, claimed that the reports were all due to optical illusions. Not surprisingly, in view of Wilson's remarkable photograph, he later changed his mind. He wrote in 1939 that:

The Loch Ness Monster was photographed once. The original picture showed just what I expected – the dorsal fin of a killer whale (Orca). A killer's dorsal is six feet high and curved. It would make a wonderful neck for a sea-serpent. Doubtless the whale had made its way through the narrow gate of the loch from the open sea. It may have gone in and out several times.

Doubtless.

It seems strange that while scientists often expect laymen to know their facts, they themselves do not bother to acquaint themselves with those of such outré cases as the Monster. What Andrews suggests about the picture and the loch is untrue, as a little research would have told him. By 1939 the animals there had been photographed not once but more than nine times. The object is clearly not a fin of any kind; and a

† This seems to be common practice with newspapers, as negatives of other photographs are similarly lost to us. No photographs should be sold to them in future.

whale could not just come and go as easily as that from Loch Ness.

But there was one scientist who greeted the monster as an old friend. Back in 1892, the Dutch zoologist A. C. Oudemans had written the definitive book on the sea-serpent. He had concluded then that there were several types, but that they were all related animals, giant long-necked seals with four flippers and a long tail. When the Loch Ness monster was reported in 1933, he realised at once that it was a sea-serpent, and he wrote a pamphlet about it showing it was one of his long-necked seals. As we have seen, there is a lot of evidence to support his theory. Except, of course, that the animal in Loch Ness does not seem to have a long tail. That, as we have also seen, was a mistaken idea based on Arthur Grant's drawing. (One of the great collections of material on Loch Ness, which I have had no opportunity of consulting, is in Dr Oudemans archives at Gouda in Holland: seven large box files of clippings and letters.)†

Further support for the monster came in June 1934, when Rupert Gould published a full account of his investigation in a book, *The Loch Ness Monster and Others*. He gives accounts of 47 sightings by 69 people, including four reports of the monster seen between 1923 and 1932. The reports represented the monster in all its queer protean variety. Its shape alters from account to account, some seeing a single hump, others a series of humps, usually two or three. On two occasions seven humps, and even eight to nine were seen. (These are actually likely to be reports of two animals together, thought to be one, as the nine humps were seen in the middle of a December snowstorm!) Others saw the head and neck, some merely some large object in a patch of foam. It was not, the scientific community thought, very convincing.

E. G. Boulenger, reviewing the book for the *Observer* (July 1, 1934) said he "repudiated the whole business as a stunt, foisted on a credulous public and excused by a certain element of low comedy". There had been some comic moments, but they were all in the past. Nothing had been really foisted on

† He also suggested the authorities should kill the creature in the cause of science and install it in a museum; he can't have had much idea of Loch Ness, if he thought that would be an easy task.

the public. And those who took any interest in the affair
beyond a cursory glance at a probably inaccurate newspaper
paragraph, were convinced that there was an interesting
scientific problem to solve at Loch Ness. But the scientists
were not, and it was mainly interested amateurs, like Gould,
and their friends who did the work.

In his book on the sea-serpent, Rupert Gould had quoted an
account by a friend of his, another naval officer, F. E. D.
Haslefoot, of an animal he had seen while surveying Black
Deep in the Thames Estuary, during the summer of 1923.
Captain Haslefoot, inspired by his friend's latest book, visited
Loch Ness in the summer of 1934. It would be hard to accuse
a man of such experience of a "stunt".

On July 12, he was walking along the disused railway lines
which lead from Fort Augustus to the old steamer Pier on
Inchnacardoch Point. The surface of the loch was grey, but the
noon sun was shining. Two objects caught his attention out
in Borlum Bay, about 400 yards offshore. These were oval
black humps about eight feet apart, rising about a foot above

Fig. 12. Captain Haslefoot's monster.

the water, and moving slowly towards the shore. Then, perhaps
scared by a nearby rowing boat, the monster took fright,
turned, and made away up the loch for about 200 yards. He
could see a distinct white "feather" as it moved at a speed of
about 10 knots.

Here it turned and swam slowly towards the shore at a
speed of about three knots. For one brief moment I saw its
head come out of the water. The head appeared to be black
and spade-shaped, neck and head black and about 4 feet out

of the water. The "flick" back into the water was distinctly sideways and very rapid. The creature swam leisurely towards the shore and submerged when about 50 yards from the shore.

He made an estimate of the animal's size: width between humps, about 6 to 8 feet; humps, low and similar; head, maximum width about 4 feet. (Later, he reduced the size of the head, telling Gould it was about 2 feet long.) "The front hump," he noted, "only produced the 'feather', which leads one to expect that the creature has a broad body. This point seems most important".

Captain Haslefoot has in mind that the "feather", as he calls the wash thrown up as the animal moves, was produced by flippers, which would have to be supported by a wide breast bone. This is exactly how a sea-lion or walrus is built, which use their limbs for propulsion as well as walking on land. Such a feather can be seen in the still from the Irvine film. His reasoning is suggestive. He also has the unique distinction of having seen both the Loch Ness monster and the sea-serpent.

One of the happier effects of Gould's book was to suggest to Sir Edward Mountain, the insurance magnate, that it might be worth keeping an intensive watch on the loch. From nearby Beaufort Castle, which he had rented for the summer of 1934, he organised a team of men to keep a complete surveillance over the whole length of the loch. All were equipped with field glasses, and a few with cameras. The watch, beginning on July 13, lasted five weeks. During that time there were 17 sightings; 11 of these were of humps.

Among the rest there were two sightings of exceptional interest. On July 30, William Campbell saw the monster only 25 yards from the shore. The head was kept down in the water, but the neck was slightly arched over the surface to join the large body. The egg-shaped body was moved forward at a

Fig. 13. Animal seen by William Campbell.

walking pace by two front fins. Campbell's sketch makes it
clear that this egg-shaped body is the same shape others have
described as resembling an upturned-boat.

The other sighting was reported by Patrick Grant. On August
12, near Abriachan Pier, he watched the monster for five
minutes. The head reminded him of a goat's, with two stumpy
horns like a sheep's broken off short. The eyes were mere
slits, like darning needles. Where the neck joined the body
there was a large swelling like "a fowl with a full crop". He
also saw fins, but these were pointing straight forward and were
not moving. The colour was dark brown, and lighter underneath. What Grant means by "a full crop" can be seen in the
Wilson photograph, where the neck can be seen to swell out at
the water-line. I wonder, was the animal Campbell saw grubbing
along the loch bed for food, as a swan does?

The expedition obtained five photographs and a few feet of
film. Four of the photographs show some very indeterminate
wave patterns, which could easily be the wakes of boats. The
fifth, however, shows a long dark hump with spray thrown up
over the back, much as in Hugh Gray's picture.

The film was taken by Captain James Frazer, the leader of
the survey, at 7.15 a.m. on September 15, a misty morning. He
used a 16 mm camera fitted with a 6 inch telephoto lens. The
object was photographed at a distance of three quarters of a
mile. Sir Edward arranged for the film to be shown to a small
group of zoologists early in October. They were invited to send
their opinions of the film to the *Field*, and six of them did so.
Martin Hinton and his colleagues were certain the film showed
a seal. The correspondence columns of the next few issues
carried letters from several Scottish readers deriding this
theory. If the animal in Loch Ness were a seal, they said, its
habits were unlike those of any seal known around the shores of
these islands.

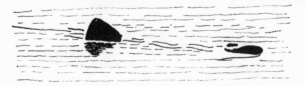

Fig. 14. From a film by Captain Frazer.

A few weeks later Sir Edward showed the film to the annual meeting of the Linnaean Society of London. He gave a brief account of his expeditions and the results obtained. Six of his men had reported two or three humps; one had seen one hump; four, the head and neck, and four a pattern of heavy wakes.

Commander Gould was also present on this occasion, and after outlining the results of his own researches, mentioned that Dr Barron, the editor of the *Inverness Courier*, had re-marked that some of those London scientists must think the Scots were half-witted if they did not know a seal when they saw one, when many of them saw more seals in a month than a Londoner would in a life time.

Sir Arthur Smith-Woodward pointed out that whatever the animal was, it was not a prehistoric reptile, because no fossil remains of such mezozioc creatures had been found in tertiary deposits. (Actually this is not a completely convincing argu-ment, for there are several "living fossils", known from even earlier periods, which though not found in later deposits, are still alive; the coeleacanth is the most famous example.)

In general the meeting was divided in its opinion. Only two speakers held out for a seal. Another thought the animal's movement's suggested a whale, another that it was an otter. One thought that Kodak's estimate of size – about 8 feet – was too big. With forthright honesty, Dr Stanley Kemp, one of the *Discovery* party, said he did not think it was a seal or whale – in fact, he couldn't guess what it might be.

These scientists had mostly reasoned backwards. The film showed what seemed to be a large animal swimming in a freshwater lake. What could the animal be? The only large animal found around the shores of Scotland which could get into the loch would be a grey seal. Therefore the animal in the film must be a seal. This, of course, was what they had wanted to show anyway. Yet the animal in film did not swim like any known seal.

So, by a similar process, those photographs showing the neck were said to be pictures of a killer whale's fin. W. R. Gregory of the American Museum of Natural History, who visited Loch Ness during the summer of 1934, came away convinced that the presence of a killer whale was the real explanation of the reports. He had bought some amusing postcards in Inverness showing great scaley reptiles crawling out of the loch. These he used to illustrate a facetious article in *Natural History*, which debunks the whole affair yet quotes not one single solitary eye-witness account of the monster. Rupert Gould and Edward Mountain had laboured in vain.

Bernard Heuvelmans has remarked that the Press made such a laughing stock of the Loch Ness monster that no scientific commission has ever dared to tackle the problem. But it seems to me that the papers were quite open minded about the affair, and that the scientific community closed its mind on the subject quite early.

As an example of the sort of scientific prejudice that has bedevilled this problem for over 30 years, a series of articles on the monster in *Nature* – then as now, the country's leading science journal – provides a good example of the attitudes of the scientific establishment. The articles are all anonymous, except for one signed "J.R." whom I have identified as James Ritchie, the ex-curator of the natural history department of the Royal Scottish Museum.

His first note about the mystery appeared in December 1933. He had spent one whole morning in July watching at Loch Ness and had seen nothing. As a result he was deeply sceptical about the existence of "the alleged monster". The witnesses might well be describing something unfamiliar to them, but "the variations in the descriptions suggest either a fertile (if unconscious) imagination, or the observation of different phenomena". He makes much of the seeming variations in descriptions and the equally various explanations, including such "impossibilities" as the plesiosaur, "sea-camel" and sea-serpent of the middle ages. The only suggestions put forward by professional zoologists – an unstable mass of peat, a white whale – were not likely to be correct for other reasons. These reasons are not specified.

Ritchie was just as sceptical about the evidence put forward in the *Times* by Rupert Gould. "To a zoologist, Commander Gould's acceptance and analysis of at any rate some of the evidence appears to be uncritical and even credulous, and his conclusions unjustified". Yet here again the writer's own objections are not specified.

Nor was he much impressed by Hugh Gray's photograph. Dismissing the retouched version of it, which was fair enough, he says he would have to examine the original negative before giving an opinion. The article concludes with a paragraph of impenetrable obscurity, in which he seems to suggest that he thinks the animal in the loch might well be a grey seal.

This theory was clarified in a second note published on January 13. He had by now examined the negative of the Gray photograph. He thought it was not taken at a distance of 200 yards – which no-one had ever claimed; 30 feet would be more accurate. It showed "no animal known to science", the implication being that it was not an animal at all.

He goes on then to deal with the latest sensation, Arthur Grant's midnight adventure, and his speculation that the animal he saw was a plesiosaur. Ritchie will have none of this. "The sketch and the description of the beast and its movements are more reliable than the identification. Without analysing these in detail, for they are wonderfully accurate considering the physical light and the mental atmosphere which surrounded the creature, one has little doubt that the object figured in the Scotsman and seen and sketched by Mr Grant in the early morning of January 5, was a large grey seal." This species, he goes on to point out, is common round the Scottish coast, but lacks the long neck which is such a feature of the evidence.

A third article (initialled this time) appeared on August 18, 1934. The animal was now world-famous and many more descriptions were to hand. "The situation is without parallel in the records of the observation of Nature", he writes, "and it is of some interest to analyse the results".

But that is just what he does not do. He begins ominously by wilfully misrepresenting an account of the monster seen near Glendoe. So that I do not fall into the same easy habits, the two passages are given here. First Ritchie's version of the incident:

Clearly not all the recent records are of equal value. On July 4, a worker at Glendoe sawmill observed the creature emerge from the loch: as it emerged propelled by flippers, five humps were seen, twelve distinct humps as it wormed its way ashore, head smaller and thicker than a horse's, neck heavily made, body fully 30 feet long, but not very thick. It was seen to feed upon weeds and water plants growing on the shore (a previous observer had seen it or another carrying a lamb in its mouth) and as the monastery clock struck 10 a.m., it wriggled back into the loch, having been under observation for an hour. A drawing representing this apparition accompanied the newspaper account. (*Nature*, August 18, 1934)

It is most unlikely that many readers of *Nature* would have been able to turn up the original report in the *Scotsman*, even though Ritchie provided the date. Those who did might well have been dismayed. Here it is:

I was working on the Glendoe Eastate about 9 a.m., and from a small hill overlooking the loch I saw the calm surface suddenly broken by a most amazing beast. It was at least 30 feet long, and as its length continued to emerge, I could distinctly see a number of humps. I was looking almost straight down on it when it first appeared and I counted twelve humps, each a foot out of the water. It moved off towards Glendoe Pier, and on one occasion lifted its head and neck out of the water and shook itself. I then saw something extending for about 4 feet from the head down the neck, dark coloured, rather like a mane. The day was so clear that I could distinguish drops of water as they fell when the monster shook itself. It reached Glendoe Pier and stretched its neck out of the water where a stream enters the loch. It did not actually come ashore but seemed to be hunting about the edge and I cannot see how it could move as it did without using flippers or feet. (*Scotsman*, July 6, 1934)

What could be clearer than that. Yet Ritchie has it all so garbled that one wonders if he was even able to read. While appearing to deal critically and analytically with the evidence, he merely glances over the contents of a few newspaper paragraphs, repeats the hoary old legend about the monster with a lamb in its mouth and adds a few ill-informed comments of his own on a couple of badly printed photographs. In the one case where he does quote real evidence, he seriously misrepresents this, making it fantastic rather than commonplace. Though the busy academic readers of *Nature* were given the gratifying impression that they were getting a critical account of an extraordinary affair, Ritchie's methods are entirely unscientific and his conclusions reached on *a priori* grounds. These articles were as non-sensical as anything published in the much abused popular press.

The press by now was losing interest in the monster. The scientific establishment was unstirred. Though their results had proved inconclusive, Rupert Gould and Sir Edward Mountain had been generous of their time and money at a period when the monster was little more than a joke. It was an opportunity lost that no scientists were stimulated to investigate the problem properly for themselves. But they were not. And it would be 28 years before another expedition would investigate Loch Ness, 28 years in which more pressing events eclipsed the Loch Ness monster.

3

The Loch Ness Enigma—In Eclipse

The case of the Loch Ness Monster . . . a few years
ago . . . which attracted a number of believers.
Scottish Anthropological and Folklore Society,
Proceedings (1953)

THE FAME OF the Loch Ness Monster, having been created by
the newspapers, languished when they turned to newer sensations. Though the London papers were no longer greatly
interested, the animal continued its appearances. Scottish
papers remained loyal and often carried reports as mere matters
of fact. The *Glasgow Herald* (the only Scottish paper indexed)
published 51 reports of the monster between 1934 and 1956.
Occasionally one of these might make its way into some
London paper, but not often. The keen interest was dead: the
general attitude was that of the Scottish Folklore Society, one
of disbelief.

The last spark of the great sensation was in August 1934,
when another photograph of the monster was taken. This
was published in both the *Daily Mail* and the *Illustrated
London News*, getting a half page in each, much more than the
Wilson picture got. The name of the photographer was not
revealed, and perhaps because of this anonymity this photograph has sunk into obscurity. I believe it was taken by a
Londoner, Mr F. C. Adams, from Urquhart Castle on August 3.
This is the first time it has been reprinted since (see plate 9).

Again we have some difficulty making out the shape of the
animal. Maurice Burton (who produced a travesty of the
photograph as a drawing in his book) says the object looks
"uncommonly like a trunk or branch brought up from the
depths by an underwater explosion". But then he only shows
the dark part projecting from the water. To my eye the photo-

graph shows more than that: not merely the long dark object, actually the neck in shadow, but also the outline of a large body. Unfortunately the image has been greatly enlarged with a resulting loss of definition. With the neck so completely shadowed, no details of the head can be made out. In this the picture contrasts with the graceful poise of the animal in the Wilson photograph. It mav be that the head is turned away from us, as is suggested by the way the neck seems to curve. Comparison with a photograph taken in 1960, of which more later, suggests this is indeed an authentic photograph.†

Though spaciously reproduced, this photograph seems to have made little stir at the time. The monster was stale copy on the newsdesk. Yet despite this growing lack of interest, the monster was still reported, and "a number of believers" were still interested enough to record them. Some incidents of the late 1930's, which got little or no attention at the time, actually throw a great deal of light on the mystery of the monster, especially its numbers and breeding.

Fig. 15. From an anonymous photograph.

A friend of Oudemans', Count G. A. Bentinck, a well-known Dutch naturalist, came in person to investigate the Loch Ness monster. He stayed at the Half-Way House at Alltsaigh for three successive summers, and saw the monster seven times. In August 1934, he saw the animal's head flush with the surface of the water (as Mr Palmer had); from its mouth "a kind of steam came forth, but was blown back by the wind". Afterwards he wrote an article for a Dutch science journal, concluding that "my observations were sufficient to satisfy me that

† A photograph taken at Fort Augustus appeared in the *Scottish Daily Express* on June 10, but it showed little more than a shallow hump (See Fig. 15)

the animal is a mammal; it is one of the family of pinnipedia described by A. C. Oudemans in his *Great Sea Serpent"*. A sound theory, as we have seen, but not widely accepted, especially in Britain.

To properly investigate this enigma lurking in the black depths of the loch, one needed to live in Inverness. Luckily one of the monks at St Benedicts Abbey was attracted by the mystery. Dom Cyril Dieckhoff was a Russian emigré with an artistic bent; a mural by him (including a self-portrait as one of the saints) can be seen in the small chapel of the Abbey. He also spoke gaelic, which was of inestimable advantage to him on his pastoral duties in the Western Highlands, where he picked up rumours of other monsters. He long intended to write a book about these monsters, and took every opportunity to interview eyewitnesses. His diaries, still kept by the Abbey at Fort Augustus, contain some remarkable stories.

He himself saw the Loch Ness monster twice. On August 30, 1934, he saw from a window of the Abbey a neck about 600 yards out in the loch, behind which there soon appeared a round black hump. Six years later, in May 1940, he and two other monks saw a wash moving across the loch towards Glendoe Pier, which became smaller and more circular as the object lost speed and finally sank. (Such a round wash can be seen in the Wilson photograph.)

At first Dieckhoff thought the monster might be some sort of large fish. But after he had discussed his sighting with Commander Miecklem, who pointed out that whatever it was he had seen off Cherry Island, it was not a fish, Dieckhoff came round to the idea that the monster was a plesiosaur. It seems to have been a lightly enough held conviction however, and did not stop him setting down evidence which pointed to the animal being a mammal.

In October 1933, he records an attempt made by an employee of the Glendoe Estate to assassinate the monster, while some of the boys from the school watched it swimming – showing one large hump – in Borlum Bay. The monster survived this unseemly assault, for it was seen again in May 1934, by another member of the community who had served with the Royal Engineers. Brother Horan was working in the pumphouse near the shore when he heard a noise. At first he took no notice as he was near the entrance to the canal and it could have been a boat.

When he looked up he saw the animal swimming only 30 yards away from him, parallel with the shore and its head turned towards him. Apparently it had no ears at all, its muzzle was rather blunt, approaching that of a seal – but it was not a seal. It had a graceful neck 3½ feet in length, held at an angle of 45 degrees to the water with a broad white stripe down the front.

It moved about, changing direction from time to time. Slowly turning towards the S.W., it found a rowing boat in its path. It stopped for a fraction of a minute, causing great commotion in the water. From this point, until it sank, there was a curious motion in the water behind the animal as if a propeller were working; during this period the animal was lower in the water than before. Finally it dived with a real plunge causing a terrific upheaval (*not* merely sinking).

After its disappearance the track, resembling that of a torpedo, continued in a N.E. direction.

I doubt if any other account so well establishes, not only the monster's very animal reactions to human beings, but also its seal-like nature. The propeller action at the rear, commented on by others, shows that the rear flippers are its main means of propulsion; the front ones being used largely for stabilising the large body.

In his diary for June 5, 1934, Dom Cyril records the details of yet another shore sighting, the second that year. The incident was not reported in the papers at the time, so we are lucky to have this account.

One recent Sunday morning, at about 6.30 a.m., Margaret Munro, a maid with the Plimleys at Kilchumein Lodge, beside the loch overlooking Borlum Bay, glanced out of the dining room window. About 300 yards away, on the shore of the bay, she saw a large animal, "the largest she had ever seen". She watched the creature, which was not quite clear of the water, through a pair of Mr Plimley's binoculars for 25 minutes. She later described it as having a "giraffe-like neck, and an absurdly small head out of all proportion to the great dark-grey body".

The skin was grey like an elephant's. She could see clearly the two short front flippers or short legs. The animal turned itself this way and that, arching its back into two or more humps. At last lowering its head, it entered the water and swam away.

Being new at her job and anxious to keep it, Miss Munro did not like to wake her employers so early in the morning. Later, when she told them of what she had seen, the Plimleys hurried down to the shore. They found a slight impression in the heavy shingle, into which a small branch had been pressed down.

It might be claimed that this story owes something to Arthur Grant's more sensational report of the monster ashore. But the details are so different that there seems to be no connection at all. No effort was made to publicise this sighting. Dom Cyril knew both the Plimleys and the girl's father, the local miller, and had no doubts about her story. The most interesting point in the report is the flexing back. The animal seems almost to ripple its shape. These changes are not, I think, structural, but merely superficial.

The notion of one, presumably immortal, monster in Loch Ness is absurd. Going on the reports alone, it is clear that there is a whole range of animals in the loch, including at least one old bull. Yet the occasions on which two or more animals have been seen together are remarkably few.

On June 29, 1933, a farmer whose land overlooked Urquhart Bay, had his attention drawn by his labourers to a black hump in the water below them. He was then surprised to see another hump further out in the loch, moving at considerable speed.

Cyril Dieckhoff was able to discover other instances. Miss Fraser of Inveroich House told him, in June 1934, that she had seen two monsters, one smaller than the other, swimming side by side. In 1937 C. B. Farrell, a personal friend of his, told him that the monster had been seen at Foyers, and then, a quarter of an hour later, in Borlum Bay. Either it had a prodigious turn of speed, or these were two different individuals. And in January 1943, another old friend, Sandie Grant, related how he and a Mr Scott, who was then in charge of Inchacardoch House, had seen from there one animal moving down the loch to Corrie's Cave. This vanished, and then another began to disturb the water near the Horse-Shoe, one of the deeper parts of the loch.

Later there were other reports. In 1939, near Brachla, Mr Hunter-Gordan, an Inverness businessman, and an Admiralty civil servant travelling with him, observed two humps moving up the loch, about 300 yards out, on parallel courses several yards apart. Now and again, smooth black humps 4 to 5 feet long broke the surface.

But this did not equal a sighting two years before from a Brachla house. On July 13, 1937, the Stevenson family and four visitors were sitting down to breakfast, when one of the children drew their attention to the loch outside the window. Running to the door they saw, about 300 yards away out in the loch, three monsters swimming past up the loch.

In the centre were two shining black humps, 5 feet long and protruding 2 feet out of the water and on either side was a smaller monster, one of which made a great splashing noise as it disappeared towards the opposite shore. The largest monster and the other smaller one then travelled together in the direction of Urquhart Castle.

If this were the old bull with two cows, we might expect them to be only part of a breeding colony numbering perhaps 15 individuals. That summer of 1937, there was reported an incident which might well indicate the herd was actually breeding.

In May 1937, the Abbot Sir David Hunter-Blair, had tried, with the help of some schoolboys specially invited up from Manchester, to capture the monster, without success. However in June two of his own pupils at the school had a strange experience. Later Dom Cyril Dieckhoff interviewed the two boys, Andrew Smith and Anthony Considine, separately, and found that their stories tallied.

They said they had been out on the lake, amusing themselves in a small boat:

As they looked into the water from the stern of the boat the boys noticed three small creatures swimming away from the stern wash. They were rather like eels except that they had four rudimentary limbs and distinct necks; the boys also

compared them to large lizards. Each was about 3 feet long.
The front limbs were flipper-like and had merely a waving
motion, while the rear limbs were held close to the body and
used for pushing. In colour they were dark grey.

The first thing that comes to mind on reading this story is:
are they babies at all? They might well have been fully grown
otters, though it would be unusual to see three together,
especially in daylight. The distinct neck and the description
of the flippers and their use certainly suggests the animal we
are more used to in larger sizes. Yet much as I would like to
claim these were young monsters, I have to admit that on the
present evidence it is doubtful.

The school seems to have taken their claim quite seriously.
Not only did Dieckhoff take pains over their story, but the
science master went so far as to claim that the boys had seen
"Baby prehistoric monsters". He, too, it seems was keen on
the plesiosaur theory.

This theory seems to have been first raised in *The Northern
Chronicle* on August 9, 1933. The plesiosaur, in England at
least, was a long established explanation of the sea-serpent.
Gould had settled for it in his book about the mystery beast in
1930, and it was perhaps inevitable that it would be applied to
the monster in Loch Ness.

Superficially it has a great deal to recommend it. The plesiosaurs seem to have lived both at sea and in fresh-water
estuaries, so it would not be surprising to find them in a freshwater lake. They had long necks and flippers, as it seemed the
Loch Ness monster had. But they also had tails, which no-one
except Grant thought the monster had, and he was probably
mistaken about that point. Aside from the whole question of
whether such an animal could survive the cold waters of such a
northern lake, there was the more difficult one of whether they
even survived their own proper geological age. Attractive as
it was, the theory was fraught with difficulties, which was why
Gould dropped it in favour of his enlarged newt. Nevertheless,
at one time or another every supporter of the Loch Ness
monster has held this theory. Some, it seems, still do. I think,
though, by the time we are done with all the evidence the theory
will look a little tattered.

The tale of the baby monsters created a small flutter of interest in the monster again. But it was not by any means the most important, or most interesting, event of the period. For in 1936 Malcolm Irvine had obtained another film of the monster.

On Tuesday, September 22, 1936, Malcolm Irvine stationed his assistant opposite Inverfarigiag, while he went 2 miles further down. Both had cine-cameras fitted with telephoto lenses. The conditions were good with only a light swell from the south-west, with a light breeze.

At 3.30 Irvine saw the monster emerge from the Foyers area. He packed hurriedly and sped round the bay at Invermoriston stopping at a point about 2 miles away where he had previously selected a suitable position. He could see the monster with the naked eye, moving swiftly about half a mile away. When everything was ready to film, its line of travel had changed to north-west. Irvine started filming, panning after the animal at the same time. It was difficult. The great magnification of the telephoto lens exaggerated every movement, and he could not keep the panning steady. At least the monster was in the picture, "a unique record of a unique animal".

This film has also been lost, it seems, so once again we have to depend on a contemporary report. The film showed the head and neck parallel with the surface, and rising and falling with the movement of a huge body. The humps were also to be seen rising and falling gently as the flippers moved beneath them. A "rubber-like tail" is clearly seen.

Irvine told a reporter that the monster was still "a biological mystery", which could not be placed in any category at the moment. The film was distributed as part of a newsreel, along with an interview with Margaret Munro who described her land sighting. Eric Foxon, Fellow of the Linnean Society, was also interviewed and asked his opinion after seeing the film. He could not say what the animal was, but "henceforth everyone will be required to admit that there is something in Loch Ness".

At this point the film itself becomes a mystery. As late as 1955, a copy was in the possession of Fr J. A. Carruth at Fort Augustus Abbey. Mrs Whyte was able to obtain some stills from it, one of which she printed in her book. Others she has kindly passed on to me. However, as she explained to me, she does not now set much store by the film, as there is some suspicion of fraud: a mechanical device is said to have been used for some sequences. The stills that do survive certainly show some large object in the water. But what?

On May 28, 1938, yet another film of the monster was taken, this time by a South African, Mr G. E. Taylor of Natal, who was on holiday in Scotland. The monster was lying stationary opposite Foyers, about 200 yards from the northern shore. Mr Taylor noted in his diary at the time:

> Its body was large and rounded, with a tapering down to the neck which dipped under the water, becoming visible about 18 inches away, rising in an arch to about 6 inches above the water before dipping again. Where this arch re-entered the water it had every appearance one would associate with a head. The body showed about one foot above the water. Its colour was very dark.

That was at noon. Mr Taylor drove off, but returned at 12.45 with a friend to find the object was still in sight, but fifty vards nearer. The bright sun now gave it what he called a straw colour. Mr Taylor filmed it again on this occasion.

Maurice Burton, who recovered this film, gives a long analysis of what it shows in his book *The Elusive Monster*. He admits that:

> It cannot be too strongly stressed that the object seen in the film does have a resemblance to an animal . . . Indeed the (second sequence) suggests nothing so much as a light chestnut horse bucking and prancing in the waves with only the back and occasionally parts of the head and neck appearing above the waterline. A real water horse in fact!

Yet he concludes that the "monster" is an unknown inanimate object.

This conclusion is based on a dubious inspection of each frame of the film. A series of drawings showing the variations in the image appear in his book, and very unconvincing they are. The small frame of the film, the tiny image of the monster, and no allowance made for the effect of the film grain, all affect the accuracy of his analysis. Mr Taylor's actual impressions suggest that it was more than likely that he filmed the real monster.

But we cannot really know. I must mention that Dr Burton has refused me any stills from the film. And he has even refused to allow it to be seen by the Loch Ness Investigation Bureau, so they could get another expert opinion on it. A great pity, and most unscientific.

The last exchange of opinion on the Loch Ness monster of any note before the war were two broadcasts from the BBC in 1937. In the first one, E. G. Boulenger, in discussing the problem, was glibly dismissive of both the sea-serpent and the Loch Ness monster. "This humped back giant animal with eyes like motor lamps", he said, "deserves a closer study if only because it is a good example of mass hallucination". Again a scientist is guilty of misrepresenting the trend of the evidence. Again he is mistaken about the nature of mass hallucination: hardly ever were the conditions right for such a deception of the senses.

And, as Rupert Gould replied in a later broadcast, the evidence for both animals was such that mass hallucination just would not do as a complete explanation. For the Loch Ness monster, especially, there was the photographic evidence, to which Irvine's new film had just been added. (A still was used to illustrate Gould's talk when it was published in the *Listener*.) The monster was still being seen – he then quotes his friend Haslefoot – and being similarly described. "No, those who regard the Loch Ness monster – and sea-serpents in general – as an exploded joke cannot have the faintest idea of the overwhelming strength of the evidence for their 'existence'. But as the astronomer Horrocks once said: 'It is easier to teach the ignorant, than those who will not learn'".

The honours here went, I think, to Gould. This debate seems to have inspired the BBC to produce a radio programme about the monster in August 1938, which included the recorded voices of eye-witnesses. It seems to have been most memorable for the simple dignity with which they told of what they had seen, particularly one old man who said the monster "remembered me of an old horse".

1938 was also the year that Captain D. J. Munro suggested that a limited company be set up to investigate the monster on a permanent basis. A series of camera stations along the loch shores would be manned by trained men, sailors, of course, being his own choice. This scheme failed to attract enough support, as he thought £1,500 would be needed. But it drew some very divided letters to the *Times*, where the old arguments about birds and otters were trotted out again, only to be rebutted once more by Rupert Gould.

During all this, the monster was continuing his casual appearances. In October 1936, Mrs Marjory Moir and some friends had an excellent sighting three miles outside Foyers,

Fig. 16. Marjory Moir's sighting.

when they watched the monster for 14 minutes. As in the Taylor film, it was resting on the surface of the water. They thought it was about 30 feet long, though this was difficult to judge, as a slight drizzle was falling on the grey loch.

> There were three humps, the middle one the largest, the one behind the neck the smallest. The neck was long and slender, the head small and without any discernible features. Quite often the head dipped into the water as if the creature were feeding, or perhaps amusing itself.

Then it suddenly raced off across the loch towards Urquhart Bay, with a tremendous wash, turned and came back to the same spot. There it settled down in the water. Mrs Moir lamented that they had no camera to record the fantastic sight.

Writing years later to Mrs Whyte, Marjory Moir recalled that when she was a child, her grandfather who lived by Loch Ness, had warned the children not to play near the water's edge because of the "Water Kelpie".

At Easter 1937, Alastair Erskine-Murray, one of the Edinburgh students who had investigated the site of Arthur Grant's adventure, saw the monster again.

We saw three humps about 800 yards out in the loch (from the road near Invermoriston, where the road is about 50 feet above the shore). They appeared to be solid, and about the size and shape of the hump on a railway engine. After a few minutes they moved up the loch and submerged, and a few minutes later a heavy wash came in on the shore below us.

A quite different monster? These more sharply raised humps, however, do seem to be part of the same animal.

On July 27 that year, an architect and his family had a more crisply described sighting: "Pillar-like neck and small head – held erect – terrific speed – like a motor boat – great commotion – wash like that from a large steamer".

Useful as the reports of visitors are, those of local people are often more interesting, partly because of their greater experience of wild life, partly because they get into spots where the monster comes closer to the shore.

For instance, in June 1937, John MacLean had a remarkable sighting, due mostly to the fact that he could keep still. He was preparing to fish at the mouth of Alltsigh Burn, when the animal appeared less than 20 yards away. First only the head and neck were visible. The neck was over 2 feet long, and about 9 inches thick. The head reminded him of a sheep's with the ears cut off, with a pair of narrow oval eyes to the front. The animal seemed "to be champing away at something", or at least its mouth was opening and closing, and it would throw back its head as if swallowing.

After two minutes it put its head down and the hump and "the tail" came into sight. The animal submerged, and when it surfaced again, it was further away. He saw no limbs or flippers. The skin had the appearance of a well-groomed horse's, smooth, sleek and well-polished, dark in colour fading to a pale straw on the belly. The second time the animal's whole length seemed to be on the surface, and was about 20 feet long. Then it dived suddenly and he didn't see it again.

Curiously, though he realised it was not the seal or otter he had first taken it for, it did not strike him it was the monster. Did he perhaps expect that fabled creature to be some scaley dinosaur, whilst this was all too patently some warm-blooded and not too frightening animal? He was not aware of any fear, only of astonishment. A sketch of what he saw appeared in the *Daily Record* at the time.

Alex Campbell recalls another of his sightings, from the late 1930's, when he saw the head and neck emerge from the loch covered, it seemed, in some entangling substance, which the animal shook off. One cannot help noticing how both the man and the animal arrived at Alltsigh Burn to hunt when the fish were rising. Clearly the animals are creatures of habit. Doubtless Campbell's animal had got itself covered in weeds, grubbing along the bottom.

A few weeks later, the *Liverpool Echo* reported that two catholic priests from that city, Fr George Grime and Fr Malcolm MacKinnon, while rowing on the lake, saw a hump speeding through the water. The *Daily Mail* reported on August 18, 1941, that "the loch Ness monster was out again". It had surfaced near Glendoe Pier, showing "a long snakey neck and fifteen to eighteen feet of body shaped like an upturned boat". It was in view of a large crowd for ten minutes, during which time it was said to have covered seven miles, speeding around so fast that it threw up spray for several feet.

For most of the war years, the monster was not reported at all, though there were several sightings. One of these was made by Cyril Dieckhoff's friend, Mr C. B. Farrell, who was then a member of the Royal Observer Corps, watching for enemy bombers. It was just after five in the morning when he saw the animal, only 250 yards away. Through his binoculars (ironically a pair made by Zeiss) he could see its every movement clearly. The eyes seemed very prominent to him. The graceful neck was about 4 feet long, and down the back of it was a curious "fin". It appeared to be feeding, as it would slowly put its head underwater, then quickly raise it, vigourously shaking its head. Finally it disappeared, without any splash, by just submerging without a ripple. (This habit of shaking the head can also be seen in swans, as they feed along the weedy bottoms).

Farrell had been affected by his new duties, as he describes the animal's colour as "dark olive and signet brown on the flanks": had the monster camouflaged itself against bombers? Certainly the Italians, eager for any victory, claimed one of their aircraft had bombed and killed it. But the monster managed to survive such hazards of war, emerging once more in the balmy days of peace.

In August 1946, while taking their first holiday for many years, the Atkinsons had a puncture near Dores. While Mrs Atkinson was admiring the lake, there was an upheaval in the water near the edge of the shore, and up came a long swan-like neck with a small head, followed by an elephant-grey body with two humps. She called her husband and they watched in astonishment until it disappeared underneath the water. Writing of this over ten years later, she said "God knows what else the Loch holds. The very thought of it makes me turn cold".

The next year, Arthur Grant and his wife saw the monster's one hump, this time in the water. In April the Town Clerk of Inverness, Mr J. W. MacKillop and his son saw the monster's neck and a large wake. It was not an extraordinary sighting, but at the next meeting of the County Council, standing orders were suspended so he could give an account of his experience.

In December 1948, Mrs Russell Ellice and her two children were driving into Inverness, when near Brachla they saw a head and long neck standing up in the water, and though the loch was like a mill-pond, there was a considerable commotion behind it. "It was really a huge creature and we were all thrilled beyond words," said Mrs Ellice. "Until then I had never really believed in its existence".

The difficulty was, neither did many other people. Reports could appear in the press, sightings could continue, but no-one would really believe in the monster's existence, until some more systematic record were attempted.

Dom Cyril Dieckhoff died in 1950, his book on the monster still unwritten. The monster's other champions were also dead, Oudemans in 1943, Rupert Gould in 1948. Luckily there were others already continuing where they had left off. Mrs Whyte was starting to collect eye-witness accounts, and Fr J. A. Carruth published a little booklet on the monster for the benefit of tourists. In August 1950 the *Scotsman* urged that an investigation be undertaken, and Dr Maurice Burton reviewing the evidence in the *Illustrated London News* felt that there was something in Loch Ness "which cannot be explained".

More importantly, in 1951 another photograph was taken of the monster. On July 14, Lachlan Stuart went out at 6.30 a.m. to milk his cows. He noticed an object out on the loch opposite Whitefield, ran back to the house for his camera, calling on a friend who was staying with the family to follow him. Running down to the shore, they saw three triangular humps moving in a line towards the shore. As the humps passed by about fifty yards from them, Lachlan Stuart took one photograph. A few moments later a head and neck appeared, which was raised and lowered several times. Because of a defect in his camera, he was not able to photograph this. The men retreated into the trees along the shore as the animal came closer in shore, but it soon swam away and disappeared 300 yards off shore.

The photograph is slightly fuzzy, but considering the early hour at which it was taken, the quality is quite good. The three humps are clearly those described by other witnesses, however peculiar they may seem as part of an animal. Mr Stuart and his friend estimated the neck and the head to be 6 feet long, and the length of the humps to be 5 feet at the water, with a space of 8 feet between them. 15 to 20 feet behind they could see what they thought was the movement of a tail. This works out at roughly 42 feet long, which seems an excessive length. The humps were blackish without any features to show it was indeed an animal.

Mr Stuart was certain it was an animal, but one unlike any other he knew of. When pressed, he said it was like "well, perhaps a prehistoric monster. A lot of them never existed. Just fairy stories. Or that's what I used to think".

Eric Palmer, curator of the museum of natural history at Glasgow University, was asked what the animal might be. "The representation in the picture might be three abnormal sized seals chasing and playing with each other, but this seems unlikely". It does indeed. But Mr Palmer assumed the photograph showed some animal, a change from the opinions of scientists on earlier photographs. In this case, it is an opinion not everyone might agree with, for this remains an unlikely picture of a live animal.

A booklet on scientific research, issued by the British Museum in 1954, seems to have the Stuart picture in mind when discussing the evidence for the Loch Ness monster.

The most famous case of the unsubmitted specimen is that of the Loch Ness monster, in which the ingenuity of the suggestions as to the nature of the animal concerned has been equalled only by the powers of imagination of some observers.

The only scientific evidence the writer could point to was an "experiment" made with a theodolite by Mr Andrew MacFee (which was reported in the Glasgow *Sunday Post* on July 27, 1952). What he took at first to be humps when observed with the naked eye, were found to be shadows when examined with the aid of the theodolite. "The phenomenon", the writer concludes sententiously, "would therefore be one of waves and water-currents". And from this we are to conclude, it seems, that the humps in the Stuart picture are also shadows. I suppose this effort was the only "scientific evidence" they choose to recognise because of its result.

Incidentally, the monster is by no means the only unsubmitted specimen, as they call it. That distinction could equally well belong to any one of the forty-odd animals described by Bernard Heuvelmans in *On the Track of Unknown Animals*. He argues that sometimes we have to be content with reports only, for specimens cannot be obtained. As evidence, Mr MacFee's observations are no better or no worse than countless other reports of the monster, a few of which have been quoted, which leave little doubt that the monster is something more than mere shadows.

This elegant piece of dissimulation was dismissed by Maurice Burton, then on the staff of the Museum.

Loch Ness must indeed be a remarkable stretch of water if shadows upon its surface can move at great speed, down one side of the loch, cross over, and move up the other side, can disappear in a flurry of foam, can cause a strong wash on the shore and can produce, on at least half-a-dozen photographic negatives, an appearance of a solid body.

Seeing that scientists were generally hostile to the monster, it is not surprising that many people never mention their experiences. The following incident would be unknown but for Mrs Whyte.

In August 1952, Mrs Greta Finlay and her son were camping in a caravan on the south shore of the loch, half a mile west of Aldourie Castle. On August 20, about noon, her attention was caught by splashing on the loch shore. Walking around the caravan, she was surprised to see, less than 20 yards away, one of the smaller monsters. As she told Mrs Whyte:

I was so taken up with the strange appearance of the head and neck that I did not examine the rest of the animal at all closely. There were two or three humps and the total length visible would be about 15 feet.

The neck was held erect, and where it met the water it enlarged to join a bulky body. The head and neck together were 2–2½ feet in length, the head alone being about 6 inches

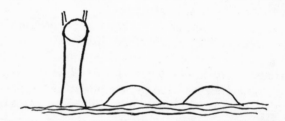

Fig. 17. Harry Finlay's version of the head and neck.

long and of about the same width as the neck. What astonished me, apart from the hideous appearance of the head, was that there were two six-inch-long projections from it, each with a blob on the end. The skin looked black and shiny and reminded me of a snail more than anything.

A drawing of the animal was made from memory by her son, Harry Finlay, a few days later. This is one of three references to "horns" on the head of the monster. Mrs Finlay had no doubts about them: as she asked Mrs Whyte "could it have been an enormous snail?" The Spicers, remember, had also thought the monster they saw was reminiscent of a snail.

There were exceptions to the general reticence of witnesses, such as David Slorach, who described his sighting at great length in an article for *Harper's Magazine* in 1957. Perhaps

because it was published in America, this interesting account
has not been noticed before.

Early in 1954, Mr Slorach was travelling on business in
Scotland. On February 4, having an appointment in Inverness
at 10 o'clock, he had set out early from Fort William. Beyond
Fort Augustus, he put on speed.

Here the road curves sharply, rises and falls, so I had little
chance to admire the view of Loch Ness, now on my right;
but in occasional side glances, I observed that the surface
of the Loch was smooth and that I could see the far shore
quite clearly. Then ahead of me, at a considerable distance,
I noticed an odd object in the water. It was about 400 yards
from the shore, and from where I was it looked like a rounded
body on stilts, as if two storks were standing on a rock in the
water.

The shape struck me as odd, and I kept glancing at it. As
I came closer, the form changed its appearance. Now it
looked like a tree trunk sticking up about three feet out of
the water and surmounted by a boss or enlarged piece. Its
shape now reminded me of a comic ornament popular at one
time – a china cat with a long neck. The thing ahead of me
looked exactly like the neck and head part. One black floppy
"ear" fell over where the eye might be and four black streaks
ran down the "neck". It was these I had previously mistaken
for the legs of storks. The rest of the object was a curious
dead white colour.

A few moments later I threw another glance in the direction
of this amusing looking object and noticed that some yards
nearer to me lay a second dark object like a barrel or buoy.
By now, I was nearly abreast of both objects, and at the speed
I was travelling I could give them only a hasty look. Suddenly
out of the corner of my eye, I caught a glimpse of movement,
and checked my speed to look again. The object in front and
the barrel-shaped object were travelling through the water
at great speed, throwing up a huge wave behind. I slowed to
around 35 mph, but the object raced ahead and was soon
out of sight behind a clump of trees.

When he drove past the trees there was nothing in sight. It

occurred to him that the object might have been towed by a boat which he had not noticed, but he neither saw or heard one. Now there was nothing in sight and everything was quiet. Only when he reached Castle Urquhart, did he realise that the object he had seen must have been the famous Loch Ness monster. Some people, expecting something really monstrous, are surprised at how ordinary the animal looks. On the back seat of the car was a loaded camera: another opportunity had been missed. But other kinds of evidence were now available.

Towards the end of December 1954, the Peterhead drifter *Rival III*, passing down Loch Ness at midday, obtained an echo-sounding of a large object at a depth of 480 feet. The recorded graph was examined by technicians from Kelvin and Hughes, who said it was not a shoal of fish, but seemed to be one solid object of large size.

Echo-soundings indicate merely the presence, size and density of an object under water. It needs skill and experience to read the soundings, which do not show the shape of the object. Even now, however, one sees it claimed that asdic has shown the monster – because of the odd shape of the recording – to have a large bulbous head and eight legs, a sort of underwater scorpion. Echo-sounding has been tried since, but with disputable success. (In 1958 a BBC crew obtained another anomalous reading, showing the presence in the loch of a large body.)

On July 29, 1955, Mr P. A. MacNab parked on the road above Urquhart Castle. He was just about to photograph that picturesque ruin, when he noticed a "bulging" in the water and a widening eddy. He fitted a telephoto lens to his camera and photographed "a long dark moving body passing from left to right up the loch under the shadow of the castle.

As the photograph shows the tower of Urquhart Castle, which is exactly 50 feet high, some have calculated that the monster is at least 60 feet long. The photograph shows two humps, the front one much the larger, but what no-one has observed is that when examined carefully the picture shows that there are two quite distinct wakes. This is not one immense monster at all, but clear photographic evidence for the existence of at least two smaller monsters, one about 25 feet long, the other about 15, perhaps a bull and his cow, or a cow and her calf. The importance of this evidence cannot be underestimated: we know for a fact that there are *two* monsters.

Since Sir Edward Mountain's investigation in 1934, there had been no intensive research done on the Loch Ness monster. The dismissive attitude of the Scottish Folklore Society, that the monster was only believed in by a few cranks, was the common one. There was no solid body of evidence to counter it. What reports there had been since Rupert Gould's book were all buried in the backfiles of newspapers. But in 1949 Mrs Constance Whyte began to collect some of these, and other accounts from eyewitnesses living around the loch, to write a short article on the monster. An educated woman with an interest in Scottish history, she is married to the then manager of the Caledonian Canal, and thus she was intimately concerned with Loch Ness, which is part of that waterway. In 1951 she published an expanded version of her article as a pamphlet. Maurice Burton, reviewing it in the *Illustrated London News*, felt that Mrs Whyte made a case for the monster which deserved further investigation. At this time, he seems to have been the only British scientist to support the monster.

Mrs Whyte industriously gathered more information on the monster, and in 1957 she published her book *More Than a Legend*. She seems to half-accept the theory that the monster might be a plesiosaur. This was not a new suggestion, and there are many who think it an unlikely one. Zoologists do not believe that plesiosaurs could have survived from the Mezozoic, and palaeontologists point out that the most recent reconstructions of the plesiosaurs do not fit the descriptions of the monster. For one thing, they now think that the plesiosaurs rode higher in the water, with more body exposed than is usual for the Loch Ness animal. Anyhow, could a reptile survive the cold water conditions of Loch Ness?

Mrs Whyte's book stimulated several lines of research. Burton thought her case was "as convincing as we could wish for in a phenomenon which has never really been investigated". At Oxford University, Denys Tucker lectured his students on the problem of Loch Ness, which he suggested was well worth the eager attention of young zoologists. On March 22, 1959, Tucker himself saw a large hump travelling across flat calm water between Inchnacardoch and Gledoe, achieving something Gould, Burton and Whyte never did. He is convinced it was an unknown animal, probably a plesiosaur.

Dr Tucker was hoping to stimulate field research. But during the winter of 1959, Tim Dinsdale took an analytical approach to the problem. He broke down the details of the 100 or so reports in *More Than a Legend*, and constructed from them a statistical picture of the monster: small head, long neck, large body with varying humps, four flippers, and short rounded tail. In his opinion this outline confirmed the theory that the monster was a plesiosaur. The crucial point in this analysis was his point about the tail. As he admits this is mentioned in only 11 per cent of the reports, and then only in very general terms. The main evidence for its existence is again Arthur Grant's. Certainly movement and splashing are seen behind the monster, but it cannot be assumed this is caused by a tail, as it could just as well be caused by flippers (as I believe).

But Dinsdale was eager for more than a statistical picture of the monster. Early in 1960, he went up to Loch Ness hoping to film the monster with a 16 mm camera he had borrowed from Maurice Burton. By chance on his last day, April 23. he did obtain a few feet of film. He had positioned himself on the

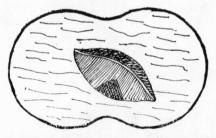

Fig. 18. What Tim Dinsdale saw before filming.

hillside above Foyers, and filmed the single hump crossing the Loch directly away from Foyers. Then it turned aside to the right, then left and moved parallel to the opposite shore. Only a single hump was visible, reddish brown in colour, "with a back like an under-fed horse".

The film was shown on the television programme *Panorama*,

where it was seen by many millions of viewers, creating a great sensation. In his book, published later that year, Dinsdale describes both his research and adventures, as well as his theory. All this was naturally a further stimulus to investigators.

Yet what did the film show? Dr Burton is convinced (having moved to the opposition camp) that it shows a boat moving across the loch; the protuberances being "a row of sou-westers" worn by several men sitting in line from stem to stern in a 15-foot dingy – no uncommon sight on Loch Ness". This theory bears no real relation to the size and shape of the object in the film. More recently he has claimed it was a heavily-laden red motor boat belonging to a Foyers man named Jack Forbes. All this is very interesting, and how convincing the production of a personal name makes it sound. Nevertheless, it is all fantasy on Dr Burton's part.

Forseeing just such a critical interpretation, Dinsdale had purposely filmed a motor-boat following the same course as the monster a short while later. Even to the naked eye, the two objects were very different and the motor-boat could clearly be seen for what it was on the television screen. Dinsdale could, with satisfaction, claim that his film was "the first scientifically valuable piece of evidence ever obtained on film of this phenomenon". We shall shortly see what a more rigorous analysis was to make of the object on the film.

1960 was a year of great activity around Loch Ness. Early that year the monster was seen ashore once more, by a man who had dedicated the last years of his life to trying to identify the monster. His name was Torquil MacLeod. On February 28, 1960 he was driving to Fort Augustus. Two miles outside Ivermoriston his attention was caught by something on the far side of the loch.

Upon turning my glasses on the moving object, I saw a large grey and black mass (I am inclined to think the skin was wet and dry in patches) and at the front there was what looked like an outsize in elephant trunks. Paddles were visible on both sides, but only at what I presumed to be the rear end, and it was this end (remote from the "trunk"), which tapered off into the water. The animal was on a steep slope, and taking the backbone as an approximate straight line, was inclined

Fig. 19. Torquil MacLeod's animal ashore.

about 15–20 degrees out of my line of sight: the "trunk" being at the top and to the left, and the tail at the bottom, in the water, to the right.

He was able to fix both his own position and that of the monster very accurately by means of a small stream marked on the map.

For about 8 or 9 minutes the animal remained quite still, but for its "trunk" (I assume neck, although I could not recognise a head as such) which occasionally moved from side to side with a slight up and down motion – just like a snake about to strike; but quite slowly.

It seemed to be scanning the shores. Then it lurched to the left, swinging round its neck, then flopping off the edge and disappearing into the deep water. As the animal turned he glimpsed a large squarish flipper, forward of the large pair. The animal's tail was never out the water, so he never saw that part of it; yet in a drawing which he later supplied to Tim Dinsdale, he drew in the by now traditional long sturdy tail.

His powerful binoculars were graduated, and in later consulting the almanac, he estimated that the animal was about 45 feet long at least, and allowing for the angle it was seen at, perhaps 50 feet. An enormous animal certainly, and here the figures are perhaps a little more acceptable than those estimated by Lachlan Stuart, though it is not clear if the length of the assumed "tail" was added in.

There was hardly a time during the summer months of 1960 when someone was not attempting to photograph the monster (They were not, however, encouraged to do so by MacLeod's story, as it was not published for a year.) There were two expeditions of importance: a group led by Maurice Burton, and a party of students from Oxford and Cambridge.

Their arrival at the loch was preceded by the publication of an extraordinary photograph, which has caused much discussion. This had been taken on May 27 by Peter O'Connor, a member of a party from the Northern Naturalists Association which was camping on the shores of Loch Ness. He had come out of his tent after 6 in the morning to find the monster riding high in the water near the shore. Watched by a friend he waded out into the water and took a flashlight photograph from within 25 yards of the animal. That was his story anyway, as told to the *Weekly Scotsman* in June.

The paper described the photograph as "the clearest to date of Nessie," and at the time it got quite wide publicity in the press generally. Tim Dinsdale gave it a prominent place among the illustrations in his first book—it even appeared in *Reader's Digest*. It seemed that it was to become a classic image like Wilson's photograph of 1934. But it did little to solve the secret of the Loch because the photograph itself became something of a mystery. The object shown was one mystery; how the picture was taken became another.

The picture shows a low curving back, about 16 feet long according to O'Connor's own estimate, which was about $2\frac{1}{2}$ feet high. At the far end, after a $3\frac{1}{2}$ foot gap of clear water, there rose a neck about 3 feet long and a foot round. The head at the end seemed to be about the same width as the back of the neck and was not readily distinguished. The over-all colour was dark grey. All these details seem consistent with what we already know.

But were they too consistent? Maurice Burton has alleged in print that the photograph is a hoax, that when he visited the site a short time afterwards he found a long pole of wood that might have done for the "neck" and a large polythene bag, which, weighted with stones and inflated with air, would have made the "body". This accusation has not been answered (so far as I know) by Peter O'Connor, and the Loch Ness Investigation no longer use this picture in their publicity. Nevertheless Dr Burton would have to produce evidence for the existence of that all too easily found polythene bag before I would believe *him*.

O'Connor's photograph resembles only one other Loch Ness picture, that anonymous one taken in August 1934 at Castle Urquhart. The shape of the body and the neck are almost the same in both, leaving me with little doubt that they are pictures of the same object. In neither is the head of the animal readily made out, as it is in Wilson's profile shot, but then many witnesses have commented on how the head seems little wider than the neck in some individual monsters.

The Burton team were at Loch Ness only for five days, from June 19 to June 27. As Dr Burton had only the assistance of his sons and his daughter Jane, the animal photographer, they restricted themselves to keeping a watch from the area around the mouth of the Foyers river. They had two sightings of an inconclusive nature. They tried to tempt the monster to the surface with a rubby-dubby bag, a sack filled with offal and fish oil, but had no success. One of the sightings was of a single hump which emerged in a patch of foam over a mile away and was impossible to photograph. Dr Burton did not see this himself. However on June 22, he and his son saw a pattern of ripples approaching them about half a mile away. As these varied from side to side, it struck him that this might be caused by a long neck being thrust from side to side. The movement then changed direction, and a dark object about 2 feet long appeared, leaving a series of concentric ripples with about fifteen feet between them. For a moment, Burton's attention was distracted, and he missed the final moment before the object disappeared, but his son said the black object gave way to 2 dark humps, the front one about a foot long, the second about 2 feet with one foot of water between.

This may not seem much of a sighting, but it is of importance. Later, Dr Burton was to write that this wake represented something very unusual. It was not an otter, but some animal swimming at a faster rate, yet merely cruising. These ripples, on mirror calm water, were not however noticed by others on the shore near them, which may explain why the monster is not so often reported. Mere ripples are not associated with it. (The pattern of ripple rings which he saw also appear in the Wilson picture, though in Burton's case the animal merely touched the surface with its head rather than rising right out of it.)

The students were luckier: they had two significant sightings. The first was on July 4. The expedition members were on Tor Point near Dores, when the monster surfaced on the opposite side of the loch. It was too far away for them to photograph, and no boat was on hand to put out after it. So for two hours they could only watch and sketch the monster from a distance. On July 10, Mr Bruce Ing observed a single hump, 5 to 10 feet long, rising two feet out of the water, for about 20 seconds, moving across the wind with a small creamy wake.

Dr Burton writing in the *New Scientist* (September 22, 1960), produced his new theory of vegetable mats to explain 95 per cent of the evidence. Yet there still remained those obstinate accounts of a long neck and head seen at close quarters, which "cannot readily be dismissed as motor-boats, vegetable mats or even otters".

In his book *The Elusive Monster* published soon after, Burton described his researches. This book was the culmination of nearly 30 years of interest in the monster, and as a case study Dr Burton is almost as interesting as the animal itself. In December 1933 he suggested to a reporter that the monster might well be a walrus, though if Gray's photo were a real one "it showed some animal unknown to science". Over the years he kept an open mind on the subject, as was appropriate for a scientist. In the early fifties he suggested the novel theory that the monster might well be a giant eel (some of whose larvae had in fact been discovered in the Atlantic), and that the humps were caused by it swimming on its side. (Not that this would explain the long neck). Then he thought it might be merely reports of otters. Mrs Whyte's book converted him to the idea that it might be a plesiosaur, a notion he maintained till 1959. Then he became persuaded that floating mats of vegetable matter was the real explanation.

This chief theory is maintained with some force in the book.

He reproduces there a photograph taken at Loch Lomond in 1937 which does indeed seem to show how like a monster a load of rubbish can be.

Yet the theory has never really been a satisfactory one; like so many of his earlier ideas, it explains too little. Dr Burton continues to hold it with complacent obstinacy. On my visits to Loch Ness I have made a point of examining the beaches. Unlike many of the lakes I know in Ireland, there was hardly any vegetation around the shore of the loch. There were hardly any twigs, reeds or sticks on the water-line. Nor were there, as far as I could see, any large clumps of rubbish that might have been stranded vegetable mats. Sources for masses of vegetable matter are limited to the swamps. The Water Bailiff at Fort Augustus, Alex Campbell, who began it all in 1933, recalls seeing such a mat only twice in all the years he has known the loch. And those he easily distinguished from the animal he called the monster.

Actually months before his book appeared, Dr Burton's theory had been discussed at length by Peter Baker and others in the *New Scientist* (November 24, 1960), and, though he does not mention the inconvenient fact, had been shown to be untenable. The only likely source where such mats could form would be in the peaty sediment on the bed of the loch. It is unlikely that such mats, if formed, would reach the surface, for they would be blown apart by their own gases expanding on the way up. Even if a rare one did reach the surface, it would not be capable of the sharp directional movements described by witnesses.

One has only to read one or two of the more recent reports to realise that the monster is something more than a gas bag of rubbish. For instance, Mrs Stanley Hill of Inverness, was one of a group of 14 people who saw the monster on August 11, 1961, from the lake-side hotel *The Clansman*.

It was fine day and the loch was quite calm. When we saw the monster it was just quietly loping along through the water 25 yards from the shore, which made it 70 yards from us. We saw three humps each about 6 feet long, and twice we saw its two near-side flippers come out of the water in a paddling motion. We didn't see any head or neck, but I could make out the shadow of a submerged part of the body about two feet deep in the water. It was going as fast as a rowing boat going a good pace, but very leisurely with no fuss or wash at all. The humps were very dark charcoal grey in colour and rose about two feet above the waterline. I am sure they were solid humps like a camel's and not undulations. We watched it for five minutes and then it submerged.

And on May 11, 1962, Mrs Christie saw the monster from the window of a neighbouring cottage at Alltsaigh. "The weather was nice and clear and the loch flat calm. Suddenly I noticed a big commotion in the water – a tremendous lot of foaming and spray and the monster in the middle of it. The animal was about 160 yards away, and about 60 yards from the shore. It had an egg-shaped head on a neck 4 to 5 feet long.

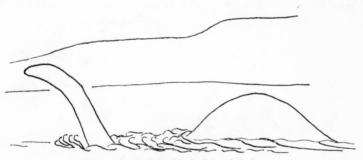

Fig. 20. Edith Christie's sighting.

Six feet behind the neck was a patch of disturbed water, then one hump, 'greenish-black", about 2 feet long. The monster was moving north up the loch parallel to the shore, 'at the speed of a fast motor-boat', with 'a terrific bounding motion'", which Mrs Christie demonstrated to a reporter as an exaggerated breast-stroke. Just such a bounding motion is visible in the Dinsdale film of the monster as well.

No: vegetable mats won't do. "Hence", as Peter Baker concluded his *New Scientist* article "it seems that some other explanation is required and on the present evidence an animal, of an unusual kind, seems most likely". For many people that unusual animal still remained a plesiosaur. Only more intensive investigations would show what it really was. And eventually such an investigation was undertaken.

4

The Loch Ness Enigma—
Under Survey

They sought it with thimbles, they sought it with care;
 They pursued it with forks and hope;
They threatened its life with a railway share;
 They charmed it with smiles and soap.
                    Lewis Carroll: *The Hunting of the Snark*

WHAT HAD BEEN lacking in the efforts to investigate the enigma of Loch Ness was some central organisation. Early in 1962 David James, a member of Parliament, Mrs Whyte, Peter Scott and Richard Fitter, then the nature correspondent of the *Observer*, formed a company called *The Loch Ness Phenomena Investigation Bureau*, which was to sponsor exploration of the loch on a continuing basis. Their work is voluntary, and any profits will eventually go to the World Wildlife Fund. Captain Munro's abortive scheme of 1938 had come to life again. The Bureau is gathering an archive of evidence; reports, tapes, films and photographs. "We claim no proprietary rights in Nessie", David James announced. "If any individual or group wishes to pursue an independent line of research, all information available to us is at their disposal". The Loch Ness Investigation is now dedicated to identifying once and for all that "unusual animal" in Loch Ness.

During the summer of 1962, from June through August, the *Observer* supported the work of two groups on the loch. One was an expedition led by H. G. Hasler, the founder of the Transatlantic Race. He brought his junk-rigged *Jester* to Loch Ness, and with the aid of a party of young volunteers began a series of systematic sweeps around the loch under sail. He thought a silent sailing boat ought to have a better chance than a power boat of coming up on the shy monster unawares – just as Thor Heyerdhal on the *Kon Tiki* saw animals which never approached ships. The boats were fitted with underwater microphones to pick up any underwater sounds, such as animals using echolocating "sonar" might make.

Some success was had by the group. They heard a clear, irregular tapping on three occasions over the low frequency hydrophones, while sailing down the loch. But they did not observe any animal. On June 28, Hasler wrote in his diary that he was "concerned at the total lack of results after nearly four weeks work".

But the next day, June 29, they saw some humps and eddies near the south shore opposite Castle Urquhart, which they associated with a strong clicking noise like a typewriter coming in on the high frequency hydrophones. Also there was a small disturbance in the water 20 yards behind the boat, which was followed by the appearance of two separate disturbances about 8 or 10 feet apart.

Later in the day, at the mouth of Urquhart Bay, three expedition members saw, at a distance of 50 feet, "two small rotating eddies 8 to 10 feet apart", shortly followed by a smaller one forming a triangle with the others and a similar distance away. A very dark hump then appeared in the place of each eddy, round in shape and oval in plan. These were 2 to 3 inches high, 6 inches long and three inches wide. Twice that day eddies and humps were seen, but further away from the boat. Altogether a busy day on Loch Ness. "These appearances", Colonel Hasler wrote in the *Observer* (August 19, 1962), "would suggest the presence of a large animal swimming or floating lazily just below the surface, and the small black humps were the extreme upper parts of it".

This cruising behaviour is similar to that which Burton observed, and is probably associated with the animal's hunting habits. But the recordings of underwater sounds associated with the appearance of the monster does not seem to have caused much comment. It may be most important, however. Sonar is used by only one group of aquatic animals, all of which are mammals, like dolphins, whales and seals. These sounds help them to locate each other and their prey. The fact that such sounds have been recorded at Loch Ness, where there are

no seals, would seem to indicate the presence of some other
echo-locating mammal. Yet the fact that an animal producing
such sounds *must* be a mammal was not even mentioned let
alone emphasised by Colonel Hasler.

At the end of June, a university expedition returning to Loch
Ness for a second year under the leadership of Peter Baker
and Mark Westwood, took over from Hasler. They now had
four motor-boats, which were also fitted with asdic with which
they intended to sweep the loch from end to end. Any large
creature would have to pass through their screen at some time:
they hoped.

The University group searched the loch for 480 hours. During
that time they had only three unexplained sightings. On two
occasions "a pole-like object" rose two or three feet out of the
water. The third time a light brown hump four feet long was
seen near Achanhannet. They examined this through 7×50
binoculars: it was similar to the one seen in 1960. These
sightings, they felt, indicated the presence of a large, unusual
animal in the loch.

Six sweeps with the asdic were completed. During these only
one echo of an object bigger than any fish known to be in the
loch was obtained, but this was of particular interest as it was
obtained just before a pole-like object surface in the same area
of the loch.

After a few days the asdic was transferred to a silent sailing
boat. Two strong "monster" echoes were recorded: one off
Foyers, the other in Castle Urquhart Bay – both places from
which sightings have often come, and which the animals
seem to hunt through fairly regularly. These may only have
been a large group of salmon, or they may have been one large
animal.

An opportunity seems to have been lost here to combine the
asdic sweeps with underwater surveillance by hydrophones.
The tapping sounds might have turned out to be associated
with the large echo-located object.

Besides work with the echo-sounder, the expedition also
took samples of the water in the loch and of mud from the
bottom. They discovered that the almost flat bottom was
composed of a layer of dark green diatamaceous mud, three
feet thick and in a remarkable state of fluidity. The water at the

bottom was fresh, and not salt, as had been suggested. (This work was done by a group under Dr R. Murray from Birmingham University.)

Work was also done to investigate phenomena that might be mistaken for a monster. Wake effects and birds were found to be the main causes of deception. Wakes from passing boats (there is a steady traffic of fishing boats through the loch) would persist for half an hour after the boat had gone by. The rise and fall of the waves could give the impression of two or more large humps to the naked eye. These would not, however, survive telescopic scrutiny – as Andrew McFee had found with his theodolite. Birds swimming in line, or taking off across the water, could also give the impression of a series of humps, or a long neck, and left a much larger wake than had been expected.

But Baker and Westwood were careful to point out that not all reports of the monster were so easily explained.

During the whole of the Cambridge expeditions's 480 hours vigil, phenomena which might be mistaken for monsters were observed on 16 occasions. Eight of them were wake effects; six were caused by birds, one was an otter and one almost certainly a large salmon. No large fast-moving objects were seen, and only wake effects compared in size with the huge manifestations of the 1930's.

Summing up their two years of work on the loch, they wrote:

We cannot say with conviction that the Loch Ness monster does not exist. Indeed, the small pieces of evidence we have all suggest that there is an unusual animal in the loch. However, we consider that the "monster" is much smaller than many people have claimed, and that the huge humps are wake effects.

Basing their conclusions on eye-witness accounts and reports of the monster seen closely, they thought it was at least 10 feet long – a cautious estimate – and was extremely elusive. With that we can easily agree; but not that the humps are wake effects. Possibly some of the large humps reported are the wake effects of trawlers and other boats passing through the loch. (Some of the photographs taken by the Mountain expedition look suspiciously like wakes.) But Lachlan's Stuart's photograph, and the Dinsdale film, show humps similar to those often described. However, there is little doubt that the monster is closer to 20 feet than the 50 or 60 feet that some have claimed for it.

Baker and Westwood were also impressed by the rarity of sightings of the monster. A well-organised expedition, it seemed, had as much chance of seeing the monster "as a tourist driving from Inverness to Fort Augustus on the A82 has". This being so, there was no point in being disappointed in the seemingly meagre results of these expeditions. Though they ended on a note of confirmation that was cryptic, these investigations were an indication of a changed attitude. The Loch Ness monster is no longer the silly season joke it once was, but a serious problem receiving careful investigation.

During October 1962, David James led a large party to the loch. With the idea that the monster was nocturnal, they patrolled the loch by night in boats mounted with searchlights which were played over the surface to attract the monster. And twice they picked out unusual objects momentarily. On the night of the 19th, Michael Spear caught in the beam "a finger-like object 6 to 8 feet out of the water".

On another night they picked up a dome-shaped object, which was filmed. This object was seen twice again by day. A long dark shape was seen on October 19, and a similar on the 25th, for a longer time but at a greater distance. David James later described what what happened in the *Observer* (May 17, 1964):

> After a week we had to cannibalise one searchlight to keep the other one going and thus on the afternoon of October 19, 1962, we had not only three watchers on Temple Pier in Urquhart Bay, but also five people engaged in searchlight repairs.
>
> The afternoon was flat calm and at first it was only the watchers who became aware of the sudden activity of the red salmon and sea-trout congregated in the Bay to catch the first spate up the rivers. Gradually, however, the mechanics downed tools and went to the end of the jetty as the aimless

jumping of the fish turned into a concerted rout with everything "scuttering" out into the middle of the loch.

Eight of us saw a length of back six to eight feet long break
the surface about 200 yards away and cruise slowly after the
fish. We shot about 50 feet of film and eye-witness statements
were taken from all concerned that evening.

Here again a familiar pattern repeats itself: the monster on
the prowl for food, cruising the bays where the fish are gathered.
The film of the object "feathering" through the water 200 yards
away was taken by John Luff. He had never seen anything like
it during his naval service and if he had would have altered
course rapidly. He estimated it was 10 feet long. This film was
subsequently analysed by experts at the Joint Air Reconnaissance Centre (JARIC), who reported that "It is not a wave
effect, but has some solidity, is dark in tone and glistens . . .".

This evidence was placed before an impartial independent
panel, and their conclusions were presented on a special television programme on February 2, 1963. The panel of four, who
were scientists and naturalists, were sufficiently impressed with
the evidence to conclude their report:

We find that there is some unidentified animate object in
Loch Ness which, if it be an animal, reptile or mollusc of any
known order, is of such a size as to be worthy of careful
scientific examination and identification. If it is not of a
known order it is scientifically desirable to investigate it also
on that ground.

Encouraged by this cautious approval, the Loch Ness
Investigation Bureau mounted an even more elaborate expedition during June 1963, with volunteers manning ten stations
overlooking most of the loch. Experiments were made with
blasting charges to recreate the conditions during 1933–34,
when the new road was being built. Whether because of this
or not, there were over 40 recorded sightings that summer to
add to the Bureau's archives.

The expedition itself, however, only had four brief sightings
and two longer ones at great distance. These last ones were
recorded on film. One was a hump, two or three feet high,

The Loch Ness monster of legend, according to a contemporary postcard

Loch Ness at the turn of the century—the steamer is the one Alexander MacDonald saw the monster from in 1889

Daily Recor

The first real photograph of the monster, taken by
Hugh Gray in November 1933

Still from Malcolm Irvine's film of the monster, December 1933

From Irvine's second film, November 1936

(a) first sequence

(b) second sequence

Dinsdale's film: the black hump starting to move across the lake

The very different wake configuration made by the motor boat filmed a little later

Photograph taken by Mountain Expedition: spray rising over a hump?

Another Mountain photograph: the monster or merely a wave?

"Steep shored mountain lakes"—the example of Lago Lacar, Argentina,
is typical of the lakes inhabited by monsters

Loch Shiel, another monster-haunted lake, where animals have come ashore (the tower is a memorial to the ill-fated rebellion of 1745)

"The Ghost of the Lough Bray monster": windrows photographed by the author shortly after a monster was reported there

The Beasts of Nodens—long-necks from a Roman mosaic at Lydney Park made about the second century A.D.

Tiamat, the monster of the Babylonian epic from a cylinder seal

British Muse

forging slowly through the water at a range of one mile, under difficult conditions for photography. The other, which wildly excited them all at the time, was a disappointment. Over a distance of 2 miles and 313 yards, they filmed a substantial object that emerged from the loch and wallowed in the shallows on a conspicuous beach.

James departed for London claiming that "the head and neck are in the can". But the beach, a small stony one nearly opposite Castle Urquhart, had been just too far away, and little was to be made out on the film. The RAF experts who examined it estimated, however, that the black object was only 17 feet long.

Another panel of experts, of which Dr Burton was a member, cautiously concluded that the frequency and consistency of the reports "warrants fully qualified scientific examination" and that the short films, poor though they were, remained unexplained. The panel was divided on the evidence as a whole.

> In the end [writes Dr Burton], we agreed that the word "animate" should be used if only to denote that there do occur in Loch Ness phenomena which result in moving humps being seen, although these could as well be caused by physical phenomena as by living objects.
>
> Moreover, when we agreed that the reports of the monster "warranted fully qualified scientific examination", my agreement to the inclusion of this sentence, and that of the other naturalist on the panel, was because we felt it was high time this nonsense about a large unknown animal in the loch was laid by the heels.

Burton strongly urged that the film taken of the dome-shaped object should be submitted to experts in hydrodynamics for analysis, "since in the opinion of at least two of these it could not possibly be an animal". This does not seem to have been done.

Dr Burton was now quite adamant that there was no large unknown animal loose in Loch Ness, and since he is the only scientist who has gone to the trouble of writing a critical analysis of the evidence, his views carry great weight in the scientific community.

In his book he had reached the fair conclusion that there was an outside chance that "there may be an unusual animal in the region of Loch Ness". But in the emotional exchanges over the question since 1960, his position has gradually hardened.

In July 1963 he published an article in *Animals*, illustrated with a full-page photograph of an otter's muzzle and headed: "Is this the Loch Ness Monster?" Dr Burton announced that he now had little doubt that the animal behind the reports from Loch Ness and the other lakes around the world were of quite ordinary otters. He points out that the European otter can grow to 6 feet. (A claim of such a length was indeed made by an anonymous correspondent in the *Field* in 1867, mentioning an otter of 5½ feet. A previous correspondent (also anonymous) mentioned one killed in Inverness which was "fully six feet". Better evidence than this for the existence of the monster has been rejected out of hand.) The activities of such a giant might well look like those of a monster. The eccentric swimming habits of otters could give a distant observer the impression of a series of humps, or one large hump.

There may yet be proof [Dr Burton concluded] that large monsters of unknown species inhabit our lakes, awaiting discovery. We can only put forward our individual opinions, based on somewhat tenuous evidence. It does seem possible that the known behaviour of otters could very well be responsible for some of the reported phenomena, either by their own appearances at the surface or, more often perhaps, by the results of the disturbances they cause in the water.

So it seemed that the existence of a large unknown animal in the loch was not so happily established as David James had announced. He and his associates had still to prove to some critics that the monster was there. This was not going to be easy, as later expeditions found.

The Loch Ness Investigation Bureau, during the 1964 season, logged 18 sightings, only 4 of which were by expedition members. On May 21 two of them, Peter and Pauline Hodges, photographed a pole-like object off Achnahannet. It was merely a dark outline about 2 feet high. When Mr Hodges slammed the car door it dived, and moved off with a considerable wake.

When it turned to go down the loch, Mrs Hodges noticed at the side "a paddling effect". She took about 4 feet of film (8 mm) of this, while her husband took two or three 35 mm photographs, which clearly showed the wake but no details of what was making it.

Despite the vigilance of the expedition members, some of the most interesting sightings were lucky encounters by others in the off-season. On the evening of March 30, 1965, Mr J. M. Ballantyne was out for a walk with his girl friend when they saw the head and neck of the monster. Mr Ballantyne later described the incident in a report for the Bureau.

The head was completely similar to that of a python, or indeed of a large conger eel, and was held at right angles to the neck. The neck was very elongated and slim, thickening to a point 1 foot or thereabouts above the water. The head and neck stood some 4 to 6 feet above the water, something like a cobra standing up when charmed by an Indian piper.

Fig. 21. Head and neck seen by J. M. Ballyntyne.

The summer season of 1965 on Loch Ness was hampered by bad weather and little was done. Two good sightings were made by Ted Holiday, the fishing writer, who has since described them in detail in his own book. On July 15, the monster's single hump slipped past the camera rig at Achnahannet. When he noticed it, the hump was already too far away to film, so he chased after it in his car.

End on, as he saw it, the yellowish-brown hump resembled the upper part of a gothic window. Though it was impossible to take any photographs, "in one sense, this sighting of the Orm (as Holiday calls the animal) made Loch Ness history, since it seems to have been the longest continuous sighting on record. Moreover, during part of the time witnesses unknown to each other were pursuing the creature down the opposite shore. A local policeman and a surveyor had seen the hump from the south shore, and later described the upturned boat shape to Holiday.

On June 21, at Whitefield, Holiday missed a photograph by a few second delay. He and a couple named Eaves had been surprised by the sudden appearance of a black hump out of the loch before their eyes. He got his camera ready and focused on it, and was about to press the release for filming "when the hump collapsed in a sort of muscular spasm", and the animal dived out of sight.

The season was not a complete failure however. On August 1, a short film (263 frames) was taken at a range of 1,282 yards of two separate wakes. These moved together from 70 to 9 feet. A JARIC report on this film "strongly suggests that there is more than one of these creatures". This was encouraging, and doubtless the expedition needed all they could get of that.

The year 1966 will probably be looked back on as a turning point in the investigation of the Loch Ness monster.

Much impressed with the analyses they had done of the films taken by the Loch Ness Investigation Bureau, David James arranged with Tim Dinsdale for his 1960 film to be sent to the Joint Air Reconnaissance Intelligence Centre. The JARIC report was sent to the Bureau on January 24, 1966: it was startling.

The technicians had examined the original 16 mm film by optical enlargement, first to establish the size and speed of the object, and secondly to interpret it. One thing they found it was not, was a boat with an outboard engine – nor a motor-boat. The film was found to show:

a solid, black, approximately triangular shape, with NO impression of perspective. If the shape is assumed to be a plane triangle . . . it is a triangle with a base 5.5 ft approx. and height 3.7 ft approx. . . . A reasonable assumption would be that during the complete film sequence the object was travelling at or approaching 10 mph.

As to what it was, they considered it could be neither a boat nor a submarine vessel, "which leaves the conclusion that it is probably an animate object . . . with some body . . . Even if the object is relatively flat bellied, the normal body 'rounding' in nature would suggest that there is at least 2 feet under the water from which it may be deduced that a cross section through the object would be NOT LESS than 6 feet wide and 5 ft high".

This seemed quite conclusive, coming as it did from experts skilled in interpreting the most difficult of photo images: proof that there was indeed a large unknown animal in Loch Ness. But the report found critics. In a letter to the *New Scientist*, Maurice Burton wrote:

Careful reading of the report shows that it starts with three uneasy premises and after several assumptions and presumptions arrives at the tentative opinion that the object was possibly animate.

That, of course, is not exactly what they say, but "it is probably an animate object". The emphasis is more positive than Dr Burton suggests. He continues:

The key sentence is, however, in the penultimate paragraph where we read, "Further discussion of wake and wash patterns should be left for those more familiar with fluid dynamics". Since the wake and wash are the only clear features in the film this is an important omission. All the dozen or so specialists in fluid dynamics with whom I have discussed the film have been in no doubt that the wake and wash of the alleged monster are consistent with those made by a dinghy with an outboard engine.

It is not clear whether these experts had seen the film or not, for it is quite clear from the shots of the monster, and of the boat taken a short time after, that the pattern of the wake and wash are very different. JARIC were emphatic that the "hump" was not a boat: Dr Burton was emphatic that it was. Yet another impasse.

What strikes one again and again in the debate on the monster is how often statements are made in print about either films or photographs which are not reproduced, and about which the reader is in no position to make up his own mind. In such a context a firm statement from a scientist can be very convincing to those unfamiliar with the details of the evidence he is discussing. It is a sorry manner for a scientific debate to be conducted.

During 1966 the Bureau collected 29 reports; but only 8 of these were from members of the expedition mounted during the season from May to September. During the winter David James had taken the best reports since 1933, and had looked up the prevailing weather conditions. He found that some 90 per cent of the sightings were in flat calm weather. It seemed that afternoon sightings were infrequent because conditions tended to be windier than in the mornings and evenings. I am not sure that this is very sound. Fine weather is more likely to bring out people than animals, and the higher frequency of sighting in the morning and evening is more probably due to the animals nocturnal habits. As we have seen, it hunts shoals of fish, and these are active in the early morning and late evening.

He concluded that calm periods were in general the best time to watch. An exception to this was a report of the head, neck and humps of the animal seen in the afternoon on March 27, off Dores. He was unable to film the monster because of the heavy snow driving into the camera lens! Two other sightings during 1966 were by moonlight, confirming the monster's nocturnal habits.

Another important development of the year was the arrival of help from America. In September Dr Roy Mackal of the Biochemistry Department at the University of Chicago arrived at Loch Ness. He had become interested in the monster the year before while on a holiday in Scotland. He was instrumental in obtaining aid for the Bureau's efforts from America.

The Chicago Adventurer's Club donated $5,000, with the promise of eager volunteers for expeditions. Dr Mackal added his scientific support to that of Denys Tucker in stimulating the interest of the scientific community in the monster. At this time he thought the monster might be a sort of giant sea-slug, a boneless mollusc capable of contorting its body into a series of humps. If it had gills it would spend much of its life under-water, which would explain the comparative infrequency of sightings.

Periodicals in Britain and America were now giving the monster a good, if sceptical, press. *Science Digest*, a popular magazine published in New York, had a long article in the issue for January 1967, which reported Dr Mackal's most unlikely theory as a serious possibility. But a writer in the London *Financial Times* in February, said he had yet to be convinced that there was a monster in Loch Ness, but he was most impressed with the evidence for David James's existence. "Were it not for his success as managing director of EDW Holdings, one might be tempted to place James in the 'crackpot' category". "Monsters", the paper concluded sagely, "are serious business".

Such serious business indeed, that in March the Highland Development Board granted £1,000 to the Bureau towards the cost of the next expedition. "These expeditions have proved a major tourist attraction over the past five years", a spokesman for the Board said. But the Provost of Inverness, Mr William MacKay, was rightly angry. He thought "this investigation has been going on long enough on public subscriptions without success. I could have found a better use for the money. I think we should propagate the myth, and not investigate it".

But if the Provost was afraid the Bureau's effort would put an end to a prime tourist attraction, his fears were needless. The summer of 1967 passed with no spectacular evidence being obtained.

A full and detailed case can be argued against the existence of the Loch Ness monster; Maurice Burton attempts this in his own book *The Elusive Monster*. I have no intention of playing the Devil's advocate, for the question has been debated already: on the BBC television series *Your Witness*, in July 1968.† The

---

† It was quite a monster-ridden night on the BBC; earlier Peter Cushing had starred in *The Abominable Snowman* by Nigel Neale.

motion was that the Loch Ness monster had been seen and should be believed, was argued by two able advocates, who called on several witnesses to support their cases.

Attempting to prove the proposition, Robin McEwen claimed that sightings by reliable witnesses, photographic evidence and serious attention from academic circles, indicate the presence of a substantial and remarkable creature in Loch Ness. His witnesses were Tim Dinsdale with his film; Alex Campbell, a hardy and convincing old witness indeed; and Ted Holiday, sporting the proofs of his book, which contained accounts of his sightings. Dr Roy Mackall, a youngish American, with a slightly fanatical attitude about the monster, aired a few unlikely scientific theories in conclusion.

Another of Mr McEwen's witnesses was Gavin Maxwell, who described an unusual incident from his own experience:

It was in September 1945. I was driving from Inverness to Mallaig. The weather was dull, drizzle, flat calm, and about five or six miles on the Inverness side of Invermoriston I stopped to relieve myself. There was a knoll about 80 feet above the loch. While walking round the broom bushes on this knoll, I noticed what appeared to be a line of stones, a submerged wall stretching out from the shore, perhaps 20 to 30 feet in all, shining wet. Perhaps two minutes later I returned. The "stones" were not there: there was only a slight disturbance in the water which subsided very quickly. I waited half an hour and saw nothing more.

Not perhaps, as Maxwell admitted, a spectacular sighting. But then, not every appearance of the monster can be monstrous.

The case against me, McEwen concluded, is that people are suggestible, they will believe anything they want to. My case is that once you've made up your mind that something is impossible, then nothing will persuade you that the facts are other than you have decided them to be.

For the opposition, Anthony Lincoln contended that there is insufficient "scientific evidence" to support a belief in the existence of a monster in the loch, and that all the alleged sightings can be explained in terms of normal phenomena: "A non-monster is boring, a monster is news".

Actually it turned out that what in fact the BBC thought boring was the detailed presentation of evidence. While the case for the monster left much unsaid, the case against it was a sorry confusion of muddled intentions. Mr Lincoln was clearly uncertain about the details of some of the evidence he was trying to refute. Maurice Burton claimed that Kenneth Wilson had washed his hands of the picture and doesn't believe in the monster. Strictly, that was merely hearsay, and irrelevant to that actual photograph, which he again claimed was the tail of a diving otter. Vegetable mats were raised and deflated once more, and otters in large groups again performed their remarkable (but so-far unconfirmed) antics of imitating monsters to fool the tourists. The final touches were added by the production of a professional psychiatrist, Christopher Evans, who repeated the by now familiar, and ill-considered, nonsense about witnesses' fantasy desires.

I had not realised before what a shambles the supposedly established opinion was. When the matter was put to a jury of solid young professional types, the motion was carried by one vote. Though the public was still divided on the question, it seemed the monster had gained a slight edge of belief.

When critics speak glibly of scientific evidence, what is it they mean? Scientists are often satisfied with less than physical evidence: for instance, what is the physical evidence for antimatter? For the Loch Ness monster there is more than enough judicial evidence, there is even evidence enough to satisfy the scrupulous historian. Scientific method should properly begin with the observation of phenomena. Any theory is consequent to such observations. However improbable it may seem to some, the theory that there is a large unknown animal in Loch Ness explains observed phenomena which cannot be accounted for otherwise.

Even while this debate was going on, however, a group of scientists were at work to provide fresh evidence of the animal's existence. During August 1968, another sonar probe of Loch Ness (the first since 1962) was attempted by a team from Birmingham University. Nothing was said about the experiment till it was complete and the results analysed.

The sonar had been set up on Temple Pier in Urquhart Bay, facing out directly across the loch. On August 28, some interesting patterns were filmed from the cathode ray display tube. These were later published in the *New Scientist* (December 19, 1968), where the engineer Hugh Braithwaite discussed them. Three objects appeared: one, stationary in mid loch, was probably an echo from a rock. The other two, objects A and C in the quotation below, moved from the bottom of the loch to the surface and down again.

Since the objects A and C are clearly comprised of animals, is it possible that they could be fish? The high rate of ascent and descent, Braithwaite thought

> makes it seem very unlikely, and fishery biologists we have consulted cannot suggest what fish they might be. It is a temptation to suppose they must be the fabulous Loch Ness monsters, now observed for the first time in their underwater activities.

This was all very fine indeed, even if it was not (as a matter of fact) the first time sonar echoes of the animals had been obtained. The author added a cautionary warning that the data were inadequate to settle the matter. As usual, further investigation was needed.

But were the two objects really the monsters? A correspondent in the *New Scientist* (January 9, 1969), suggested that the same echoes might be had from masses of peat raised by their gases from the bed of the loch, which sank when the gases had escaped. Just because the sonar showed *animate* objects rising from the bottom of the loch did not prove they were *animals*. The writer concluded that monsters were reported from large lakes elsewhere, and in some of these the "animals" had turned out to be "Burtonesque vegetable mats". "Perhaps, in time, Nessie may be shown to be, literally, a load of old rubbish".

Though Mr Odds has a happy turn of phrase, his facts are not quite sound. Burton, as we shall see, has produced only *one* instance, and that from Norway, of a monster turning into "a load of old rubbish". Which leaves how many other episodes to be explained?

A new explanation of many of them (judiciously selected to

prove his case) was forthcoming in December, when Ted Holiday's book appeared as *The Great Orm of Loch Ness*. Holiday was lucky enough to have seen the monster or, as he styles it, the Orm, on two occasions, which have been mentioned in passing. The purpose of his book was to explore his theory that the monster is a sort of giant worm, which preys off fish deep in the loch and exudes a corrosive slime. His idea is that this horror is related to a unique newly discovered fossil from America called the Tully Monster. The fossil is six inches long. Though he explains it all with enthusiasm, and a display of scientific panoply good enough to carry it, the theory is just a little too far-fetched for me. Any resemblance between the tiny fossil and a 20 foot monster seems to me to be merely the long arm of coincidence. (It seems that Mr Holiday himself also thinks his theory is wrong: in a recent book [and article in *Flying Saucer Review*] he says all monsters are – if I read him rightly – psychic phenomena related to the saucers from Mars!)

The book got excellent and, of course, uncritical reviews, and was an immense success: it just slew them in Milwaukee.† All an indication of how attitudes have changed about the business of monsters and their hunters.

Meanwhile, in America, Dr Mackal was having second thoughts about the monster being an invertebrate. He now thought that a sort of sea-cow adapted to fresh water would better fit the descriptions. Curiously enough the only anomalous carcase that has come to hand recently in any monster-ridden lake was at Lake Okanagan in Canada in 1914: it was identified as a "sea-cow". Could it have been, instead, one of the monsters, unrecognised out of the water?

This change of mind was not unconnected with the recent appearance in America of Bernard Heuvleman's book on the sea-serpent, where the theory that lake-monsters, or at least some of them, are mammals is briefly discussed. Heuvlemans contends that the type of sea-serpent he calls the "long-neck", is a mammal also found in many steep shored lakes in the cold-temperate regions of the world. It has all the character-istics which witnesses have mentioned, except perhaps that

---

† "A must for anyone who relishes the thought that this trampled earth may yet hold dark and terrible secrets". *Milwaukee Journal.*

problematical long tail. It is, he believes, a form of long-necked seal. This is the guiding theory of the present book.

By this time the Loch Ness Investigation was permanently established at Achnahannet, where Clem Skelton was technician in charge. During 1969 the Investigation was involved in a series of efforts to solve the mystery of Loch Ness.

In May, a young American oceanographer named Don Taylor brought a small yellow submarine to Inverness, financed by a large American corporation. Mr Taylor's submarine, *Viper Fish*, was beset with mechanical difficulties, and in the end he failed to sight let alone photograph the monster. He went away, complaining that no-one had explained to him before he arrived that visibility in the loch was only 12 inches!

Another submarine, the Vickers *Pisces*, was also in the loch at this time, undergoing trials and assisting in the making of a Sherlock Holmes film in which the monster had an important role. A monster made of wire and PVC had been made for the film, but this sank under tow and was lost. When they obtained an echo-location on a 40 foot object they assumed it was their monster, rather than the real one. In deep diving trials, however, they discovered an unsuspected trench in the loch over 800 feet deep.

In the autumn the Bureau and Independent Television News co-operated on a large scale probe of the loch. Using a newly developed camera, ITN anchored a balloon over the loch to take time-lapse photographs of the surface. If the monster was there, it ought to appear sometime. Using a sonar beam also, they hoped to get a location on the monster during the fortnight.

The *Daily Mail* was associated with this highly publicised search, and sent its veteran writer Vincent Mulchrone to Loch Ness to send back colour pieces on its progress. Almost inevitably, the pranksters also turned out. An immense bone, nearly five feet high, was reported to the *Mail* by two fishermen "who wished to remain anonymous". As well they might. It transpired, after the paper had spread the picture of the bone over the column widths of half the world's press, that the bone was part of a whale's jaw, and had been lifted from a rock garden in York, where it had been dumped by the local natural history museum. The *Daily Mail* had egg on its face for the second time. A disgruntled Mulchrone returned to El Vino's claiming they had found nothing in Loch Ness because there was nothing to find there.

Nor had ITN had any news for its viewers on the monster's identity, and the Bureau had to content itself with recording 19 sightings, a decline from the 29 in 1966. In their annual report published in June 1970, David James said that though "there is growing evidence of a living creature in the loch, they were no nearer identification".

Before the Investigation could even begin their 1970 season, a lecturer in visceral physiology at an Osteopathic college in London, claimed that samples of water he had taken from the loch's feeders indicated that the monster's life was threatened – not by railway shares as the Snark was but certainly by soap. Pollution was ruining the loch. Loch Ness he advised should be made a conserved natural area. However, Holly Arnold of the Loch Ness Investigation said his claim was rubbish. Only the day before, on July 26, there had been a sighting in Urquhart Bay by a local man well known to the Investigation.

During the summer, Dr Robert H. Rine from Massachusetts tried to measure the monster's sexual response. The American claimed that shy though the monster might be, it was quite a sexy brute. A mock monster made of plastic buoys and covered in salmon oil had been run off with one day and had never been seen again. More sonar evidence of a large object was obtained. Dr Rhine, in reporting these findings, said that the monster was albino white, about 35 feet long and probably blind due to living in the murky gloom 200 feet down. The animal probably belonged to the eel family, and breathed in the same way as eels – on the surface, with gills, or through its skin! Whatever about this giant eel theory, the idea that the monster is white contradicts every report since 1933. It seems that even its best friends don't know the monster very well.

September found yet another American team, financed by a whiskey firm, and led by Jack Ullrich, a consultant to the Smithsonian, trying to photograph the monster with infra-red cameras which would be able to penetrate the gloom that had defeated Don Taylor. Sonar sweeps and acoustic monitors were also to be used. Ullrich rather fancied the idea that the animals were plesiosaurs, despite the difficulty of the low

temperatures in Loch Ness. "The Loch Ness monster is no
longer a myth but a reality supported by substantial scientific
evidence", he told reporters. However, his efforts were not able
to add much to that evidence. They had no luck with the sonar
or the infra-red cameras, but Ullrich himself photographed a
wake which was quite inexplicable as wind or a passing boat.
(A photograph taken near Foyers in August 1969 by Mrs
Jessie Tait, which seems to show a series of black shallow humps
in the water, is quite clearly two boat wakes crossing each
other.)

The annual effort at Loch Ness has now become an established feature of life in Inverness. Tourists passing on the A82
drop in at a permanent exhibition about the monster and its
history. Research is being done on the loch, even into quite odd
aspects of it. In 1970 it was discovered that temperature
differentials caused a rocking motion about 200 feet down,
which would send an underwater wave 100 feet high racing up
and down the loch. Despite what seems after almost ten years
of investigation to be a discouraging lack of concrete progress,
the Investigation are not discouraged. Fanatics never are. Tim
Dinsdale, now full-time field director of operations, in presenting the report for 1971, was still optimistic. And this despite
the fact that when he had been in charge of five telephoto
cameras, he had been too shocked to move when the monster's
head and neck emerged from the water 200 yards away. The
water horse still casts an ancient spell over mere mortals.

> It is no use [he told a press conference] scientists saying there
> is no monster: there jolly well is. For me the job of proving
> it is a matter of principle, like defending the truth, no less.
> I just have to do something about it, and that is what drives
> me on.

No, the fanatic heart is never discouraged.

Near Dores, an ex-soldier living with his cats in a tent,
patiently searches the surface of the loch daily in the chance of
taking the all revealing full-frontal of the monster which he
expects to be worth £5,000. Meanwhile he lives on £7 a week,
and opens another tin of cat food, a sane man lodged in the
wilderness, remote from war, and rumours of war.

Mr Searle's perseverance has recently been rewarded. On July 27, 1972, he photographed two shallow humps breaking the surface near Balachladoich Farm. At the front there is a patch of broken water where we might expect the head to be; at the rear what I take to be the tip of the rear flippers rises from the water. An interesting picture, even though it shows us nothing of the head and neck.

Mr Searle seems to think this as well. A few months later, on October 20, he took another set of photographs. This time, as well as two humps, a short neck and large head rise over the water. I do not believe that these photographs in fact show a living animal, nor am I fully satisfied with his account of how they were taken. He claims that the monster, having posed for one photograph, swam under his boat and came up on the other side where he photographed it again. Yet, to my eye at least, it seems quite clear that the object in the different pictures is the same and has not moved at all. Rather the boat has been rowed around a quite static object. It seems a pity that Mr Searle has chosen to discredit his earlier photograph by perpetrating such an obvious hoax.

The *Daily Record*, which published Searle's pictures, was inspired by this last coup to offer a reward of £1,000 for tracking down and capturing the Loch Ness monster. This seems a generous offer, but a reward was still on offer at the time from Black and White Whiskey of a *million* pounds for the capture of the monster alive, conditional on the British Museum accepting it as a genuine monster. (The mind boggles at their careful deliberations on that question.) Both are likely to keep their money: coming to grips with the monster is still a difficult feat.

*   *   *

I knew Loch Ness only from books and maps while working on much of this book. But in the summer of 1967 I visited the loch during an extended tour of the Highlands. Inverness town is not a large place, but it was crowded with English holiday makers. Funny postcards were for sale, with the monster being mistaken for a mother-in-law and other ripe samples of British humour a la Magill. Genuine photographs, usually

Lachlan Stuart's, could also be bought. Was it to attract and entertain these tourists and visitors that the monster was invented, as some still claim? Hardly. Very few, so it seemed to me, ventured out to the loch, and the tourists who did barely paused, to see if by any chance the monster was in sight, before crowding back onto the bus for the Isles. No, the monster is one baby that cannot be left on the doorstep of the Chamber of Commerce.

Late in the afternoon we drove down along the southern shore of the loch. This was on the old narrow road built by Wade after the Jacobite Rising of 1715, on which the Spicers saw their strange apparition in 1933. The first impression of Loch Ness is its size and grandeur: the sun setting over it, great dark mountains rising sharply from the mouse-grey waters on the northern shore. From Wade's road it is remarkable how little one can see of the loch because of the bushes and birch trees, not to mention the abominable pine trees of the Forestry Commission, which line the shore. Since this was the only road until 1933, it is not surprising that nothing strange was noticed in the loch by travellers.

We stopped for dinner at the Foyers Hotel. The hostess was sceptical about the monster. She said it had not been seen for about eight weeks, so far as she knew. In the hall of the hotel, beside the telephone, was a printed notice asking anyone who had seen anything they thought unusual in the loch, to report it at once to the Investigation H.Q. at Achnahannet. These notices are posted in public places all around the loch, so that now even the sightings of casual visitors may be recorded.

After dinner we walked down a beaten path to the British Aluminium Company's pier. This was now deserted and dangerously rotten. The loch was still, just the sort of weather the monster is suposed to like. Some fishermen came down as we left, but there was no sign of the biggest catch to be made in Loch Ness.

Skirted by new roads and the site of an aluminium factory, the loch might seem to be part of the modern world. But this is not really so. In some ways it belongs still to an older Celtic world, where the distinction we make between the subjects of zoologists and psychologists has no meaning. Loch Ness is a lost world of the imagination, where the spirit is still young.

To some Loch Ness has a peculiar appearance, faintly sinister and mysterious. Gavin Maxwell claimed the loch "seems to reach out at you as if it were a thing sentient and aware, creating a feeling of unease even under a summer sun". Percy Cater, one of the first London journalists to go there in 1933, wrote after a second visit in 1955:

> The Loch oppresses me as much as it did when I first saw it twenty years ago. It remains as enigmatic as the face of Mona Lisa . . . Its surface, suggestive of its sinister depths, is as forbidding as anything I know . . . In this harsh landscape it is easy to think of strange goings on in the loch.

These impressions are not mere romanticising inspired by the alleged existence of a monster in the loch. In 1773, Dr Johnson, riding along General Wade's road on his way to Skye with Boswell, was impressed with the wildness of the scene before him, the rocks "towering in horrid nakedness" above the lake.

What would Johnson have said if he had heard about the monster? Perhaps what he said on another occasion: "This phenomenon is, I think, as wonderful as any other mysterious fact, which many people are very slow to believe, indeed, reject with an obstinate contempt". He was talking about ghosts, and would have been interested to learn that Loch Ness is haunted by more than the Water Horse.

The old Celtic world was retreating from Loch Ness when he and Boswell passed. Till recently the atmosphere of that prehistoric world could still be breathed in the remoter corners of Scotland. But, as the poet Edwin Muir so sadly observed of the Orkney island where he was born, the mermaids and the fairies were now no more. "All these things have vanished from Orkney in the last fifty years under the pressure of compulsory education".

Whatever changes education may have brought to Inverness it has not driven out all the legends around Loch Ness. There was one old man who was asked if he believed in the monster. "I do not", he replied, "but I have seen the Water Horse". These legends, though mostly remembered by such old people, are not all about that legendary animal.

The loch is said to be haunted still by the spectre of Saint Columba's ship. This is a story which I have only once seen referred to in print, but it casts an odd light on ideas around the loch.

According to the water bailiff Alex Campbell, the ship is seen every twenty years: in 1902 it was seen by Finlay Frazer of Strathenick; in 1962, near Invermoriston, by an Irish tramp Thomas O'Connell. In 1942, it was seen by Colin Campbell, the brother of Alex, who describes the incident:

> It was pitch black and I could not even see the trees or rocks around me. But there, 30 yards from the shore was the ship. It had no light of its own. It was spotlighted by something fluorescent, whitish and bluish and magical. The ship was stationary, as though at anchor. I saw ropes coiled on the deck and every line of her. She looked like an ancient craft from Biblical times.

Much the same sight was seen by Thomas O'Connell.

"Up here", says Alex Campbell, "we do not tell odd stories, unless they are true. We tend to be cagey, reticent men; but this has gone on so long I feel people must be told". It was Campbell who first wrote about the monster in 1933; his brother Colin, who has seen the ship, does not believe in the monster: he has never seen it.

We had hopes of seeing the monster ourselves, as has everyone who comes near the loch. We had camped that night in a field by the shore near Whitefield. It was a curious sensation, sitting on a stump by the shingle looking out over the water, too rough really for the monster. One was quite ready to believe anything about monsters then, in that gloomy dusk: the place had a proper air of mystery. Next morning, after an early swim, I was more chastened: the monster would want to be pretty hot-blooded to live in that icy water. Nevertheless, as we drove around the loch, we kept an eye on the water, so full of deceptive dark patches and long sinuous ripples.

We followed the old road around to Fort Augustus. Foyers and Fort Augustus are two places where the monster is frequently seen. I was not surprised that this should be so, for there are stunning views over the loch at both places. In his book Maurice Burton, for instance, quotes 47 accounts of a single sighting by boys at the Abbey School. In the hotel just outside Fort Augustus (formerly Inchnacardoch House, so often mentioned in reports from the 1930's), the cocktail bar is called Nessie's Nook: I had second thoughts about catering to the tourists.

The next day we drove along the northern shore. The road here is the modern one blasted out in the early thirties, from which the monster was most often seen then, and from which Kenneth Wilson took his famous picture in April 1934. The trees and bushes have grown again since then. The volume of reports since seems to be in inverse ratio to the density of the vegetation. At a few lay-by's the bushes had been cut down by the Loch Ness Investigation to give their mobile camera cars a clear view. At these places a few people loitered hopefully. They might have been lucky. It was from a lay-by on July 23, as we later learned, that the monster had been seen by a bus driver and his passengers: four large humps speeding up the loch.

At Achnahannet we came to the Loch Ness Investigation Head-Quarters. Arranged on a permanent site were caravans for living quarters and laboratories, and parking space for a fleet of vans and cars. The expedition flag bravely fluttered out from a tall flagpole: *azure a monster argent naiant regardant.*

A small charge to visitors helps towards the now vast expenses of running the operation. In one of the caravans is a display of photographs, drawings and maps setting out the story of the monster, and explaining the various theories. Here, it seems, the plesiosaur is still popular.

That day there was among the photographs one that surprised me, and which I knew would have warmed the cockles of Maurice Burton's sceptical heart. A few days before the monster had been reported by several people near Aldourie Castle. A photograph was taken of it. When enlarged it was found to show a young deer swimming across the loch. I remembered that Dr Burton had suggested the possibility of a swimming deer being mistaken for the monster. Later, back in London, I looked up what he had written.

Having given an account of a deer seen swimming in another loch, he goes on to make a point about those small "horns":

What is significant is that the only three reports of antennae from Loch Ness were on August 11, 1933, August 12, 1934, and August 18, 1952.† The red deer stag, in its second year of life, carries a pair of short unbranched antlers. During July and August these are in velvet. [A comparison shows the antlers and the reported antennae to be similar.] In my opinion we can afford to ignore these reports of antennae.

And here was photographic evidence in support of his theory from Loch Ness itself, moreover from a spot near where one of these three reports came. It was unsettling, especially as the expedition members seemed to attach little importance to the incident or the photograph. Nor has anyone, so far as I know, referred to this incident in print. So much for scientific rigour. (However, we cannot ignore reports of "antennae", for as we shall later see they are really ears.)

We were shown the cameras set to survey the Loch. A 35 mm Arraflex with a high power zoom lens, capable of closing on an object 2 miles away. It was not in use that day as the weather, we were told, was too rough for the monster to appear. Also two aerial survey cameras, set 6 feet apart, which took 30 pictures a minute. By putting the three exposures together, a three dimensional image could be obtained.

The expedition member who showed us the cameras was convinced of the monster's existence, "that has been proved". He said their job was to gather further evidence of its habits and life. I mentioned Maurice Burton; he answered with a sneering version of the name, which escapes me now. He airily dismissed such sceptics – "or should I say septics" – as merely recalcitrant. We left before a bad case of paranoia developed. I imagine his arrogant and silly views do not reflect those of the Investigation as a whole.

When I mentioned Burton's theory about a giant otter, he replied that there were no otters in Loch Ness. This I do not believe. The 1962 Cambridge Expedition had accounted for one of their sightings as an otter, so they had no doubts about the matter. But if there is some question of their existence in Loch

† Respectively, reports by A. H. Palmer, P. Grant and Mrs Finlay, all quoted here.

Ness, why wasn't someone looking into it? Otters may be rare and hard to observe, but their play areas are easy to detect.

He also dismissed the vegetable mat theory, on firmer grounds, as only one had been seen in 30 years. That, however, was one. What with that bit of news and the photograph of the deer, Maurice Burton's theories looked more likely.

The methods of the Loch Ness Investigation seem unscientific. The existence of the animals in the loch has yet to be soundly proved beyond doubt. The burden of proof rests with those of us who believe they exist. Photography such as they are carrying out, is all very good. But it means that vital matters such as otters (that might well grow to six feet) and vegetable mats are left as matters of hearsay. These are the problems at Loch Ness. And it seems to me that, if we are going to solve this mystery, we must have a full scale scientific investigation of Loch Ness.

The young man we met that day complained that the then Labour Government (he was a Tory) gave no support to the Investigation. As they are not, at present, making any large contribution to scientific knowledge, why should there be such support? But surely the country that sponsored the *Beagle*, the *Rattlesnake*, and the *Challenger*, would support a full ecological inquiry into Loch Ness as a sample area of the British Isles? Such an investigation into all aspects of life around the loch would settle the question of the monster, and at the same time provide scientific information of great interest, should the monsters fail to be found. Then we would know about the deer, the otters and the vegetable mats.

David James has said that the only aim of the Loch Ness Investigation is photography. Their stations are arranged to survey a wide but limited area of the loch, which does not include the mouths of the rivers. Their lack of success during a decade of endeavour suggests that there is something wrong with their approach. Mere photographic surveillance has failed.

Other methods of investigation have been tried. Echo-sounding has been tried frequently, with indifferent success. When echoes of large objects have been recorded, they were often open to other interpretations. Anyhow, it is impossible to use a means to search either the bottom or the top ten feet of the loch, or very close inshore, due to the echo bouncing back off the surfaces. For this reason, throughout the sweeps of the loch, no echoes have been had from eels or otters, known to be there, because they live respectively on the bottom, and close to the shore at the top. It may well be that the monster does as well.

Another point is that animals, such as dolphins, that use sonar themselves, are painfully sensitive to manmade ultra sounds, and flee them. The evidence produced by Colonel Hasler, that the monster uses sonar, would indicate that it too would flee from the sonar search beam. Anyway, the images on a sonar display only reveal the presence of a large animal; they cannot help us identify it.

Photographs are needed for that, preferably photographs of the monster in shallow water, or ashore. The entire effort of the Investigation has gone into trying to photograph the monster swimming on the surface of the loch. Their scheme is based on the idea that the monster is an animal of the deep water, which only rarely ventures to the surface, usually in calm bright weather. This may be a false idea.

There is good evidence that the monster quite frequently emerges onto the beaches of the loch, and may even wander around ashore. One of the few films obtained by the Investigation was of a 17 foot long object wallowing on a distant shingle beach. This is much the same situation in which other witnesses, such as Margaret Munro in 1934, and Torquil MacLeod in 1960, also saw the monster.

It was unfortunate that the silly hoax in 1933 should have involved the alleged spoor of the monster on the shore. Obviously if it does come ashore it must leave some traces. We are right to be suspicious of such traces, but what few there are do seem to have a pattern.

There are the traces which the art students examined on the scene of Arthur Grant's encounter. They also found, it may be remembered, a patch of flattened grass further up the shore, where it seemed some large animal had been lying.

They are not the only witnesses. Captain Alastair MacIntosh describes in his memoirs, published in 1961, how he came upon Alec Muir, then a carpenter at the Foyers Aluminium works, on the Dores Road. Muir said the monster had just crossed the road in front of his car. They followed "a visible trail" through the woods to a clearing. "Showing in the moss was an immense depression where the monster has obviously lain down to rest". This is the same area where Mrs Reid saw her "strange animal" lying up in the bracken away from the road.

In 1962, on an isolated beach beyond Inverfarigaig, Ted Holiday noticed "at one spot there was a curious patch of bent and broken bushes several yards wide beside the water for which it was hard to think of an explanation." Later he learnt that the local people occasionally see these patches, which they associate with the monsters.

There is also evidence of the monster wandering around ashore. By my reckoning (and I think I have been through the literature pretty thoroughly), there are 17 reports of the monster ashore between 1870 and 1960. (See Table 1.) These are not a great number, but then not everyone thinks of the monster coming ashore at all. Most people, except the much-abused Maurice Burton, have assumed it is to be found in the deep waters of the loch. Burton thought his "otterlike" animal might be found ashore, in the marshes, on Cherry Island and up the burns along the shore of the loch. Ironically enough, it seems he may well be right in the long run.

Earlier I have quoted a few accounts of the monster ashore. It will now be convenient to gather up the few accounts that remain. These are mostly reports which have only recently been revealed, many years after they were made.

Sometime during the 1930's, according to Mrs Whyte, the school children at Drumnadrochit school told their master that they had seen "a most peculiar and horrifying animal in the bush swamp in Urquhart Bay". There were pictures of prehistoric animals around the walls of the classroom, and they pointed out the long-necked plesiosaur as being very like the animal they had seen.

Another, even more indefinite report is mentioned by Ted Holiday, who says that some time during the 1890's, a gypsy woman saw the monster on the road between Dores and Foyers. I do not know the source of this information.

The report of a Mrs Eleanor Price Hughes in 1933 that she had seen the monster emerge out of the bushes at Drumnachochit and vanish into the lake carrying something pink in its mouth – "are not baby seals pink?" – was dismissed as a hoax by Gould. Oudemans believed her story, though he thought the pink object must have been a piglet.

There remain three more circumstantial accounts, all from correspondents of Tim Dinsdale, who are quoted by him in his books.

The first of these is very odd. One night in April 1923, Mr Alfred Cruickshank was driving to meet a train at Speanbridge. His headlights worked off a magneto, and would fail as the car slowed down at corners. Approaching a bend on the lochside road, his lights began to fail just as an animal of great size crossed in front of him. It seemed to be over 20 feet long and about 5 feet off the ground.

> Colour, green-khaki, resembling a frog, with cream-coloured belly which trailed on the ground. It had four legs, thick like an elephant's and had large webbed feet; in reality it looked like an enormous hippo, but with arched back and long trailing tail which was on the same level as the belly, as you can see in my rough drawing. It gave out a sharp bark, like a dog, as it disappeared over the road into the water.

The sketch showed a low fat animal with a large doglike head, almost no neck, four short legs with fingers or claws, and an immense tail.

Dinsdale was nonplussed at this account, and certainly it is strange. The sharp bark of fright which the animal gave I am quite ready to accept, for though only Adamnan refers to the animal making a noise, evidence from elsewhere confirms Mr Cruickshanks' statement. Also, the dark colour and light belly are consistent with what we already know. What is not consistent is the short neck and the huge tail: what are we to make of these?

Dinsdale suggests that in the failing light of the headlamps, with the body sideways on across the road and the neck swung round to face the car, the head might well have appeared much larger and the neck been invisible. As for the tail, it strikes me that as Mr Cruickshank makes it as long as the body, he has actually seen the long trailing hind parts and not a tail at all.

Mr Cruickshank is not the only one to have compared the monster to a huge frog. An item in the *Northern Chronicle* on January 31, 1934, claimed that 45 to 50 years before, a diver investigating a small ship which had sunk off Johnnies Point, while down about 30 feet, saw on a ledge "a queer looking beast, which he described as something in the nature of a huge frog". It was as big as a goat or a wedder, and just stared at him with neither fear nor ferocity. (This story came from the divers grand-nephew, Donald Frazer, lock-keeper at Fort Augustus.)

The other incidents are more straightforward. About 1879 a group of children were picnicking on the northern shore of the loch near the old graveyard. They had nearly finished their meal when they heard a noise, and looking round saw an extraordinary creature coming down the slope behind them. It was an elephant grey, with a small head and a long neck. It turned it's head from side to side, seeming to peer at them as it waddled down into the water. The woman who told this story to Edward Smith of Sussex, said that she could hardly wait to tell their father when they got home. He listened to them, and then sent them to their rooms and came up and caned them, "Not for telling him a fairy story, but for pretending it was true".

Earlier I mentioned that, according to E. H. Bright, a man named Hossack saw the monster about 1865. Bright himself, in 1880, was walking with his cousin along the shore near Drumnadrochit, when they saw the monster emerge from the woods and waddle to the water's edge on its four legs. It left a tremendous wash. It had a long neck, like an elephant's trunk, was dark grey in colour and generally reminiscent of an elephant. His grandfather was amused at the story, but later admitted there were stories of an animal in the loch, but that the local people did not care to talk about it. On the shore where they had seen the monster, they later found several three-pronged footprints.

Three-pronged footprints? This does not seem to fit with the detailed description given of the monster's tracks by the Edinburgh art students in 1934. What it does fit in with though, are the alleged monster tracks found by Weatheral on the same beach. It has never actually been suggested in print that they were planted by Weatheral, but the affair of the "hippo" tracks discredited them. The amazing thought that they might not have been a hoax at all dawned on me at once, when I read Bright's account. If the monster has some sort of clawed flipper, that would fit with Cruickshank's flippers with fingers, and with Mrs MacLennan's curious hooves. This was all very suggestive, but highly conjectural on my part, yet we shall see that there is other evidence about the animals limbs which confirms it. I leave it there for now.

These stories, as well as the others quoted earlier, suggest to me that the monster, or rather monsters, spend more time ashore than 17 sightings in a century would indicate. If it does come ashore, as I think, it naturally does so in isolated and unfrequented places. But these are just the places which are not under camera surveillance by the Loch Ness Investigation Bureau. They are rarely visited, except, as in several of the instances above, by children playing. If we want revealing photographs of the Loch Ness monster – and that is all that will settle the matter – these are the places we should search.

In the summer of 1971, we returned to the loch to look into the whereabouts of the Irvine films and to investigate the marshes and river mouths.

This time we dropped down from the north. Drop is the right word, too. One drives along through the low hills, and there, quite suddenly the wide rift of the Great Glen opens before one, the dark band of black water at the bottom. The road weaves down the steep hillside, coming out at Abriachan, where Arthur Grant had his adventure.

We turned south, and drove on to Drumnadrochit. We found a camping place well away from the main road, in a field in an older part of the village. One of the places where the monster had come ashore in 1879 was near "the old graveyard on the northern shore". As far as I could discover, this grave-yard at Drumnadrochit was the one meant.

After eating, we thought it might be as well just to have a quick look round the graveyard, and the part of the swamp beyond. Getting through the graveyard was easy enough, but once into the trees it was difficult. There were narrow paths, so it seemed that a few people, obviously fishermen, used the place quite regularly. But as we went on further, in the growing dark, it became clear that no-one in their right mind would spend much time in this place.

Two rivers, the Enrick and the Coiltie, flow into the loch here at separate points. There are small islands covered in bushes and impenetrable scrub between the two streams. It got darker and we thought it most unlikely that we would make any spectacular discovery now, and to meet the monster in the dark was not quite so delightful a prospect as it later seemed in the snug of the hotel, drinking Glen Grant.

"It's just as well there are no crocodiles here", my friend remarked. Only to be told that there was, as a matter of fact, a queer story about a South African farmer who brought home a crocodile from Natal . . .

The next morning we set off to look over the rest of the swamps. On the way, we pulled in at the Loch Ness Investigation Bureau. The man in charge of the exhibition was regaling the visitors with a ripe tale of a diver meeting some large black object while swimming in Urquhart Bay. There was a large scale Ordinance Survey Map of the loch with the recent sightings marked on it, as well as the shore sightings. There were only seven of these. Again: so much for scientific rigour.

We drove on to Invermoriston. Here the mouth of the river is also hard to get to, and again seems to be visited only by fishermen. Most people will stop and have a look at the remarkable falls, but will not go further along the river bank. The river in the next half mile or so consists of deep pools, which run quite clear over a rocky bottom. It was here that John MacLeod saw the monster before 1907. Certainly it is a remarkable place for a sighting. If, as seems very likely, the monster hunts around the mouths of the rivers, I would imagine that the pools of the Morrison river would be an excellent place for an observation post. That day, however, we saw nothing ourselves.

The next stop was at Inchnacardoch Bay. We were able to hire a boat at the boathouse near the road (the one mentioned by Mrs Cameron, near which she and her brothers were playing when they saw the monster lurch down the opposite shore). We rowed over and landed on Inchnacardoch Point, near where the last remains of the boiler marked the wreck of the old steamer which had once plied the loch from the pier at the top of the Point.

The Point and the marsh beyond it were not quite so overgrown as I had imagined they would be. However, the belt of trees stretched far back to the road, and the area seemed quite as isolated as when William Macgruer and his small friends startled the monster into the water. While providing lots of lurking places for large animals, Inchnacardoch Point does not have any advantages for observers. After taking some photographs, showing where I thought the animals seen by Macgruer and Mrs Cameron might have been seen, we drove on into Fort Augustus.

I had written in advance to Dom Aloysius Carruth, to ask for a little of his time to learn about the Irvine films. The only time we could catch him was after he had shown a party of American visitors around the Abbey. But our visit was in vain. In an effort to learn what he knew, without revealing what I did, we sparred around each other for several minutes. But the seal of the confessional had been extended to cover Mr Irvine's mysterious strip of celluloid. If Father Carruth knew the secret of the films, he was not telling us.

In passing, we photographed the beach at Borlum Bay, where Margaret Munro had seen the monster hauled ashore. At Foyers the river flows out in two streams through a flat delta. Though many sightings have been made here, the only place for observation, as Dinsdale found, is on the hill behind. The building of a new industrial plant in Foyers village is likely to pollute the river anyway, so making it a less attractive hunting ground for the monster.

The mouth of the Farigaig, however, provides another area of scrub and marsh, but sightings from here of any kind have been infrequent. Our examination had been full of interest, however, revealing that those areas where the monster is most likely to be seen, are the very areas which are not under observation. It seems to me that the efforts of a small party might well be centred on the pools at Invermoriston. Here a camera station could be set up, equipped with sonar and hydrophones for underwater surveillance. The hydrophones would be particularly important, as I would like to see an analysis done on the sound waves, to see how they compare with those produced by other seals. If the monster is to be photographed, it is more likely to present itself here at the river mouth, while the fish are rising, than anywhere else.†

Before discussing the identity of the monster in detail, we shall have to survey the evidence, sometimes complementary, sometimes contradictory, of lake monsters in other parts of the world. Once it is realised that the animals in Loch Ness are only a few of many, some of the strangeness will leave them, and we will be better able to make sense of the reports.

A butcher near Foyers described to us a curious patch of foam and ripples he had seen on the loch near Dores.

"If that wasn't the monster", he concluded, "then there's something queer in the loch".

A commendable attitude: to deny the monster is one thing, but it can't be denied that "there's something queer in the loch".

---

† Which is where a recent photograph was in fact taken. Bob Rines and Harold Egerton, aided by sonar, photographed in August 1972 off Temble Pier what they claim to be the rear flipper of a plesiosaur. On this point Tim Dinsdale is quite emphatic, as the picture shows an aerodynamic leading edge as would have been expected. There is not much support for the mammal theory in this, but some other well-informed experts have expressed doubts about the photograph. Until it has been more widely discussed, I would prefer to reserve my opinion. An article on the photograph by Dinsdale appears in the April 1972 issue of the *Journal of the Royal Photographic Society*.

5

Highland Water Horses—Scotland

It is the same animal of which one has occasionally
read accounts in the newspapers as having been seen
in the Highland lochs.

Lord Malmesbury in 1857

THE LOCH NESS monster is not unique. Though the animals there
get most of the press attention, reports of similar beasts have
also come from other lochs in the Western Highlands. But
because these lochs are more isolated, there are not so many
eye-witnesses as at Loch Ness. The local crofters are often the
only people who watch over those remote grey reaches of
water, and they rarely speak of what they see swimming in
them. If they do speak, all too often their stories are taken, not
as reports of real animals, but as folktales of strange beasts
like the Kelpie and the Water Horse.

It is a matter of attitude. The further we penetrate into the
Highlands, the more archaic the world view becomes. (This was
certainly true till recently, but television changes all before it.)
We enter a country out of step with our urban one, where the
borders of the real world as we see it are not always distinguished. The Orkney poet Edwin Muir wrote of those islands
as a "place where there was no great distinction drawn between
the ordinary and the fabulous; the lives of the living turned
into legend".

Like all pre-literate societies, the Highlands for centuries
preserved its traditions by word of mouth. Its story-tellers
were charged with keeping to the exact words of every story, and
each could recite several hundreds. Even if the lives of the living
turned into legend, the legends would be accurately remembered
for a long time, and might even have some strong basis of fact.

We have already seen the life of Saint Columba turning into

a legend, though the account of the monster he worsted in the river Ness seems to be only slightly over-coloured. Similar traditions have been current around other Scottish lochs in the centuries since, and bearing in mind the differing attitudes, they are often quite convincing.

Stories of lake monsters are recorded in some of the early histories of Scotland. Hector Boece in his history of Scotland published in 1527, recalls that he had been told by Sir Duncan Campbell:

> that out of Garloch, a loch of Argyle, came a terrible beast as big as a greyhound, puted like a gander and struck down great trees with the length of his tail; and slew three men quickly who were hunting, with three strokes of his tail; and were it not that the remnant of the hunters climbed up in strong oaks, they had all been slain in some way. After the slaughter of these men, it fled speedily to the loch. Sundry prudent men believed great trouble would follow in Scotland because of the appearance of this beast, for such had been seen before, and great trouble always followed soon after.

This was not the only dangerous monster loose in medieval Scotland. Timothy Pont, who wrote a description of the Highlands as they were in 1590, echoes the credulity of Boece in this account of Lochaber:

> In this little country there were certain inhabitants of certain parts of Lochaber called Lochferia and Mamor foreagainst Ardgour, and they did build a house of timber in one little island which was against the mosses next to the principal town, which they had in Argour. And the said inhabitants having this island for an strength house to keep himself and the principal men of his kin and friends from their enemies. They dwelling there for a space, it fortuned on a time a monstrous being in the loch, the most part of the inhabitants being in the island, it was overwhelmed by that terrible and most powerful monstrous beast and so they all perished and were devoured.

Though this strikes me as reminiscent of the story of Beowulf cast in chronicle form, the actual incident seems to have been widely known. James Gordan, the schoolmaster of Rothiemay, writing of Ardgour in 1644, says that "the first inhabitants dwelling, as is reported, in ane isle were chased thence by a monster".

Another Scottish history *The Chronicles of Fortingale*, describing the events of 1570, records:

There was ane monstrous fish, seen in Lochfyne, having a great een in the head thereof and at times would stand above the water as high as the mast of a ship; and the said had upon the head thereof two croons ... whilk was reportit by wise men, that the same was one sighn and toekn of ane sudden alteration in this realm.

Our monster has grown from a "beast as big as a greyhound" in 1527, to a "terrible and most powerful monstrous beast" in 1590: already exaggeration and confusion are appearing, the ordinary becoming fabulous. Despite the aweful dread with which they were regarded, there was possibly more to these monsters. It is not unlikely that such animals make excursions ashore (as they certainly do at Loch Ness) and that they might well be capable of doing some damage to flimsy wattle huts and young saplings. The description of the other animal in Lochfyne suggests the "periscope" appearance of the Loch Ness monster.

On a 14th century map of Scotland, now in the Bodleian Library in Oxford, a note says of Loch Tay:

In isto lacu tria mirabilia
insula natans
pisces sine intestines
fretum sine vento†

Blaeu's *Atlas*, drawn up in 1653, observes that Loch Lomond has "waves without wind, fish without fin and a floating island". These windless waves are perhaps those strange wakes seen on Loch Ness, or the strange wave patterns such as Maurice Burton describes in *The Elusive Monster*. Recent

† In this loch three wonders: a moving island—fish without fins—waves without wind.

witnesses have commented on the resemblance of the monster's humped back to a small island, while the same smooth shape might easily be called "a fish without fin".

The compiler of the Blaeu map adds ingenuously that "The fish which they speak of as having no fins are a kind of snake and therefore no wonder". Just so indeed. Many of these early writers were rather confused about the real identity of the animals they reported. Timothy Pont, for instance, writes of Loch Awe that the local people claimed that there were giant eels in that loch "big as ane horse with ane Incredible length" and for that reason did not fish in the loch. Loch Awe is still supposed to have a great beast in it, *an Beathach Mor Loch Abha* as it is called in gaelic. (Similar stories were found among the people around the shores of Loch Rannoch.)

The next step in the growing tradition is a folk tale. During their tour of the Hebrides in 1773, Boswell and Johnson visited the small island of Rasay, where the party passed two lochs. Of one of these, Loch na Mna, Boswell records a story their guide told them:

He said, there was a wild beast in it, a sea-horse, which came and devoured a man's daughter; upon which the man lighted a great fire, and had a sow roasted on it, the smell of which attracted the monster. In the fire was put a spit. The man lay concealed behind a low wall of loose stones, which extended from the fire over the summit of the hill, till it reached the side of the loch. The monster came, and the man with a red hot spit destroyed it. Malcolm (the guide) showed me the little hiding place, and the row of stones. He did not laugh when he told me this story.

Though Boswell and the Doctor were hardly pioneers, it was not until the 19th century that the Highlands became fashionable for tourists: Queen Victoria made popular in England both Scotland and Scotch. These early tourists were duly followed by the Victorian folklorists, who heard traditions of such creatures as the Kelpie and the Water Horse, which fade eventually into the first modern reports of monsters.

John Leyden, on a tour of the Highlands in 1800, when riding past Loch Vennachair, discovered that "the people of the vale

had been a good deal alarmed by the appearance of that un-
accountable being, the water-horse (Each Uisge)". This monster
was held responsible for the death by drowning of a party of
children crossing the loch a few months before. James Hogg,
in a note to one of his poems in *The Mountain Bard*, wrote in
1807 that "in some places of the Highlands of Scotland, the
inhabitants are still in continual terror of an imaginary being
called the Water-Horse". Though the water horse was mentioned in 1893 by a novelist as "a fabulous goblin", another
writer in *Bradford Antiquities* (July 1903) hinted at a more
sinister origin behind the Highland belief when he claimed that
the water horse is "a sprite that demands at least one life
annually".

There is no doubt that the water horse was thought to appear
in the shape of a horse: the kelpie is more difficult to place.
The etymology of the word is obscure. The gaelic word cailpach
or calpa, meaning a colt or a bullock, is suggested, but, according to the *Oxford English Dictionary*, "positive evidence is
wanting". Anyhow, the Kelpie was the Lowland Scots name for
a water monster which appeared on the surface with a black
back like a large animal. It was said to haunt streams and rivers,
drowning careless travellers. Collins in his *Popular Super-
stitions of the Highlands* (1747) speaks of a man being drowned
by the Kelpie's wrath, and we learn from a letter of Robert
Burns to his friend Cunningham (September 10, 1792) that the
kelpie haunted nearby fords and ferry-crossings in Ayrshire.
Though Walter Scott mentions it in his *Lay of the Last Minstrel*
in 1805, by 1813 James Hogg tells us in *The Queen's Wake* that:

The darksome pool . . . was now no more the kelpie's home.

In the remoter Highlands, however, such legends remained
more than poetic conceits, the water horse something more a
myth. From Walter Scott, who was one of the first to take a
serious interest in his country's traditions, we hear some
interesting evidence of its existence. Writing to Surtees in 1810
(March 23) he says

If I could for a moment credit the universal tradition respect-
ing almost every Scotch loch, highland or lowland, I would

positively state that their water-cow, always supposed to dwell there, was the hippopotamus.

Nor would I be at all surprised, considering the uniformity of that tradition both as to the nature and appearance of the animal, if upon their drawing some of these lochs, which the rage for improvement will one day bring about, we should come upon the skeleton of this Egyptian behemoth.

Five years later, writing to Lady Compton, Scott was a little more explicit.

A monster long reported to inhabit Cauldshields Loch, a small sheet of water in this neighborhood, has of late been visible to sundry persons. If it were not that an otter swimming seems a very large creature, I would hardly know what to think of it, for a very cool-headed, sensible man told me he had seen it in broad daylight – he scouted my idea of an otter and said the animal was more like a cow or a horse.

Sir Walter "by a sort of instinct" took his rifle with him when he next went walking around the loch.

Finally, in his journal for November 23, 1827, he noted the following anecdote:

Clanronald told us, an instance of Highland credulity, that a set of his kinsmen – Borradale and others – believing that the fabulous "water-cow" inhabited a small lake near his house, resolved to drag the monster into day. With this in view, they bivouacked by the side of the lake in which they placed, by way of night-bait, two small anchors such as belong to boats, each baited with the carcase of a dog, slain for the purpose. They expected the water-cow would gorge on the bait and were prepared to drag her ashore the next morning when, to their confusion, the baits were found untouched.

This was not to be the last effort to fish out a monster. Nor indeed an exclusive example of "Highland credulity".

John Francis Campbell of Islay, one of the earliest collectors of Scottish folk tales, wrote in 1860 that "in the Highlands of

Scotland people still believe in the existence of the water-horse" and in Sutherland and many other parts of the country many believed they had actually seen these "fancied creatures".

> I have been told [he continues] of English sportsmen who went in pursuit of them, so circumstantial were the accounts of those who believed that they had seen them. The witnesses are so numerous, and their testimony agrees so well, that there must be some deeply-rooted Celtic belief which clothes with the dreaded form of the Each Uisge every dark object.

If only the explanation were so simple as that. Two years later, Campbell himself recorded a very curious story about a mysterious animal which he calls "the Boobrie", which seems to have been a sort of sub-variety of water-horse which was seen in a loch in Argyle.

An aquaintance of Campbell's waded out after it one cold February morning, getting within 85 yards before it dived out of sight. It was like a Great Northern Diver to his eye, with the exception of a white streak on the neck and breast. The neck was "two feet eleven inches long" and "twenty-three inches in circumference" which are surprisingly certain estimates in the circumstances. The bill was about "seventeen inches long and looked like an eagles at the end", meaning, I suppose, that the upper part overhung the lower. The legs were short, black and powerful; the feet webbed till within five inches of the toes, with large claws. Footprints, as measured in the mud at the north end of the loch, covered a space equal to thst contained by a pair of large antlers. The voice was like the roar of an angry bull – a most unbird-like sound – and it was said to live on lambs and otters. Campbell laments that his friend did not have a bow, for then a specimen of the Boobrie might have been taken. Others, he says, had also seen this creature.

It is most unlikely that this was actually a bird – what bird, except perhaps a form of giant extinct penguin, would measure perhaps 13 feet long? Other witnesses have thought that the long neck of these lake monsters is very like a swan's – or a Great Northern Diver, a more vivid comparison for a Scot as those are large long-necked black birds. A remarkable drawing of a marine long-neck seen off the Orkneys in 1919, was given a remarkably bird-like profile by the witness Mr MacKintosh Bell. The rest of the description – voice, claws, footprints and shape of head – fit with the long-necks seen elsewhere. I have quoted this story at length to show that not all that is called folklore is fantasy. Indeed English visitors were also persuaded by the evidence that monsters existed in the Highlands.

And why shouldn't they be? For in 1856, the *Times* in its edition for March 6, carried at the bottom of an inside page a short paragraph, very discreetly headlined "The Sea Serpent in the Highlands". This is the earliest report I have been able to find of a Scottish lake monster in the columns of the national press. Here it is in full:

The village of Leurbost, Parish of Lochs, Lewis, is at present the scene of an unusual occurrence. This is no less than the appearance in one of the inland fresh-water lakes of an animal which from its great size and dimensions has not a little puzzled our island naturalists. Some suppose him to be a description of the hitherto mythological water-kelpie; while others refer it to the minute descriptions of the "sea-serpent", which are revived from time to time in the newspaper columns. It has been repeatedly seen within the last fortnight by crowds of people, many of whom have come from the remotest parts of the parish to witness the uncommon spectacle. The animal is described by some as being in appearance and size like "a large peat stack", while others affirm that a "six-oared boat" could pass between the huge fins, which are occasionally visible. All, however, agree in describing its form as that of an eel; and we have heard one, whose evidence we can rely upon, state that in length he supposed it to be about 40 feet. It is probable that it is no more than a conger eel after all, animals of this description having been caught in Highland lakes which have attained huge size. He is currently reported to have swallowed a blanket inadvertently left on the bank by a girl herding cattle. A sportsman ensconced himself with a rifle in the vicinity of the loch during a whole day, hoping to get a shot, but did no execution.

That intrepid gentleman was no doubt one of those Campbell

had in mind above. Strangely enough, this item was copied from (of all papers) the *Inverness Courier* – where it appeared some 70 years before the Loch Ness Monster did! Sometimes it would seem to be worthwhile knowing the files of one's own paper.

As I say, this seems to be a unique report. There was no more about the monster in the *Times*, which is a little surprising, as this was not long after the *Daedulus* sea-serpent affair, and the Victorian newspaper readers had then shown an avid appetite for monsters of many kinds. No communications with Lewis were doubtless the cause of this lapse.

A London correspondent, signing himself "W.P.", who read this item, wrote to the *Inverness Courier*, confirming the report:

I beg to inform you that when shooting in that island in September 1821, with four gentlemen, we saw the same animal, and probably in the same loch; and for several hours endeavoured to get an opportunity of shooting at the creature, but without success. We dined that evening with Mr Mackenzie, at Stornoway, and mentioned what we had seen to him. Mr Mackenzie expressed considerable surprise, but stated that the report was current in Lewis Island when he first came there, that such an animal had been captured in that very lake, and that it resembled in appearance a huge conger eel, and it required one of the farm carts to convey it to Stornoway. The capture of this creature must have occurred seventy or eighty years ago.

An event supposed on such hearsay to have occurred before 1780 is a little beyond our belief. But this is not the only report of the capture of such an animal. A Mrs Cameron of Corpach, near Fort William, writing to Captain Lionel Leslie, claimed that when one of the locks on Caledonian canal at Corpach were being cleared at the end of the last century, workmen killed an animal they found in it. "In appearance it resembled an eel but was much larger than any eel ever seen and it had a long mane". They thought it might have come down from Loch Ness, even then the rumoured haunt of such queer animals. But this also seems a vague claim which remains unsubstantiated.

To return to our Victorians. Lord Malmesbury, an English politician with estates in Scotland, write in his diary, between accounts of Cabinet affairs and news of the Indian Mutiny, about the water-horse he was told about while staying at Achnacarry during 1857:

> *October 3rd.* – This morning my stalker and his boy gave me an account of a mysterious creature, which they say exists in Loch Arkaig, and which they call the Lake-horse. It is the same animal of which one has occasionally read accounts in the newspapers of having been seen in Highland lochs, and on the existence of which in Loch Assynt the late Lord Ellesmere wrote an interesting article, but hitherto the story has always been looked upon as fabulous. I am now, however, persuaded of its truth. My stalker, John Stuart, at Achnacarry, has seen it twice, and both times at sunrise in summer on a bright sunny day, when there was not a ripple on the water. The creature was basking on the surface; he saw only the head and hind quarters, proving its back was hollow, which is not the shape of any fish or seal. Its head resembled that of a horse. It was also seen once by his three little children, who were walking together along the beach. It was then motionless, about 30 yards from the shore, and apparently asleep, and at first they took it for a rock, but when they got near it moved its head, and they were so frightened that they ran home, arriving in a state of greatest terror. There was no mistaking their manner when they related this story, and they offered to make an affidavit before a magistrate. The Highlanders are very superstitious about this creature. They are convinced there is never more than one in existence at the same time, and I believe they think it has something diabolical in its nature, for when I said I wished I could get a shot of it, my stalker observed very gravely, "Perhaps your Lordship's gun would misfire". It would be quite possible, though difficult for a seal to work its way up the River Lochy into Loch Arkaig.

Sir Herbert Maxwell, the distinguished grandfather of the writer Gavin Maxwell, writing over half a century later, had a very different account of a "monster" in Loch Arkaig. Four gentlemen were crossing the loch in a steam pinnace when a large animal came to the surface. It seemed to be in a struggle with something, and the waves from the commotion passed over the wake of the boat. One of the party, "a trustworthy and intelligent man", not given to romancing, later told Sir Herbert that they had seen "a large unknown animal". Sir Herbert was inclined to believe his old friend.

However, three weeks later, he met the stalker who had been with the party, and asked him about the incident. Yes, the stalker had seen the animal before the party had. "What did you think it was?" Sir Herbert asked. "It was an otter". The stalker had heard the members of the party speculating about their "large unknown animal". But he had not been asked for his opinion, and as was the custom of those days, it was not his place to offer it unasked.

Was the water horse described to Lord Malmesbury also an otter? It hardly seems likely. But otters may account for some reports of lake monsters. They have a habit of swimming in line behind each other, and in leaping, dolphin-like, through the water in pursuit of fish: both of which could give the impression of a "large unknown animal". But I am satisfied that not all accounts can, by any means, be explained away in this fashion.

I have not been able to trace what must be an interesting article about the Assynt monster by Lord Ellesmere, who died in 1857.† Lord Malmesbury's reference to occasional accounts of water horses in Victorian newspapers is most tantalising. I have traced one or two of these, from the year before he wrote, but are there others? If these could also be traced they would be of great interest. English visitors brought back stories of the water horse in Loch Beiste on Greenstone Point in Western Ross. As it was mentioned (I believe) in *Punch* during the 1850's, perhaps this is another of the accounts Lord Malmesbury read.

The landlord on whose estates Loch Beiste lay was an Englishman named Bankes. He attempted to capture the water horse by draining the loch (just as Scott had predicted someone would eventually). When that failed, he tried to poison it by

---

† Loch Canish, which flows into Loch Assynt, is also said to have monsters, one of which was seen in the 1930's by a Kenneth MacKenzie of Steen; a long neck with a head like a hind, but without ears, rose over the stern of his boat one evening.

charging the water with quick lime. That also failing, he fined his tenants a pound each to punish them. Damned peasants!

Skye was the scene of another effort to capture a water horse, this time one in Loch nan Dubhrachan on the Sleat. In 1870 (according to Mary Donaldson, a Skye writer who heard all about the affair from an old man) the local laird, MacDonald of Sleat, tried dragging the loch for the beiste. It had been seen on the shore once, and had been mistaken for a dead cow, until it took to the water and swam out with its head under the water. The event was a great holiday, children were let out of school, crowds arrived by cart and trap, "there was more whiskey than at a funeral". And there was fun for all. Two boats dragged the loch with a long net. When it caught on a snag, thinking the monster had been netted, the crowd fled in fear. In the end the laird caught for his trouble only two pike. Damned fish!

The geologist Sir Archibald Geike mentions in his *Scottish Reminiscences* (1904) that he discovered lingering traces on Skye of a belief in water horses and water cows in some of the lakes south of Strath. The water horse was said to run off with young girls, but he never actually met anyone who claimed to have seen one of the creatures.

Others did. Fr Allan McDonald, then the parish priest on the island of South Uist, was lucky enough to interview a man who had seen one quite recently. As I have said, folklorists seem to have taken for folk stories what may really be reports of unknown animals. This story (quoted in a recent book *Strange Things*, by John Lorne Campbell and Trevor Hall) is drawn from one of the priests folklore notebooks.

On June 5, 1897, one Ewen MacMillan described to Fr Allan how he had gone out one day in June four years before to look for a strayed horse. There was a foggy haze over the island, when he came to Loch Duvat on Eriskay:

He saw an animal in front of him on the north side of the lake which he took to be his own mare and was making up to it. He got to within 20 yards of it but he could not distinguish the colour on account of the haze, but in size it appeared larger than a common Eriskay pony. When he came to within 20 yards of it the creature gave a hideous or

unearthly scream (sgiamh gránda) that terrified not only
MacMillan but the horses that were grazing at the West
end of the lake, which immediately took flight. MacMillan
ran the whole way home and the horses did not stop till
they reached home.

Fr Allan calls this animal a "water horse", and because of his
keen interest in the occult, thought it was some sort of spirit
creature. But there is really nothing in the story to suggest that
the animal was other than flesh and blood. It may well have
been unusual, but not unreal and I think we can assume it was
an animal similar to the Loch Ness animal. As we have seen
there is evidence that these may not be larger than 20 feet.
That unearthly cry, which adds such a neat touch of horror to
the story, will be heard again.

This is an interesting story also because it shows us how, in
Muir's words, the ordinary turns into the fabulous. This unusual encounter, dressed up by repetition, might well become
one of those exaggerated stories we have read here. It seems
that by the end of the last century, Scotland was well known
as the haunt of strange lake monsters. We will now cast around
to see what traces of them have been found recently.

It seems appropriate to begin on the island of Lewis, where
the earliest report came from in 1856. Norman Morrison, a
zoologist, reported to Cyril Dieckhoff in 1941 that an animal
was sometimes seen in a small loch on that island. In appearance
it was like an upturned-boat, and was called by the local
people *Searrach Uisge* (Water Colt).

More recently, on July 27, 1961, two anglers saw a monster
in Loch Urabhal, near the village of Achmore. Two teachers,
both locally born, Ian McArthur and Roderick Maciver, were
fishing at the shallow end of the loch. Maciver jumped to his
feet, shouting "There's something in the loch". The animal
was about 45 yards away from them in shallow water. It appeared three times on the surface. It had a hump and there
was either a small head or fin about 6 feet from the hump. It
swam like a dolphin, that is, up and down in undulations, but
was much bigger. The sun was bright and the loch calm.
McArthur just had his camera ready for a picture when it
submerged for the third and last time.

Loch Urabhal is a freshwater lake and McArthur thought it most unlikely that any sea animal could have got into it. His father told him there were no legends attached to that lake, and they had probably seen an otter. But McArthur pointed out that the animal did not swim like an otter.

The Lewis historian, Dr Donald MacDonald, told a reporter that he had heard of no traditions about that particular loch. The only loch in Lewis reputed to have a monster was Suainbhal, near Uig, where lambs had once been thrown into the loch to feed the monster. Loch Suainbhal seems to be the lake of the 1856 sensation.

Back on the mainland of Western Scotland, Loch Treig below Ben Bevis was supposed to be the home of particularly fearsome water horses. These hidden terrors of Loch Treig were revived in 1933. Mr B. N. Peach, an engineer in charge of a hydro-electric scheme on the lake, claimed that some of the divers working on the project had surfaced with stories of monsters in the depths. Some men as a result had gone to other jobs.

From other lochs with traditions of water horses have also come other new reports. Writing in 1724 of Loch Lomond (where the "floating island" was said to be), Alexander Graham of Duchray claimed that "in this Loch at the place where the River Enrick falls into it, about a mile west of the church of Buchanan, its reported by countrymen living there about, that they sometimes see the Hipotam or water-horse".

On September 22, 1964, a Helensborough couple, the Haggertys, saw a long humped back moving up the lake. The same summer a railway engineer and his fireman, emerging in their train from the tunnel onto the stretch of track above the loch, had seen a huge object "bigger than a long boat and moving fast – just like a torpedo", swiftly crossing the water.

A few lochs have no traditions (so far as I know) yet do have monsters. Loch Quoich is one of these. A certain lord used to fish there, and on one occasion he was with two gillies, when they saw the monster lying on the shore close to the water. When the story got around as gossip, the peer swore his servants to secrecy lest they all be accused of being drunk. At about the same period the monster is said to have been seen swimming under the water by a fishing party crossing the loch by boat.

A special correspondent of the *Northern Chronicle* produced
some stories of this same animal in 1933; but these seem to be
little more than unfounded rumours. Cyril Dieckhoff heard
evidence of a monster in Loch Lochy, and the same correspondent had stories about that animal as well.

In 1930 a man living in Lochyside warned his wife not to
wash the linen in the lake any more. When pressed he revealed
that he had seen a strange animal in it, and though it might be
harmless, it was as well to take no chances. And in 1929 two
gamekeepers of long experience saw what they thought was a
log slightly rounded in the centre. But with the aid of a telescope they soon saw it was some large animal, whose movements
they were able to follow for a mile before it dived.

I don't know what evidence Dieckhoff had, but there is now
some doubt that the monster is still there. In March 1960,
Maurice Burton received from a correspondent a photograph
which had been found in the family album, apparently of a
monster surfacing in Loch Lochy. "An enlargement of the
picture," he writes in *The Elusive Monster*, "shows a dark
irregular mass in the middle of the foam, with something like
a group of bubbles". The object disappeared a few seconds
after the photograph was taken. Dr Burton concludes that the
"monster", in this case anyway, was one of his masses of slimey
rubbish.

But on July 15, 1960, Mr Eric Robbins, his wife and a friend,
saw what they took to be a "monster" at 7.25 in the evening.
First they saw two stationary waves – doubtless those "waves
without wind" mentioned on Blaeu's atlas – and as these moved
off across the loch they rose out of the water forming a broad
back. Then the object began rolling over. Watching through
binoculars, the trio saw "a fin or paddle on the side of its body
as it turned". The underside was lighter in colour. The back was
about 15 feet long, and they estimated the total length of the
creature – which was 250 yards offshore – to be 30 to 40 feet.
By then nine other people were watching the turmoil in the
water and the waves breaking on the beach at their feet.

The evidence from Loch Oich, which lies between Loch Ness
and Loch Lochy, while strong at first seems on investigation a
little vague. It seems generally agreed among writers on this
question that there are traditions of a monster in Loch Oich.

"There is a tradition in the Great Glen of Scotland", wrote Alister MacGregor in 1937, "and indeed in Inverness generally that a strange beast inhabits the depths of Loch Oich, but although many of the natives and not a few travellers profess to have seen it, the beast has been overshadowed by its more famous neighbour in Loch Ness". Although he himself does not actually quote any evidence, it is quite strong.

Oudemans in an article on the Loch Ness monster in 1934, quotes an odd little story about Loch Oich which is worth having on the record. A deep pool in the Garry River which flows into the loch is called locally "The Children's Pool".

Tradition has it that many years ago some children residing at Inchlaggan were playing on the loops of the Garry at this spot when a huge "beiste" in the shape of a deformed pony appeared on the bank of the river. Curious to learn whether the creature was not a real pony on which they could enjoy a ride, the children went up to it, and, the story has it, that they found the "Beiste" so docile that one of them ventured on its back. No sooner had the child done so than the "beiste" plunged into the pool with the rider at the same time carrying with it a child clung to its mane. No trace was ever found of the bodies thus mysteriously drowned.

Though most of us would think that merely a piece of folklore, Oudemans seems to have taken it seriously enough. And on consideration given that these animals are in fact some kind of large mammal related to the seals, there is nothing inherently impossible about the story. A deformed pony with a mane describes well enough the animal we are now familiar with. From my own experience, however, I doubt if much light would be thrown on the story by local inquiries.†

One of those travellers MacGregor mentions had seen the monster in the summer of 1936. Mr A. J. Robertson had been

---

† Oudemans quotes a story from the same district, about "a huge serpent" which was said to be sometimes seen in the deer forest of Guischan in Glenmoriston. His source recounts the tale from an old crofter: "It was of the dimensions that are usually attributed to the sea serpent, but what chiefly disturbed me was the fact that the fearsome creature had a huge hairy frill or mane round its neck". Could this have been yet another of our animals wandering ashore?

boating in the south-western end of the loch, towards Lochy. He first noticed a commotion in the water. Part of a huge black snake-like body rose to the surface, then the head appeared about a yard in front of the humps. The head was vaguely dog-like.

Loch Oich is connected by a river with Loch Ness, so it is just possible that an animal could make its way into it from the larger loch. One of the first journalists to investigate the Loch Ness monster in 1933, J. W. Herries, continued to take an interest in the problem. On a later visit he looked into these rumours of another monster in Loch Oich.

I interviewed three young men who had seen this object making its way from Loch Ness into Loch Oich. Afterwards I saw the lock keeper at Loch Oich (that is, the keeper on the Caledonian canal lock at the southern end leading into Loch Oich), who had a close-up view. His daughter called his attention to a strange animal in an almost land-enclosed bay close to their house. He went out and saw swimming about an animal six feet long, something like an otter, but much larger. He told his daughter to bring his gun; but before she could do so, the stranger had submerged. He was knowledgable about the water and its denizens, but could liken what he had seen to nothing in his previous experience.

There is little doubt that the keeper would have recognised the animal for what it was had it been an otter. Yet he saw at once that it resembled such an animal in its adaption to an aquatic life. The small size of Loch Oich makes it eminently suitable for further investigation.

I should mention here a suggestion made by Angus Ross of Edinburgh University, in a letter to the *New Scientist* (December 1, 1960). He claims that some years ago a creature was reported from Loch Oich.

The eye-witnesses were unimpeachable, but their accounts were not as clear as might have been desired. The drawings made, on the other hand, show a creature remarkably like what we generally term a giant squid. The differences between the Loch Oich creature and a squid might be real, but might equally well be due to defective drawing.

He suggested that there was little doubt that Loch Oich contained a squid, and that the Loch Ness monster was also one.

This is not an original theory: Henry Lee used it in 1883 to explain away the sea-serpent. Whatever its merits in that context, it won't work for lake monsters, because giant squids could not survive in fresh water. I have not been able to trace these drawings he mentions, but I guess that they showed a "string of buoys" effect, a series of humps with what might be a head at the front end. It would be interesting to know if these still exist.

Lately, however, the Loch Oich monster has fallen into disrepute. On July 8, 1961, the Scottish *Daily Express* published a photograph of what was archly called "Wee Oichy". This "monster" turned out to be only a clever hoax. The journalist Jonathan Routh and some friends had contrived a device which ran through the water giving the impression of a large animal. Having gone to great trouble to have it photographed and reported, the hoaxers were chagrined to have their monster stolen from them by a student group who claimed the credit for the whole affair.

It was unfortunate that the hoaxers had to choose a loch with both old traditions and modern reports of a monster. Now all reports from Loch Oich will be looked at twice, and then probably be rejected.

On my second trip through the Highlands, I thought it would be worth while trying to find out more about the lock keeper's sighting. We had no difficulty finding the cottage of the man now in charge of the lock, but he had only come to the job in 1939. He had, however, been an assistant for a few years before that. He had no memories of any reports of a monster in Loch Oich. Now there is no doubt that the English visitors had seen something back in 1936. Was this a case of the local people keeping quiet, we wondered? The matter then became even more complicated, when it turned out that the previous lockkeeper had had no daughter. Could the girl have been his niece? we were asked. The matter then vanished into a complexity of family relationships impossible to follow, even with an Irish training in these things. No light was cast on the sighting, except that below Oich Bridge there was an almost land-locked pool: Herries had been right about that anyway.

Since returning from Scotland, I have discovered that the lock keeper at Oich Bridge was wrong. The Loch Oich animal was indeed seen in 1936 by one Simon Cameron, the canal bridge keeper at Laggan, Invergary on September 19. Mr Cameron said the animal rose to the surface beside his house, and with quick powerful strokes of its forelimbs travelled briskly in an easterly direction, passing out of his sight. The animal was six feet long, with a furry-looking body and a dog-like head. Asked by a reporter if he thought it might have been an otter, Cameron replied that "There is no otter on earth anything like that". So Herries was right about the witness as well. So much for local knowledge!

Over on the western sea-board, around Loch Shiel and Loch Morar, the traditions are more circumstantial, the reports more recent and authentic.

Dom Cyril Dieckhoff, for his book about the Loch Ness monster, availed himself of every opportunity to record accounts of other monsters in the Highlands. While on his pastoral duties about the Western Highlands, especially in the Catholic district about Morar, he came by several stories of the monster in Loch Shiel.

In December 1933 he was told by an old man who lived near Shiel Bridges that "gum faca fear beist loch Seile faisg air Dalilea", that a man once saw the Loch Shiel beast near Dalilea. Later the same month he was told by the Glenuig postman of an old woman who had seen the animal about 1874, who described it thus: "Bha 3 cnaip aice; bha e dol gle luath", there were three humps on it and it was going very fast.

Ewan MacIntosh, the keeper on the Cameron-Head estate at Inverailort, told him about a sighting in 1905. MacIntosh, two young boys and an old man called Ian Crookback were out on the lake in the steamer *Clan Ronald*, opposite Gasgan, when they saw three humps rise out of the water which they all examined through a telescope.

In 1926, according to one Ann Mor MacDonald, her brother Ronald MacLeod saw *an Seileag*, as the animal is known locally. The old woman's gaelic is slightly obscure on one point. MacLeod she says saw the animal "tighinn amach as an uisge aig a' Rudha Ghainmheach", coming out of the water at Sandy Point, between three and four o'clock one afternoon. He

watched it through his telescope – he was a former head-keeper
– and reckoned it was bigger than the *Clan Ronald*. The neck
was rough and long, the head broad with a wide mouth, and
there were seven "sails" on the back, the largest in the centre.
At other times he saw only three humps, though again the
largest was in the centre.

Did Ann Mor MacDonald mean that her brother saw the
animal actually crawling out of the loch onto the shore of
Sandy Point? It seems she did. Mr Francis Cameron-Head
spoke to the two witnesses Ronald MacLeod and Sandie
MacKellaig about their sightings. Sandie MacKellaig had once
tried to shoot an Seileag from his boat when he was giving a
lift to two tinker women, who warned him not to as it had done
him no harm. A nephew of Sandie MacKellaig, who owned the
hotel at Glenfinnan at the head of the loch, told Dieckhoff in
1933 that his uncle and cousin said "that the monster came on
land occasionally".

Both Loch Shiel and Loch Morar are strange places, their
long shores without houses, their great depths unexplored. Loch
Morar is actually the deepest loch in the British Isles, an odd
and daunting place. Again Cyril Dieckhoff records some of the
earliest information about the Loch Morar monster, which is
locally called a' Mhorag. He records in his diary:

27th March 1934. Charlie MacDonald (one of my Glenuig
friends) at that time keeper at Letter Morar, went out to
look after the deer and being near the hut saw some animal
suddenly coming out of the water. It shot up with its neck to
about the length of his arm. It reminded him of an eel
except that an eel never shoot up like that. He judged
it must have been a very big animal to cause so much
commotion.

Traditions about a monster in Loch Morar go back a long
way: "Who has not heard of the Mhorag?" a local writer
James MacDonald asked in 1907. It too was a portentous
beast. A diligent young man on the *Guardian* discovered a
rhyme about the creature in an old collection of Scottish
songs:

> Morag, Harbinger of Death,
> Giant Swimmer in deep-green Morar,
> The loch that has no bottom . . .
> There it is that Morag the monster lives.

The monster was supposed to appear before the death of a MacDonnell; and indeed, three weeks after the Morag was seen by a whole boat-load of visitors one of the last of the Brinogary MacDonnells died.

The writer James MacDonald was thankful for his own name when he encountered the beast. This happened one night in January 1887, when he was crossing the loch to poach deer on the slopes above Raitlan. The creature appeared in three parts on the surface, said to represent by local tradition the death, the coffin and the grave of a MacDonnell.

Fateful though the monster was many people are said to have seen it during the 1880's, but the first solid account we have of it is from 1895. That summer Sir Theodore Brinckman and his wife were out fishing with their stalker MacLaren, when Mrs Brinckman described a long dark shape like an upturned boat and asked if it was the launch they were expecting. No, said MacLaren, "it'll just be the monster". And he explained to them that the animal was well known, though only seen from time to time.

The Loch Ness affair brought Morag to the attention of the outside world, but then she was promptly forgotten about. However, in 1946 Mr Alexander MacDonnell was taking a party of schoolchildren from the *Comunn na h-Oigridh* summer camp at Inverailort from Morar to Meoble in the Lovat estate boat. As the boat was passing Bracorina Point on the northern shore, some of the children cried out "Oh look! What is that big thing on the bank over there?" Mr MacDonnell said he saw then an animal about the size of an Indian elephant, which plunged off the rocks into the water with a terrific splash. This seems to be the only report from Morar of the animal ashore. (I think it must be the sinuous shape of the long neck, which looks rather like a trunk, as well as the dull grey colour, which brings an elephant to so many people's minds when trying to describe these animals.)

In 1948 a boat-load of tourists saw Morag, an encounter which was widely reported at the time in the press. Mr John Gillies was taking the party, mainly from Liverpool, out for a day trip round the loch. On the way back, when they were passing Swordlands, one of the visitors noticed something in their wake. "And there was the Maggie", Gillies later told Mrs Whyte, "about 30 feet long with four humps sticking out of the water about 2 feet above the surface. I did not see any head or tail as it was about half a mile away from the boat and it disappeared in 60 seconds. It had quite a good speed and wash on it".

Since then the animal has been seen around the loch quite regularly. An English couple who owned the house at Swordlands for several years after the war became so used to the thing coming and going that in the end they gave up watching for it. Most of their sightings were of "an upturned-boat".

In September 1958 Dr George Cooper, a distinguished scientist, and his family were holidaying at Morar. Dr Cooper was painting a view of the western end of the loch, showing the islands there which harbour the last vestiges of the ancient Caledonian forest. He noticed what at first he thought was a large log drifting slowly down the loch, which quite suddenly vanished after he had watched it for over an hour. At one stage he recalls that one end may have been higher than the other. The appearance was "rather like the rough or semi-rough surface of a tree trunk": it was definitely not shiny. After it had vanished he executed a quick water-colour sketch (now in the possession of the Loch Morar Survey). This remarkable painting is, as Elizabeth Montgomery Campbell remarks, "perhaps the only existing portrait of the beast of Loch Morar – or any other Scottish loch monster".

In August 1968, however, John MacVarish, a local hotel worker, saw the head and neck emerging from the water while he was travelling between Bracora and Lettermore. The neck was 5 or 6 feet long, about 18 inches wide, tapering to a flat, snake-like head which was small compared to the size of the neck. The skin was smooth and black. The animal was moving forward at a slow speed and the movements of the water at the sides suggested paddling by fins. When he started his engine to try and get nearer, the animal moved out into deeper water and settled down out of sight. (Mr MacVarish has since seen some humps and a wake.)

The next summer marks a turning point in Morag's history, due to an incident which I will come to in a moment. But first two interesting reports from Meoble Bay in July 1969. On July 8, a regular visitor to Loch Morar named Bob Duff was trolling across Meoble Bay at about 2 knots. The water at this point is very clear, about 16 feet deep with a white sandy bottom – leaves could clearly be seen on the sand. Looking over the side of the boat:

Mr Duff saw what he described as a "monster lizard" lying on the bottom. It was not more than 20 feet long, motionless, and looking up at him. The shock of seeing it caused him to rev up and get away as fast as possible so that he only saw it momentarily. As described and drawn by Mr Duff it appears he saw only the front part clearly. The head was snake-like with a wide mouth and slit eyes. As it was seen from above the neck was not visible and its length could not be estimated. It had four legs and the front legs were clearly seen to have three digits each. The body, hindquarters and tail were only vaguely seen. It was a grey-brown, the skin rough like "burnt coke".

When Duff recovered his nerve and came back to look for it, the animal was gone. However, a couple of weeks later a Mallaig shopkeeper looking over the side of a boat moving over almost the same place, saw an indistinct greeny shape on the bottom. He was certain it was something unusual but his cautious friend refused to stop and have a look.

These two reports are of exceptional interest, particularly Mr Duff's mention of three digits on the front limbs, a detail we have already heard about at Loch Ness and which we will meet again. The slit eyes are also another familiar feature of the animal. It has been noticed at Loch Ness that most of the sightings are in shallow water at the mouths of rivers. This is only natural, as one would expect a seal-like predator to lie up in such places in wait for trout, salmon and eels making their way up the river and streams. This, it will be recalled, had been Malcolm Irvine's theory which enabled him to film the monster twice. One would have thought it worth while to maintain a boat patrol in Meoble Bay to take advantage of the animal's habits. But not at all. When a cadet branch of the Loch Ness Investigation Bureau lighted on Loch Morar, they set up the same discredited camera sites along the shores. The one at Meoble Bay was set to overlook the remoter end of the loch rather than the bay itself.

The interest of this group in Loch Morar was aroused by a sensational encounter by two men on the evening of August 16, 1969. Duncan McDonnell and William Simpson were returning from a fishing trip. It was about nine o'clock when they were passing the islands at the west end of the loch in their motor boat. The kettle was on for tea. McDonnell heard a noise behind the boat and turned to see some large object moving towards them about 20 yards away. It struck the boat, unintentionally he later thought. The kettle was knocked off the stove by the impact, and Simpson went down into the cabin to turn off the gas. McDonnell was trying, meanwhile, to fend off the creature with an old oar, which broke in his hand. The body was quite solid to the touch and did not give. Simpson by now had brought up a loaded rifle from the cabin, and fired at the animal which fell astern and sank from sight. They thought it was the noise of the report rather than any wound that frightened the animal off.

As to what they saw: the animal was about 25 to 30 feet long, with three shallow humps or undulations. The skin was rough and dirty brown in colour. They saw no tail. MacDonnell while fending off the animal had seen the top of a snake-like head, about a foot across the top or so, rising 18 inches out of the water.

This was not the first time that Duncan MacDonnell had seen the monster. On previous occasions he had seen the head and neck, and once a set of humps. He was reluctant to enlarge upon these incidents for the Loch Morar Investigation (from whose reports the quotes above are taken), and said that many other people had stories to tell but would not do so for fear of being called liars.

MacDonnell was right to be cautious, for the manner in which his rather frightening encounter was written up as news was lurid enough. I first read about the affair in a wire service dispatch published in the *New York Times*. According to this report from United Press International, which must have appeared in countless other papers, the episode was even more exciting, with the monster biting off the end of the oar in a rage and having a great hole blasted in its side by Simpson's shotgun. Americanisms betrayed the blue pencil of a New York sub-editor. This dispatch is typical of the sort of back-page filler the wire services provide to add a little colour to the daily news. In other chapters similar stories will often be quoted, which have not all been personally authenticated. The reader can, if he likes, on this warning, take them all with a large pinch of salt. But remember MacDonnell and Simpson *did* see the Morar monster, despite the added lurid details.

The Loch Morar Survey set up its own investigations at Morar in 1970, '71 and '72. On three occasions members of the expeditions had sightings of a large hump, on the second only missing by a moment a photograph of it. A full account of these investigations and their background can be found in a recently published book *The Search for Morag* by Elizabeth Montgomery Campbell and David Solomon. The group have now decided against any further investigation, at least for the moment. They feel that only a fully financed and officially supported expedition would bring the final results desired. So, at Loch Morar, that is that for the time being.

Loch Ness, as I say, has absorbed the attention of most investigators, and there at least some progress has been made towards the solution of the enigma. All the same, these bits and scraps, and odds and ends of evidence from other Scottish lochs should not be ignored or neglected.

It might be argued that the tradition of water horses in so many of these lochs casts some doubt on recent reports of monsters: people may only be seeing what they are expected to see. But in my opinion the contrary is true: the modern reports show that there is some truth in the old traditions of the kelpie and the water horse after all. And that elsewhere, when we find such old traditions of lake monsters, we are likely to be on the track of some unknown animal.

The Loch Ness animals are not unique, either in Scotland or the world. The more attention given to reports from other places, the sooner the real existence of these animals will be completely established. To some of those other places we will now move on, beginning in Europe itself with Ireland and Scandinavia.

6

Pooka and Piast: Ireland

But one old serpent
Sternly refused to be so servile
And leave Lough Allen his habitat,
Although it flapped as the holy habit
Of the saint with rage. He showed his fang.

Austin Clarke: *The Last Irish Snake*

LAKE MONSTERS, ACCORDING to the naturalist Robert Lloyd Praeger, are "an accepted part of Irish zoology (section mythalia)". Recently, however, some of these monsters have been asserting themselves in a most unmythical manner.

In his invaluable book on Irish place names, the historian Dr P. W. Joyce observed that "legends of aquatic monsters are very ancient among the Irish people". He shows that a large number of places in Ireland now have names which indicate a once widely held belief in water monsters such as the water horse, the piast and the pooka. He quotes Adamnan's story of the monster seen in the River Ness: as there now seems to be a basis in fact for that legend, might there not be more to these other traditions as well? Might not monsters belong to some other zoological section?

One tale in the Fenian cycle of ancient Irish sagas tells how Lough Derg in Donegal got its name. The hero Finn slaughtered there a monster which had swallowed some of his followers. Finn overcame the monster, and two hundred warriors, now naked and hairless, came out of its belly alive. The lake became known as Lough Derg, the Red Lake, because of what the ancient poet calls "this wonderful slaughter".†

† Captain Lionel Leslie, who has been investigating reports of Irish lake monsters for some years now, was told several years ago by an old man that there was still a water horse to be seen in Lough Derg. One cannot help but speculate on the connection between these legends and the origin of Lough Derg as a place of pagan and Christian pilgrimage.

Water monsters appear in other saga stories as well. These stories, so reminiscent of classical myths, are a curiously common motif in early Irish literature. We must be wary, however, of reading anything of value to natural history into them. Many of these swallowing-monster myths will probably have belonged originally to rituals of kingship or of tribal initiation, the hairless nakedness of the warriors signifying their rebirth. These myths are only to be understood in their true context, and divorced from their proper rituals now seem absurd to the zoologist.

The water monster motif is often found in lives of Irish saints, also. Another Irish scholar, James Carney, has suggested that the stories in the sagas were added to them by the monastic scribes who recorded them in early Christian Ireland.

Some examples: in the seventh century *Life Of St Mochua of Balla*, we are told how a stag took refuge from a royal hunting party on an island in Lough Ree on the River Shannon. None of the hunters dared to follow it "on account of a horrible monster that infested the lake, and was accustomed to destroy swimmers". One of the hunters was brave enough to swim across to the island "but as he was returning the beast devoured him".

Saint Colman of Dromore saved someone from a worse predicament: a young girl washing her nightdress in a river pool was swallowed by an aquatic monster, but by his blessing the saint brought her safe from the monster's belly.

And once when Saint Molua was at Druimsnachta (now Drumsnatt in Monaghan), two boys went for a swim in a local lake. While they were playing *apparuit bestia terribilis valde, cujus magnitude erat quaci magna scapha*, a frightful creature appeared which was quite as big as a large boat. The echo here of a familiar description of the Loch Ness monster as "an upturned boat" reassures us that we are not dealing with completely fanciful stories.

In Ireland, as in ancient Greece, animals were supposed to have their counterparts in other spheres: Pegasus on Olympus, the Water Horse in the sea-waves. The country people supposed that this world was reduplicated underwater. They told stories of cows, bulls and dogs from that other world. Sometimes these were even captured: water horses came out of lakes and were broken to the plough; strange cows in byres where poor families milked them were said to have come up from pastures under the water.

But besides these harmless creatures, true monsters called variously piast, peist or ollpheist, haunted some lakes. St Patrick, when he banished the snakes out of Ireland, is said to have chained the most terrible – such as the one on Lough Allen – to lake bottoms, allowing them to appear only every seven years. Such legends easily become localised, and people will soon claim to have seen huge animals jumping in a neighbouring lake.

Or so the folklorists claim. But as we go through the early accounts of Irish lake monsters we shall find that there is often only a superficial covering of fancy, often the work of the collectors, and that real animals are clearly behind some of the stories.

In the last chapter I quoted several early Scottish historians. Here now is a comparable Irish story from *A Description of West or H-Iar Connaught* (1684) by Roderick O'Flaherty. Writing about the general features of interest around the shores of Lough Mask, he remarks in conclusion:

There is one rarity more, which we may term the Irish crocodile, whereof one, as yet living, about ten years ago (1674) had sad experience. The man was passing the shore just by the waterside, and spyed far off the head of a beast swimming, which he took to be an otter, and took no more notice of it; but the beast it seems lifted up his head, to discern whereabouts the man was; then diving swam under the water till he struck ground; whereupon he run out of the water suddenly and took the man by the elbow whereby the man stooped down, and the beast fastened his teeth in his pate, and dragged him into the water; where the man took hold of a stone by chance in his way, and calling to mind he had a knife in his jacket, took it out and gave a thrust of it to the beast, which thereupon got away from him into the lake. The water about him was all bloody, whether from the beast's blood, or his own, or from both he knows not. It was the pitch of an ordinary greyhound, of a black slimey skin, without hair as he imagines. Old men acquainted with the lake do tell there is such a beast in it, and that a stout fellow with a wolf dog along with him met the like there once; which after a long struggling went away in spite of the man and his dog, and was a long time after found rotten in a rocky cave of the lake when the waters decreased. The like they say is seen in other lakes in Ireland, they call it Dovarchu, i.e. water-dog, or anchu which is the same.

What are we to make of this quite remarkable story, presented to us as it is in such a commonplace way? Here the difficulties begin.

In the edition of O'Flaherty's book which was published in 1866 by the Irish Archaeological Society in Dublin, the editor James Hardiman adds in a footnote to the story the information that "In these Western parts, this animal is generally called Each Uisge, which means a water-horse, and he is described as having a black shining skin and switch tail without hair. The story related by our author is yet told in the neighbourhood of Lough Mask".

There seems to be some confusion here. The word *dovarchu* does sometimes mean an otter in Irish. But Hardiman seems to be mixing up two creatures which are carefully distinguished in the folk tradition. In 1843 the author of *Wild Sports of the West* observed that in Connaught "animals of extra-ordinary formation, and strange virtues, are supposed to inhabit lakes and rivers. Among these are the *sea-horse* and the *master-otter* are pre-eminent. By a singular anomaly, the first is said to be found in certain island lochs, and his appearance is imagined to be fatal to the unfortunate person who encounters it".

O'Flaherty's Irish crocodile is presumably the *master-otter*, while the *sea-horse* is the each uisge of gaelic stories. The water horse is the same animal that we have searched out in the Highlands; perhaps the master otter is the Kelpie. It has often been suggested that some reports of lake monsters could be sightings of large otters, and Maurice Burton once suggested that the Loch Ness animal might be a long-necked otter-like animal. In fact there is such an animal among the sea-serpents, one quite different from the Merhorse and the Long-neck. Whether these are the animals that Connaught peasants were trying to distinguish is hard to say, but certainly the description of the Lough Mask animal is strongly remiscent of an otter.

A difficulty about many of these reports is that in Ireland, as in Scotland, modern writers relate as folklore curious stories which were told to them as fact. Sorting out the fancies, fictions and actual facts is difficult. O'Flaherty reports the existence of a strange animal in Lough Mask as a passing matter of fact; in the hands of the Irish writers of the last century such facts turned into fantasy.

For example, W. B. Yeats, in that youthfully charming book *The Celtic Twilight* published in 1893, writes of such miraculous creatures as the White Stag of Arthurian Romance, the magic boar of Celtic saga and the queer creatures of Irish stories. Many of these tales were told to Yeats by Paddy Flynn of Ballisodare in Sligo; others by Galway peasants Lady Gregory took him to visit around Kiltartan Cross in Galway. "Another time", one of these informants told him,

> My father told me he was in a boat out on the lake with two or three men from Gort, and one of them had an eel-spear, and he thrust it into the water, and it hit something, and the man fainted and they had to carry him out of the boat to land, and when he came to himself he said that what he struck was like a calf, but, whatever it was, it was not a fish.

Yeats comments that a friend of his (perhaps George Russell) was "convinced that these terrible creatures so common in lakes, were set there by subtle enchanters to watch over the gates of wisdom".

Lady Gregory herself provides more stories of these Gort lakes in her *Visions and Beliefs in the West of Ireland* (1922). She was told there was a monster in Lough Graney, but it was seen only every seven years. Another man said of the same lake:

> The lake down there is an enchanted place, and the old people told me that one time they were swimming there, and a man had gone out into the middle and they saw something like a giant eel making for him, and they called out, "If ever you were a great swimmer show us now how you can swim

to the shore", for they wouldn't frighten him by saying what was behind him. So he swam to the shore, and he only got there when the thing behind him was in the place where he was. For there are queer things in lakes.

Of the small lake near her house at Coole, Lady Gregory was told that it had a monster as well, though her informant had never seen it himself,

> but one day I was coming home with my two brothers from Tirneevan School, and there as we passed Dhulough we heard a great splashing, and we saw some creature put its head up, with the head and mane like a horse. And we didn't stop but ran. But I think it was not so big as the monster over here in Coole Lake, for Johnny Callan saw it, and he said it was the size of a stack of turf. But there's many could tell about that for there's many saw it, Dougherty from Gort and others.

These stories, so reminscent of recent Scottish reports, have a plausible sound despite the fact that those who collected them probably didn't believe a word of them. In the Wicklow Hills, the young John Synge (to exhaust the Irish writers of the Revival) heard a less credible story, probably a genuine folk tradition kindled with some modern touches, about a monster in Lough Nahanagan. He was told it by a young girl who had been looking after his dog.

A man was going round Ireland swimming in every lake. He came to this lake and he had a big black dog with him. He'd taken off his clothes to dive in when the girl's brother warned him to send the dog in first to try the safety of the water. The swimmer threw a stick across the water and his dog swam out and retrieved it. But then "the dog went down out of their sight, and the insides of him came up on top of the water".

This must be considered as folklore. As with Scottish lochs, even in modern accounts it is often difficult to judge what is merely folklore, though it must be remembered that folklore often has a basis in fact. And it is to more factual accounts that we now turn.

In 1934 Cyril Dieckhoff was told of a Donegal monster by

one of his correspondents Joseph Gallagher, who wrote in Irish.

May 25th, 1934.
This happened in my own time, about 1885. A young woman waded out as far as she could off the Shore of Lough Muck to pull bog-bean, and when stopped heard a splash no distance from her. She looked and there was an animal making towards her. She made for the shore as fast as she could. Then for a year or two afterwards it was seen occasionally. It would raise two humps above the water. This lough is less than three-quarters of a mile long by half a mile across. Salmon might come into it in November when spawning. Only now for the last 40 years nothing was seen in the lough. It's 45 miles from the sea. It could get no food there only brown trout. No one there could tell what kind of animal it was. The young woman that seen it first always declared that its eyes was in or about 3 inches each way.

These large eyes have occasionally been reported on the Loch Ness monster, and seem to be due to the lighter colour round the eye rather than to any great size. As Mr Gallagher intelligently points out one of the problems about many reports of Irish monsters is that they are often seen in what are little more than puddles in the bogs, where survival would seem to be difficult. Perhaps, like the Loch Ness monster, these animals can move across land.

The Lough Muck monster disappeared after a few years; others still survive. In his book *Seventy Years of Irish Life*, published posthumously in 1893, W. R. Le Fanu wrote:

That dreadful beast, the Wurrum – half-fish, half-dragon – still survives in many a mountain lake – seldom seen, indeed, but often heard. Near our fishing quarters in Kerry there are two such lakes, one the beautiful little lake at the head of the Blackwater River, called Lough Brin, or Bran as he is now called, the dreadful wurrum which inhabits it. The man who minds the boats there speaks with awe of Bran; he tells me he has never seen him and hopes he never may.

The monster's name is derived from an ancient legend that

Finn's hunting dog Bran was drowned in the lake while chasing a stag and that his ghost now haunts the place as a water-dog. Though it is small, only one mile long by half a mile wide, Lough Bran reaches the great depth of 35 fathoms in places. The Blackwater River which flows out of it is famous for its fishing, but Lough Bran is now said to be bare of fish. It is an out of the way place with only one road to it and few houses near its shores. Its monster would seem to be something more than a mere ghost. The boatman in 1893 may not have seen the monster, but others have. A local (but anonymous) resident told me in a letter (1964):

Sure there is a monster in Lough Bran lake, I have seen it. Two persons have seen the monster and he is there with years. He is about 14 feet long and has two big eyes in his forehead. O'Sullivan and O'Connor have seen him. He is like a colt and half a fish seen for years there. It's in this lake that the hound of Fionn Machumhail was drowned.

As my correspondent says, the monster has been seen recently. In 1940 a twelve year old boy was astonished to see some strange animal lying on the shore of the lake, basking in the sun. It was black, he said, with four short legs. On a later occasion a man high above the lake on the mountainside looked down to see a huge wave in the middle of an otherwise calm lake. Another man heard strange splashings on his way home past the lake one dark evening.

On Christmas Eve 1954, Timothy O'Sullivan (the man mentioned in the letter above), who farmed at Cappa near the lake, went out to bring his cattle in for milking. Passing the lake he saw what he took at first to be a couple of ducks. But then the "ducks" rose higher out of the water, and he saw that they were actually two "fins", each about 2 feet long and 2 feet high. The length between the "fins" was 12 feet. They rose and fell four times, only 60 yards offshore.

Mr O'Sullivan rushed back to his house, and much to his wife's astonishment began to load his shotgun with heavy gauge cartridges. He explained quickly and, followed by her, ran back to the shore of the lake. But the objects were gone, and the lake was still in the gloomy light of a midwinter evening.

"Some miles further on", continues Le Fanu, "between Lough Brian and Glencar, there is another lake from which a young boy while bathing was driven and chased by the dreadful wurrum which dwells in it. It bit him on the back and hunted him all the way home, where he arrived naked and bleeding". When he was asked what the beast was like, he said it "was something like the form of a donkey".

Despite Le Fanu's irony, I wonder if this might not be a true story. Would an Irish country boy run home in such a state from an encounter with an animal he was accustomed to handling all his short life? He had clearly been badly scared by something beyond his knowledge, and could only say it "was something like the form of a donkey".

The animal in Lough Brin, whatever it is, is alternatively a water-dog, a water-horse, a fish-like animal and a monster penny-plain. This seems to be merely a matter of vocabulary, and has nothing to do with the actual identity of whatever it is. Even in recent reports there is still this mixture of fact and folklore.

In one of her later books (written with the spiritual aid of Martin Ross) called *The Smile and the Tear*, Edith Somerville recalls some interesting stories from her own experience of lake monsters. Miss Somerville was stimulated no doubt by the newspaper reports that year of the Loch Ness monster, though she stays in West Cork for her own stories.

In January 1914, shortly before the outbreak of war, as everyone later noted, a snake-like animal appeared in a Lake which the author calls Lough Abisdealy (in gaelic *Loch an Beisealaig*). This seems to be actually a lake called Poul na Gurrum, which her nephew Lionel Fleming recalls as being the bottomless haunt of a worm which devoured the local sheep.

One Sunday a young lady was driving to church in a dogcart with her groom and kitchen maid.

I do not know which of the little party first saw the snake, but they all agreed that suddenly they beheld a long black creature propelling itself rapidly across the lake. Its flat head, on a long neck, was held high, two great loops of its length buckled in and out of the water as it progressed. Obviously

a snake, and a huge one. The three witnesses stared, doubtful
of their own eyes at this amazing sight. The avenue is within
a few yards of the water, so they were able to have a clear view
of the mysterious monster. For how long they gazed at it I
do not know. Unfortunately a virtuous anxiety not to keep
her scholars waiting induced the principal witness to proceed
on the way to church before the snake submerged. But her
certainty that it was a snake, and a very large one, could not
be shaken.

Nevertheless, she was wrong: from her description of its
undulations it is clearly a mammal and not a reptile. The groom
thought it was about 35 feet long. The kitchen maid said it was
the length of the scullery. Edith Somerville thought the latter
a more probable estimate, as few West Cork sculleries are
35 feet long.

According to a local Irish-speaking woman the name of the
lake meant the Lake of the Monster; on the Ordinance Survey
it appears, however, as Lough Abisdealy. There was a tradition
of a water-horse in the lake, but it was also said that a butcher
had drowned himself in the lake and his ghost had assumed the
shape of the snake. The monster was said to have appeared
fifty years before, during the Crimean War; when it appeared
in 1914, it was, of course, taken as a portent of the new war.

Miss Somerville also describes another monster, seen in a
seaside wood, but more of that later.

Another of the legendary animals said to haunt Irish lakes,
along with suicidal butchers and heroic dogs, is the pooka.
The usual form of this creature is that of a large black dog, or
sometimes a horse. Nowadays the pooka is merely a country
bogey to frighten children to bed. Many who so use it have no
idea of its origin. Kevin Danagher of the Irish Folklore Commission was told by an old man in the Wicklow hills that in
fact the pooka was the same as the *each uisge*.

The pooka has given its name to many places in Ireland, such
as Lissapuca and Rathpuca. The best known of these places
is Poulapuca, the Pooka's Pool, in Wicklow. Before the valley
there was flooded to make a reservoir for Dublin, the river
Liffey flowed over a ledge into a deep pool, where the pooka
was said to lurk ready to way-lay unwary travellers at night.

D. A. MacManus, in his book *The Middle Kingdom*, discusses
the pooka as an occult creature. His book is not an account
of local traditions such as one of our Swedish-trained folklorists might write. He claims to set down actual accounts of
encounters with fairies, leprachauns and pookas seen in the
last few generations in several parts of Ireland. A friend of
Yeats, Captain MacManus has written a late piece for Celtic
Twilight, and very entertaining it is too. (Incidentally, the
book contains a valuable account of Biddy Early, the Connaught wise woman with whom Yeats was fascinated.)

There is one story in the book of interest to us, that of the
Derry Pooka. A friend of the author, a Mr Martin, spent the
Hilary Vacation from Trinity College Dublin in 1928 at his
parents' home in County Derry. A small river flowed past the
end of the garden. One afternoon the young man was fishing
there. Looking to his right, he saw some creature come swimming round the bend 100 yards away. He could not quite make
out what it was, "whether dog, panther or what, but he felt
it to be intensely menacing". Dropping his rod, he climbed an
ash so small it bent under his weight.

> Meanwhile the animal continued paddling along, and as it
> passed it looked up at him with an almost human intelligence
> and bared its teeth with a mixture of snarl and jeering grin.
> His flesh crept as he stared down into its fearsome, blazing
> eyes, which seemed like live coals inside the monstrous head.
> Even so, he could only think of it as a wild animal, which had
> presumably escaped from a travelling circus.

The creature disappeared round the bend of the river. Mr Martin
ran back to the house for a gun loaded with heavy shot, but
he failed to find the animal.

Soon after this encounter, Mr Martin opened a packet of
Player's cigarettes, and found that the card inside, one of a
series on Irish place names, was about the origin of Poulaphuca.
The picture of the Pooka was similar to the animal he had seen.

"Until he saw the cigarette card he had no idea that it might
have been something occult", writes MacManus. He then made
enquiries among the local people, and found it was well known.
Down the years it had often been seen standing in or by the

river near the bridge, always at dusk. It was some 50 years since anyone claimed to have seen it in broad daylight. Of the animal shown on the cigarette card Mr Martin told the author, "Yes, that is just what I saw, except that it does not show the red eyes or the slavering mouth and the wicked teeth. It was as tall as the mantleshelf. The picture is so true you'd think it was drawn from life".

This strange story raises a problem concerning nondescript animals. MacManus presumes that the creature seen by his friend was occult, and that traditional creatures like the pooka and the water horse are also. He heightens the description of the incident, but actually provides little more than a vague notion of the animal itself. Doubtless Mr Martin did see some strange animal, but it was a creature of flesh and blood. What, we cannot tell on the evidence provided.

Old traditions have, however, been more strongly confirmed than in this case. The tradition of a monster in Lough Ree on the Shannon, which has already been mentioned in the story from the *Life of St Mochua of Balla*, has been revived by recent reports.

At 9.30 p.m. on May 18, 1960, three Dublin priests, down on Lough Ree for the Mayfly season, were fishing off Holly Point. Fr Matthew Burke, Fr Daniel Murray and Fr Richard Quigly had visited the lake before and knew it quite well. It was a warm summery evening and the lake was still and calm. There was no wind. They were watching for signs of the rising trout, when one of them turned to the others and said, "Do you see what I see?" All three then saw some kind of animal swimming up the lake only 100 yards away.

"It was moving", one of the priests said later. "It went down under the water and came up again in the form of a loop. The length from the end of the coil to the head was 6 feet. There was about 18 inches of head and neck over the water. The head and neck were narrow in comparison to the thickness of a good-sized salmon. It was getting its propulsion from underneath the water, and we did not see all of it". The head was flat like a python's. They were not sure of the exact length of the creature as they did not see all of it. One of the priests had the initiative to sketch the animal on the back of an envelope.

These details, clearly describing the now familiar long-necked animal, are taken from a newspaper interview published a few days later. So that there could be no doubt about the matter, the three priests even submitted an account of their sighting to the Inland Fisheries Trust. This second report is more detailed, but not all the details are the same as in the earlier version. Possibly further consideration had clarified the event in their minds.

There were two sections above the water; a foreward section of uniform girth, stretching quite straight out of the water and inclined at the plane of the surface at about 30°, in length about 18–24 inches. The diameter of this long leading section we would estimate to be about 4 inches. At its extremity, which we took to be a serpent-like head, it tapered rather abruptly to a point.

Fig. 22. Lough Ree monster.

Between the leading and the following sections of this creature, there intervened about two feet of water. The second section seemed to us to be a tight, roughly semi-circular loop. This portion could have been a hump or a large knob on the back of a large body under the surface that was being propelled by flippers. As to the dimensions of this section, if a loop, we should say the girth of a large fifteen pound salmon; if however, a round hump . . . we should put its base at about 18 inches . . . We would estimate the overall length to the two visible sections, measured along the surface from tip of snout to end of hump, at about 6 feet.

The movement along the water was steady. There was no apparent disturbance of the surface, so that propulsion seemed to come from a well-submerged portion of the creature. There was no undulation of its body above the water. It was cruising at a very leisurely speed, and was apparently unconcerned about our presence. We watched it moving along the surface for a period of two or three minutes in a north-easterly direction. It was going towards the shore; then it submerged gradually rather than dived, and disappeared from view completely. Another couple of minutes later it reappeared still following the same course . . . It reached a point 30 yards offshore, where it submerged and we saw it no more.

At about 9.30 the same evening, according to an addendum to this report, they saw a long black object about three-quarters of a mile away, about the length of a row-boat. Though the three priests associated this with what they had seen earlier, there is no real indication that this second object was an animal at all.

After all the uncertainty of detail concerning the Irish crocodile and the fantasy of the pooka it is refreshing to come at last to a sober and straightforward report by three excellent witnesses. Few reports from Ireland are as convincing as this, yet it produced almost total disagreement.

When the trio came ashore they told a local fisherman what they had seen. He suggested that "the monster" was really a family of otters at play. Though one of the priests thought this was a likely suggestion, the other two were not convinced by it.

So on the Friday all three went across the lake to see the well-known authority on the River Shannon, the late Colonel Harry Rice. Colonel Rice had mentioned the monster supposed to haunt the lake eight years before in his book about the river, *Thanks for the Memory*. A friend of his who claimed to have seen it, had told him that it looked "for all the world like a dozen barrels of porter strung together" – doubtless a reference to the appearance of several humps. Colonel Rice knew of the account in the *Life of Saint Mochua*, but he considered the aquatic monster merely a legend before the three priests came to his house that day.

I took down everything they said, he wrote later, and sent it to the local press with a request that if anyone else had observed anything strange, they should get in touch with me. I cross-examined the priests for almost two hours, and

applied all the criticisms one would normally use, but two
of them were so convinced that they had seen something
extraordinary, that I could not shake them . . . These
gentlemen are expert fishermen, and thoroughly qualified to
observe such a matter.

The following Tuesday the story made its way into the Dublin
papers, the next day into some English ones, and on Saturday
28, there was a long article on the affair in the local Athlone
paper, *The Westmeath Independent.*

By now more stories of the monster had come to light. A
retired postman, Mr Paddy Hanly, a river man of great experience, whose parents came from the Black Islands in the middle
of the lake, had a curious story. When he was a boy he had
heard about the water-monster, and 30 years before had, he
thought, nearly caught it. He and some of his family were
fishing north of Yew Point at the mouth of Bally Bay, when he
hooked something. The line, the strongest on the market
("almost a rope") stretched out and the boat was towed across
the lake. Once the other side of the Adelaide buoy, Hanley had
cut the line. He had not seen what was on his hook, but he has
heard of similar incidents down the years.

On another occasion, F. J. Waters had a similar experience
near the same place. Mr Waters was fishing off Beam Island
with a heavy line, for trout, when he hooked something which
dived rapidly to the bottom, snapping the line after 70 feet
had run off the reel. He considered the speed of the dive was
impossible for any fish to attain. Mr Waters had no idea what
he could have hooked.

In 1958 two English tourists were similarly towed around the
lake till they cut their fishing line. And in February 1960 two
net fishermen, Patrick Ganley and Joseph Quigly of Inch Turk,
were out netting pike. They caught something large in their
net, but while they were trying to haul it aboard the creature
broke the net and escaped. "It must have been as strong as a
horse", one of them later remarked. This happened in 60 feet
of water, out in the middle of the lake, half a mile from where
the priests were to see their animal.

In June it was reported that back in 1950 a cabin cruiser
had hit some object in mid-channel at a point where the water

was thought to be deep. The skipper took bearings on the shore to fix the spot, which was later dragged. Nothing was found. In Colonel Rice's book, *Charts of the River Shannon*, the spot is marked "Unidentified Snag". The surrounding water is 70 feet deep.

Another report said that two men walking along the shore of St Mark's Bay late one summer's evening saw an animal swimming parallel to the shore. Its neck was raised a foot above the surface; then there was a gap of water; and then a black hump. They thought it was a calf, but on putting out in a boat to rescue it, they found nothing, as it had submerged. Colonel Rice, who published this story, noted that the animal could not have been a calf as they keep their heads down level with the water when swimming, just as a dog does.

As soon as the Lough Ree monster became newsworthy, explanations of various kinds, and varying credibility, were put forward. These ranged from the amusing and silly through the reasonable to a plausible identification:

(a) When the matter of the monster was raised at the meeting of Westmeath County Council, one councillor said he had been told that the monster was nothing more than "Councillor D'Arcy out for a swim".

Others at the meeting thought the monster would be good for the tourist trade, something many others must have thought as well, as this is often said unfairly about the Loch Ness monster. But as Colonel Rice pointed out at the time, the three priests had nothing personal to gain by their report, and their only interest in Lough Ree was its Mayfly.

(b) At a meeting of the Irish Inland Waterways Association, of which Colonel Rice was the chairman, one member said the alleged monster was a midget Russian submarine which had been dropped from one of the jets that had flown over Athlone the week before.

(c) In *The Westmeath Independent* of May 28, it was suggested that the monster was a coelacanth. This theory was later expounded by Colonel Rice at the Waterways Meeting, and again in the June 4 edition of the paper. The Colonel's ideas about the coelacanth were a little fantastic. He said that "such a creature would be of the serpent variety, with a rudimentary alimentary tract". It would live by sucking in the mud of the lake and extracting the nourishment from it in the manner of an earth worm. Needless to say, the coelacanth is nothing like this at all: nothing more was heard of this theory.

(d) The explanation offered by some local fishermen, and favoured by some Dublin experts, was that the three priests had seen a line of hooked fish. The fishermen on the Black Islands set down several hundred feet of line with many baited hooks on it to catch pike and eels. "It is possible", said a fishing expert, "that three or four big pike caught on these hooks would fight, wriggling and twisting themselves up the dropper line to the main one and where, possibly, they would break surface. Three fish breaking the surface alone together would give an undulating impression of one fish swimming through the water".

The priests, however, had been quite specific that the animal did not undulate, and moved through the water with little wash. Nor does this theory explain the long neck that was so conspicuous a part of the evidence.

Yet another Dublin expert (there is never any lack of them) said: "I have seen these lines, and when several pike get coiled around them, they become a complete mess. It may well be that one of these could be mistaken for a big monster. However, if it were not for the fact that this thing was supposed to have been seen by three priests, I would have said it was a figment of the imagination".

The vocation of the witnesses at least assured that their report received some attentive response. As for the theory: pike or eels caught on such lines and tangled round them would make, as the man says, a great deal of splash and wave. Yet the animal moved steadily through the water, with little disturbance to the surface. This alone disposes of the theory without even mentioning the fact that such long lines are not set at that time of year.

(f) Fishermen on Lough Conn suggested that the priests had in fact seen a line of ducks. This, in view of the exactness of their description, seems unlikely. Many explanations like this are suggested by knowledgable people, who have not bothered to acquaint themselves with the details of the evidence. Such theories are curious rather than useful.

(g) A line of otters was proposed by a local school teacher,

Mr Hanley. This was also what the fisherman the priests first met had thought. It has, again, been put forward to explain the Loch Ness monster. A correspondent of mine, Mrs Anne Kinsella of Gory, writes to me (July 5, 1963):

> I was visiting my brother (who lives not far from Lough Ree) very soon after the three Dublin priests had seen the "monster". He was highly amused at the publicity it got in the press. You see, he lives quite close to a small lake and had often shot otters some of which measured 7 feet in length. Otters can move on the lakes surface without making a ripple, and all the diagrams and drawings given in the papers at the time were the antics of an otter.

Now: otters in these islands are thought not to grow beyond 5 feet 9 inches. If some specimens do indeed run up to 7 feet, they would indeed be monsters in their own right, and would provide an explanation for "the master-otter" of tradition. But such large otters will have to be produced first. Anyhow, it would have to be a large otter with a long neck to fit the priests' description. And that in itself would be an unknown animal of great interest.

(h) A deliberate hoax seems beyond even anti-clerical consideration. As does

(i) an optical illusion; though I suppose such can never be entirely ruled out.

(j) Colonel Rice after further thought changed his mind (probably because of an article in the *Illustrated London News* on a sea-serpent seen off the coast of Scotland). He now thought the monster might be a type of plesiosaur. The Colonel had reached the classic solution already proposed for both the sea-serpent and the Loch Ness monster. Personally I'd rather have one of those seven-foot otters anytime. But people can never resist the notion of a prehistoric monster.

I have given a large amount of space to this incident partly because the modern reports confirm an old tradition, and also because it is the best documented Irish sighting that I know of. Clear and precise, it echoes in every way the descriptions we have already read of the long-necked animal in Loch Ness. Not all Irish lake monsters fall quite so conveniently into the pattern.

(About this time fishermen on Lough Neagh, in Northern Ireland, reported that they had caught some large animal which had broken through their nets and escaped. I have no other details of this incident, but such a report might have been expected. The authors of the *Shell Guide to Ireland* claim that Lough Neagh takes its name, Loch nEachach, from the horse-god, Eochu, Lord of the Underworld beneath its waves. And in December 1933 the *Fishing Gazette* described the Lough Neagh monster as horse-like with "a tail like a propeller".)

Our next report concerns a very different and quite puzzling animal. Glinsk is a small remote village in county Galway, three miles from the River Suck which flows into the Shannon. This is an area few strangers visit. The fishing correspondent of the *Irish Press*, G. S. Lane, while fishing above Dunamon Bridge on the Suck was told by an old man to stay away from Lough Dubh, for it was a strange place, where "queer things had been seen from time to time in the past".

Some time around 1956, three men working on the Suck saw a strange animal swimming in the lake. They were too far away to see it distinctly, but it seemed to have been quite large. In 1960 another local man, Con Mahon, saw three animals, one large and two smaller ones, swimming around Lough Dubh, an incident he described at the time over the radio.

Then, in the middle of March 1962, the teacher at the National School in Glinsk, Mr Alphonsus Mullaney, and his young son, also called Alphonsus, had a terrifying experience on the shore of the lake. Mr Mullaney later described what happened to them to a reporter from the *Sunday Review*:

We were working on the bog after school and I had promised to take young Alphonsus fishing. We carried a twelve foot rod with a strong line and spoon bait for perch or pike, of which there are plenty in Lough Dubh.

For a while I let the boy fish with the long rod and used a shorter rod with worm bait. I got no "answer". After five minutes I decided that the fish were not there that evening, but I took the long rod and walked up and down the bank.

Suddenly there was a tugging on the line. I thought it might be caught on a root, so I took it gently. It did not give.

I hauled it slowly ashore, and the line snapped. I was examining the line when the lad screamed.

Then I saw the animal. It was not a seal or anything I had ever seen. It had for instance short thick legs, and a hippo face. It was as big as a cow or an ass, square faced, with small ears and a white pointed horn on its snout. It was dark grey in colour, and covered with bristles or short hair, like a pig.

His son had seen it for longer than he had. Apparently the animal had taken the bait, or so Mr Mullaney thought. Angered by the pain and the barking of a spaniel, it had tried to mount the bank and attack the boy. He screamed and ran in fright to his father. Later Mr Mullaney got out a picture-book of animals to help him describe what he had seen. Of all the animals, he picked out the rhinoceros as being closest to the face description.

The Mullaneys hurried away from the lake, for the boy was frightened out of his wits. Mr Mullaney sent for some local guns. The shore of the lake was searched, but no trace of the animal was seen. Men armed with guns kept watch for a time from fear the animal would take to the land.

"I never sought", Mr Mullaney writes to me, "any publicity in the matter and I repeatedly refused T.V. appearances in this connection. My child was very frightened when he saw the animal and I was more than anxious to blot out its memory from the impressionable mind as early as possible lest it should react to his disadvantage later on".

The expert opinion of the National Museum (Natural History) was sought by the *Sunday Review* when it published its interview with Mr Mullaney. After stating that the lake was too far inland for seals to get into it, and that the description baffled them, "they pointed out that recently animals not native to these shores were found near Scotland and Ireland, such as turtles, indicating the possibility of climactic changes in the Atlantic".

It is sometimes more difficult to make sense of such official statements on the identity of lake monsters than to understand the actual reports. Certainly tropical animals such as Kemp's Loggerhead Turtle have been washed up by the Gulf Stream on the west coast of Ireland, but what has that to do with the

animal in Lough Dubh? If the scientists thought, as this seems
to suggest they did, that the "monster" might be some rare
visitor to Ireland, why did they not hurry on down to
investigate?

I am not surprised though that the description baffled them.
It is certainly outside the usual pattern of reports from these
islands. The Lough Dubh monster is not one of our long-
necked Loch Ness animals, but what it is I have no idea. A
hoax is out of the question. Witnessing the appearance of a lake
monster is not the sort of publicity a state employee at the
mercy of his parish priest particularly wants.

With the next report we are back to the familiar. John Synge
was not the only writer to find traditions of monsters in the
lakes of Wicklow. The naturalist Robert Lloyd Praeger has
recounted in his book about the Irish landscape a further
legend about Lough Nahanagan; and another story is told of
Lough Clevaun. These legends have recently been confirmed.

South of Dublin, just over the border in Wicklow, are two
mountain lakes, Upper and Lower Lough Bray. They are
quite remote, visited by trippers only in the summer. The
nearest public road is half a mile away, and only a private
drive reaches the lower lake. The waters of both lakes are deep
and stained black by the peat.

On June 17, 1963, a correspondent signing himself "L.R.",
wrote to one of the Dublin evening papers to describe how he
and a friend were looking down from a height into Lower
Lough Bray on Whit Monday (June 3):

Soberly and without doubt we are convinced that we saw a
creature which could only be described as a monster. Looking
down into the lake which was perfectly clear (i.e. calm) in
the evening light we saw a large hump like the back of a
rhinoceros emerge from the water. Ripples spread out to
each side of it and then a head something like a tortoise only
many times bigger broke the surface. It came up about
three feet above the surface of the water, moved slowly
around and swam forward a few yards. As it did so the body
was clearly revealed, circular and not less than ten or twelve
feet in circumference. It was a dark greyish colour. Suddenly
and silently the creature seemed to dive and smoothly vanish

leaving an agitated swirl of water. We saw it for not less than three minutes. Comparing our stories we found them to be identical to a surprising degree although my friend thought the head was more like that of a swan.

He added that he and his friend were absolutely certain of what they had seen that evening. "It may have been a trick of the light or shadow, but to be honest nothing will convince us that such was the case".

His friend's comparison of the head with that of a swan implies that it narrowed sharply to the front, which is characteristic of the Loch Ness animals.

An anonymous report such as this should be accepted with caution, but it seems credible enough to me to be included in the dossier for the moment. When I visited Lough Bray soon afterwards, I took some photographs of the lake. On one of these the picturesque cottage on the south shore is clearly visible. On the surface of the lake itself are three dark shapes. I saw nothing myself at the time, and I have no doubt that what Bernard Heuvelmans called "the monster's ghost" when he saw the print are windrows. Even on a still day, cat's paws on the surface can create such long shadows and hump-like objects on the surface, which have the deceptive sinuous appearance of living animals.

Doubtless some people do mistake shadows on the water surface for "monsters". A good example is provided by a story in that classic book *True Irish Ghost Stories* (1929) by Seymore and Neligan. A Mrs A. V. Hunt describes how she and a friend, with two workmen, were watching Lough na Corra below Croagh Patrick one afternoon in 1911.

Suddenly the surface of the water was disturbed by a large black shape that rose and swam the length of the lake in what appeared to be a few moments. Other similar shapes appeared, and these weird things kept playing about, diving and swimming like a lot of seals. The lake is between two and three miles long and from the height on which we were, in comparison with the cattle, the creatures looked bigger than any house we could see; even with the aid of binoculars we could not distinguish any detail at that distance . . . We called the men at work of the chapel to come and watch. After a short time the creatures disappeared, one by one, and the lake resumed its former tranquil appearance.

These witnesses thought they were watching some animals "swimming like a lot of seals". Once the phenomenon suggests an animal, witnesses will assume it is indeed an animal. Yet in this case we have nothing more than a lot of black shapes seen from a great distance. Though they might have reminded Mrs Hunt of seals, there is nothing in her account to indicate they were in fact animals. They were almost certainly shadows (such as I photographed on Lough Bray) playing over the length of the lake.

But however deceptive shadows may be, they would not account for the long neck and small head so clearly seen by "L.R." and his friend. Nor, I think, would they account for the next report.

A few weeks later another monster was reported, this time from Lough Major in county Monaghan. In the last week of July three youths G. Reilly (18), Talbot Duffy (17) and Paul Pentland (12) claimed that when they were coming back from a fishing trip, they saw a "monster" splashing up and down in the lake like a sea-lion. Although they were frightened, they watched it for a few minutes, then threw a few stones at it. It made towards them and they fled. Talbot Duffy had shot plenty of otters, and was certain that what they saw was not one. They said it had a hairy head and two protruding horns. When they came back the next day they found that a dozen bream dropped on the bank the evening before had been eaten, and only a few bones remained. Another local man, Paddy Brady, confirmed the boys description, as he had also seen the animal in the lake. The next weekend people from Monaghan and the surrounding counties visited the lake hoping to see the animal. But no-one saw anything unusual at all.

This animal was also unlikely to have been a seal, 36 miles from the sea. But unlike the Lough Dubh monster falls more easily into the pattern of other descriptions, despite the lack of details.

I am not so confident however about a monster which created

quite a stir during the summer of 1968 on Achill Island, where what appear to be traditional stories have been confused by a hoax.

It is often claimed that monster stories are invented for publicity purposes. Those who claim this cannot know the lakes involved. It is very hard to imagine that any ordinary tourist would take himself out into the remote wilds where many of the monster haunted lakes are secluded. Some of the Scottish lakes have tourist appeal of coure, but no real evidence of invention can be found. Achill Island, however of all the places in Ireland where monsters have been reported is the most tourist conscious. Every summer finds it crowded with Dublin and even European visitors, doubtless all eager for a new sensation. Any reports from such a place would have to be very carefully considered.

The reports concerned Glendarry Lough in the centre of that offshore island. On the first Sunday in June 1968, a Dundalk businessman gave a lift to two young girls, Mary O'Neill from Mullingar and Florence Connaire from Galway. As they passed the lake at one o'clock, one of the girls pointed out a "huge animal" on the shore about 100 yards away. The girls were not too frightened but wanted to move on. Despite them, the man stopped to photograph this apparition with his Polaroid camera. The animal, if animal it was, seemed to be about 40 feet long with a head like a greyhound and a long tail. "It was just like a dinosaur", Mary O'Neill said later. "It moved a bit and I would say it was about 20 feet long". The photograph, when it emerged from the camera, showed exactly what they saw, there was no doubt about that, even if the animal's actual size seemed uncertain.

This encounter was reported in the Dublin *Evening Herald* on June 5, along with an enlargement of the photograph, showing a rather hideous monster grinning from behind a convenient bush. When asked in November 1970 for a copy of the photograph the paper replied that it was supplied to them for reproduction only and they had neither a copy of it or a record of the photographer's name. The photograph may very well be exactly what the two girls saw, but I am not convinced that it shows an animal. The object resembles no known dinosaur, despite Miss O'Neill, but does represent many people's imaginative notion of what one would look like. As we have already seen, if lake monsters exist in these islands, they are almost certainly mammals and not prehistoric reptiles. In this case it seems to me that someone has disguised a stack of turf as a monster and had it photographed by an unwary tourist.

But if someone has perpetrated a hoax, he chose a good place for it. The *Herald's* reporter, sent down to investigate on the spot, was able to discover several local people who had seen a monster in the lake.

Two months before, on May Day, a local part-time contractor John Cooney, and his friend Michael McNulty, were driving past the lake when an animal crossed in front of the van. According to Mr Cooney.

> It was between 8 to 12 feet long, I thought, with a long neck like a swan only much bigger. The tail was very thick. It was moving at an angle to us and we couldn't see exactly how long it really was. And it was weaving and curving. We could see it clearly. It was dark brown in colour and was slimey and scaley. The eyes were glittering. I don't know whether it actually looked at us, but it disappeared in an instant into the thick undergrowth – and we didn't stop to make further enquiries.

Now this sounds very like a slightly exaggerated account of our old long-necked friend, the long tail being the trailing bulk of its body.

Also in June a Limerick woman had seen "a log" bobbing and twisting on the lough, but it was gone when her husband came to look.

Two years before, according to Denis McGowan, an English angler came into his shop after seeing some strange animal in the lough. But he gave no details of what he had seen.

And Thomas Cooney of Graheen was said by his cousin to have seen the monster 35 years before. A Mrs Annie Calligan saw it about that time, and 30 years ago a party of women working turf also saw it. These were not the only witnesses.

Three weeks before the photograph was taken, Gay Denver, a 16-year-old trainee carpenter, was cycling home from Mass.

He had dismounted and was walking up the rise by the lake when he saw the animal near some trees 50 yards from the lough, "humping himself" along and climbing up a turf bank near the wood. "It was moving in a jumpy way, like a kangaroo. It had a head like a sheep and a long neck and tail. The hind legs were bigger than the front ones". The animal was about 12 feet long, "much bigger than any horse", and dark in colour. Gay Denver said the photo also showed what he had seen. The monster had "a humped, bumpy back, just like that, and a small head".

During a visit to Achill I bought a rather charming souvenir of the monster made by a local potter from the photograph. The local people seemed reasonably convinced of the animal's existence. Certain parts of the stories of John Cooney and Gay Denver fit with what we would have expected, and if that was all the evidence there would be a good case for the monster. But the scaley prehistoric monstrosity in the photograph is a bit much even for my credulous disposition.

If Achill Island had any hope of cornering the monster business in the West of Ireland, they were to be disappointed. Lake monsters have become epidemic in the province of Connaught, and a rival monster was soon reported from a lake near Clifden.

To the south of that town there is a wide area of bogland splattered with numerous small lakes, some no bigger than puddles. A chain of three small lakes connected with the sea by a small stream have produced several recent sightings.

In 1954 Mrs Georgina Carberry was one of a party of four who were fishing in Lough Fadda, the largest of the three lakes. They saw "a large black object which moved slowly, showing two humps. The head was about 3 feet out of the water, in one long curve. The mouth was open and set under the head like that of a shark. It was black in colour, and the skin was smooth. The whole body seemed to have movement in it". As it swung round and dived down near a rock, they saw the tail was forked, "a V-shaped tail".

This, even to the detail of the "tail", presents us again with the familiar long-neck. This story came to the notice of Captain Lionel Leslie. In May 1966 Captain Leslie, his friend Lord Massarene, another friend, and three marine biologists at-

tempted to capture this monster. As members of the Loch Ness
Investigation, their plan of action was adapted from a scheme
used in that loch by David James. They tried to flush out the
animal from the depths of the lake by exploding underwater
charges of gelignite. They had a ciné camera trained on the
lake to record whatever emerged: a strange disturbance was
observed after the explosion but not filmed.

In 1968 another attempt was made, this time to net the
animal. Professor Roy Mackal was on hand to lend his expert
aid, this time to trap the animal in a lake 130 by 80 yards. A
family of seven told the party that they had watched a black
animal about 12 feet long with the usual hump and neck
swimming around the lake. Nets were set out, and a fish
stunner employed. But though the fish population of the lake
seemed normal, no monster floated to the surface. Shortage
of time and the proliferating water-lilies prevented them from
dragging the lake. They had to conclude that the animal must
have escaped to the sea down a shallow stream. A year later,
however, Ted Holiday heard from a local shepherd that he had
seen a monster on the land near the same lake. Hurried investigation by a skin-diver cast no light on the mystery of these
comings and goings.

A farmer living by one of the lakes, Mr Tom Joyce, had seen
what were locally called "horse-eels". The nineteenth century
collector of folklore, Thomas Crofton Croker, had described
the horse-eel as being "a great conger eel, seven yards long, and
as thick as a bull in the body with a mane on its back like a
horse".

Mr Joyce thought at first that the small object he saw was an
otter, but slowly some 7 or 8 feet of back rose out of the water
to a height of 2 feet. It moved off, crushing its way through the
reeds before it sank.

Another witness, Mr Pat Walsh, said he had been out in his
boat when a head and neck emerged out of the water beside
him. He rowed swiftly ashore, scared out of his witst hat the
animal would come up under his boat and upset it. Two men
he knew had once gone down to investigate a strange object
near the shore of the lake. Though it made off into deeper
water, they said it was a gigantic eel some 16 feet long.

Inspired by these reports, in 1969 Captain Leslie, Holiday,

and three others returned in September for an all out attempt on the lake. This time they spread out nets across all three lakes, which to their surprise they found to be quite shallow, the bottom being covered in a thick fluid layer of muck. In October they had to give up due to the bad weather setting in. The animals were not swimming around the lakes, and must either be holed up in the ooze on the bottom, or have escaped, as they had thought before, down the stream to the sea.†

That conclusion seems valid, and not surprising. The long-necked animals reported from so many lakes around the world are clearly related to (if not the same as) the marine long-necks, one of the commonest of the sea-serpents. To conclude this dossier of Irish cases, and to illustrate this connection, I shall record the story of the Monster of the Woods as told to Edith Somerville.

In July 1921 Miss Somerville was visited by an old man of her acquaintance called Thady Byrne, who asked if she had heard about the "monster that was in the woods". The woods he spoke of covered some 500 acres of hills and glens in West Cork, and hung over a long and lonely inlet of the sea called Myross Bay. Thady had been making his way home through the woods when he saw the monster, which was "sitting on a rock and looking at me".

It was black, and as big as a greyhound, but it was like a cat. It had long bristles cocking out from each side of its jaws, but not a braid of hair upon its tail. It had a great gowl on it, like a bulldog, and a great wide chest and shoulders, and he tapered away to his tail. You'd hear him barking at night in the woods, and the bark was like the squel of a saygull.

Someone suggested the Thing – whatever it was – had come in from the sea. On the next Sunday Thady and some friends went hunting for it with dogs, but didn't find it. Rumours of it went around, and eventually all the local chicken stealing was

---

† A more detailed account of these expeditions can now be found in *The Dragon and the Disc* (1973) by F. W. Holiday. The reports confirm to the smallest detail—no tail and small horns included—the general picture already established, but in my view the author's theories should be treated with great caution.

blamed upon it. The animal was seen at different times for about a week, but accounts of it even from reliable men varied. One man thought it might be a crocodile, but "some men who had seen it (but from a distance) thought it might be a monkey". Some monkey!

Thady's description can be of only one animal, some sort of seal. Living near the coast he would have recognised at once any ordinary seal such as the Common Grey seal. Such an identification is unlikely. Clearly this animal was able to raise itself up on its front legs to look around it, which relates it to the sea-lions or the walrus. It can't be a sea-lion, and if it had been a walrus (some of which have been known to wander quite far south) Thady would certainly have mentioned the conspicuous tusks. We can only conclude that it was a maned sea-serpent, a long-neck with a mane and whiskers. The neck of this type may not be quite so long as the animals in Loch Ness, but this is an uncertain point. If I am right, this is a unique account of one of these animals ashore, though they have been reported along the coasts of Ireland before. In 1922 one appeared in the Shannon at Limerick while the Civil War was raging, only to be fired on by a National soldier. In 1933 another appeared, further down the river.

Because it has become so mixed up with folklore it is difficult to make sense of much of the Irish dossier. Some cases, like the monsters in Lough Ree and Lough Bray, and perhaps in Lough Abisdealy, are clear enough. Elements of fantasy and exaggeration, due doubtless to what foreigners would like to call "an irrepressible Celtic imagination", have crept into the others. The one photograph ever taken is almost certainly a hoax, though an amusing one. The few efforts to capture one of the animals have been dismal failures. Nevertheless, sufficient evidence has been produced to convince one that there are, in some Irish lakes, animals similar to those reported from Scotland. There are also some other odd things, like the Lough Dubh monster, which must remain intriguing mysteries. And then there is always the old serpent chained to the bottom of Lough Allen . . .

For those anxious to discover yet more monsters, the old Irish epic recounting the high deeds of Finn provides a generous number of clues. Finn has just slain the water monster, and the poet then quite casually proceeds to recite a long list of other such creatures which the hero has slain in the past:

What fell of monsters by Finn, till doom may not be reckoned: what he achieved of battle and exploit all men cannot number.

He slew the monster of Lough Neagh, and the giant of Glen Smpil, and the great reptile of Loch Cuilleann, MacCumhaill of the gold slew it.

He slew the serpent of Benn Eadair: in battle it could not be mastered: the phantom and the reptile of Glenn Dorcha fell by the hand of the prince.

The blue serpent of the Erne fell, and the fierce serpent of Loch Riach: he slew, though it was a stout heart, a serpent and a cat in Áth Cliath.

He slew the phantom of Loch Léin, it was a great endeavour to subdue it: he slew a phantom in Druim Cliath, and a phantom and a serpent on Loch Ree.

Finn of the great heart slew the phantom of Glen Righe of the roads: there was not a reptile in Ireland's glens but he took by the force of his blows.

The phantom and the serpent of Glenarm Finn slew, though they were valiant; so that victorious Finn exterminated every monster against which he advanced.

He slew the serpent of Loch Sileann that brought a treacherous deluge on our host, and the two serpents of Loch Foyle that made fierce attack on us.

A shining serpent on the Shannon, it broke down the defense of men: and the serpent of the fight of Loch Ramhuir, that surpassed the monsters of the world.

He slew, it was a great good fortune, the fierce phantom of Sliabh Collan, and the two serpents of Glen Inne fell by his sword.

He slew the serpent of Loch Meilge, whose prowess was not unworthy of Finn's hand, and the great serpent of Loch Cera too, and a spectre at Áth Truim.

There was a serpent on Lough Mask that gave many defeats to the men of Fál, he slew it with his victorious sword, though it was a fierce burden for his sword.

On Loch Laeghaire, in truth, there was a serpent that made flames: in payment of what he suffered of its ravages he beheaded it with his weapons.

The furious serpent of Loch Lurgan fell by Finn of the Fianna: all that it destroyed of our host may not be told till distant doom.

A serpent of the singing Bann fell by the hand of Finn of the hard encounter: we had often been wasted by its attacks until it was slain at Asseroe.

Altogether a remarkable catalogue of monsters, even if some of them are already familiar from more recent reports. It is quite impossible that these could actually be snakes or reptiles – a fact that some scholars, Anne Ross for one, do not seem to realise.

There is only one other explanation: that we have here a slightly mythical list of lakes where long-necks were known in Celtic times. That any survived to our own day after the furious onslaught of Finn was lucky indeed.

We cannot leave Ireland without mentioning the strange mystery of the Kerry Carabuncle, which is an animal and not a disease.

The story starts in 1756. Charles Smith in his *History and Present State of Kerry* was the first to hear of the legend. "The common people here-about have a strange, romantic notion of their seeing in fair weather what they call a carabuncle at the bottom of the lake in a particular part of it which they say is more than 60 fathoms deep". Smith seems to assume that by carabuncle was meant some sort of bright precious stone, and in a footnote expresses his doubts about its real existence.

But Smith had not heard the whole story. Over a century later the naturalist Henry Hart was exploring the Kerry Mountains for plants. He describes how a countryman who accompanied him on a visit to Mount Brandon in 1883, told him that in Lough Veagh, one of the lakes below the mountain, the local people often found pearl shells. These, he said, came off an enormous animal called "the Carabuncle" "which was seen glittering like silver in the water at night". The animal had gold, jewels and precious stones hanging on it. It had never been caught, though Hart expresses the ironical hope that it might soon be added to the collection of Irish animals in the National Museum.

We learn yet more about the carabuncle from another naturalist, Nathaniel Colgan, writing in 1914. On a visit to Brandon in 1888, Colgan happened to meet Hart's informant and he asked him about the legend. It seemed that the monster lived in Lough Geal, not Veagh, and was a kind of snake which made the lake shine at night, and threw off shells with precious stones in them. He had never seen it, but thought that if you could capture it you would make your fortune.

At Connor's pub in Cloghane where he was staying, Colgan heard yet more from Connor himself. He also had never actually seen the carabuncle, but had often heard tales of it. It was said to be seen only once every seven years and was "like a cashk rowlin' about in the wather". His wife added that she had always thought it was a fish, and it was connected in her mind with the pearls which some fishermen had got out of the lake years before. (Colgan surmises these were from *tinio margasitifer*). Next morning the postman confirmed that the Carabuncle lit up the whole lake and that it was the origin of the pearls. Lough Geal, by the way, is 360 feet up on the slope of Mount Brandon as you come through Connor Pass to Cloghane.

All this is strange enough, but the strangest part is yet to come. Colgan brought to light a passage in Alfred Russell Wallace's *Travels on the River Amazon*, where the explorer laments that the Amazons "must be placed with those (legends) of the Curipura, or Demon of the Woods, and the Carbuncle of the Upper Amazon and Peru". On reading this Colgan wrote off at once to the great man Wallace asking for more information about the Amazonian legend. Wallace replied that he couldn't recall it at all, but that perhaps Bates his companion might do. Bates, in turn, replied that he no longer wasted his time on such matters.†

What then is the connection between the Kerry lake monster and the legendary animal of the Amazon? Colgan wondered if some Spanish traveller had turned up in Kerry and left the name behind him, which is not unlikely given the long standing

---

† Borges in his book on imaginary beings, refers to the carabuncle. A poet Fr Martin del Barco Centenara describes in his *Argentina* (1602) seeing one in Paraguay: "a smallish animal, with a shining mirror on its head, like a glowing coal". This only seems to confuse the matter more.

connections between Iberia and Ireland. But only the name and legend? Why not a real animal, perhaps some species of red and white phosphorescent tropical fish. The real carabuncle is either a livid sore, small bright coals or a bright jewel: hence the livid red-black colours for the fish. There is also the final possibility that the fish drifted up on the Gulf stream, as happens with other tropical plants and animals, and was put alive into the lake not far from the sea-shore.‡

But what sort of fish? And is it still there? I recommend the mystery to some enterprising biology student in need of a summer project.

‡ Colgan, out on Lough Inagh in Connemara in 1897, was told by his landlord, Joyce of Cloonacartan, pointing out a grassy spit of land running into the lake, that some years before a friend of his had seen a water horse emerge from the lake there, which shook its mane before plunging back into the water.

7

Soe-Orm and Skrimsl: Scandinavia

> They are all exceedingly curious, and deserve to be
> brought together as forming a singular group.
>
> *Taylor's notes on Grimm*

FOR CENTURIES THE Scandinavians have taken their lake
monsters for granted. Their attitude seemed strange to a correspondent writing in *The Gentleman's Magazine* in 1765. "The
people of Stockholm report that a great dragon, named
Necker, infests the neighbouring lake and seizes and devours
such boys as go into the water to wash". Because of this monster
they tried to dissuade M. Huet, the bishop of Avranches, from
swimming in Lake Malern one hot summer day. But the intrepid
cleric would not be stopped and "they were greatly surprised
when they saw him return from immanent danger".

Though Bishop Huet did not encounter Necker – actually
the Norse equivalent of piast or water horse – the progeny of
that monster still survive, not only in Swedish lakes but elsewhere in Iceland and Norway.

Long before 1765 Scandinavia was the reputed haunt of the
sea serpent, known then as the Norwegian Sea Snake or Soe-
Orm. The stemposts of Viking ships were carved with fierce
dragons, such as the one on the Gokstad ship, with its beaked
mouth and long neck. One famous boat was called the *Sea
Dragon*: to continue the tradition a recently launched Swedish
submarine has been appropriately named *Sea Serpent*.

Norse mythology had its own legends, such as Sigurd killing
Fafnir, of heroes slaughtering water monsters. The Anglo-
Saxon cleric who composed the epic *Beowulf*, with those
sinister monsters lurking in the fens, turned these traditions into
literature. A critic has pointed out that for the original audience
of the poem, these monsters were real enough, but as remote

and exotic as the Komodo Dragon is for us today. Besides Grendal and her brood, however, the poet almost casually mentions "those creatures forced to swim the icy currents of abominable lakes", which I take to be a clear reference to some kind of warm-blooded lake monsters – as well as mentioning true sea serpents, which sound very seal-like in their habits.

Otherwise we have only such intriguing hints of the animals as in the legend of the God Thor fishing for the Midgard serpent. Plaques found at Uland in Sweden show warriors struggling with monsters, which are clearly made of wattle-work and similar to those carried till recently through several European towns on the feast of St George to a mock fight with the saint in the market place. These folk dramas were the last vestiges of the ancient ritual from which much of the mythology of the dragon was derived. The figure-heads on the ships may have ended as mythical monsters, but it is more than likely that they began as totems of the sea serpent.

Some of the earliest credible reports of the sea serpent to come from reputable witnesses were recorded by Erik Pontopidan, Bishop of Bergen, in his *Natural History of Norway*, published in 1752. He also claims in the same book that he would "not entirely disbelieve what is related of the water snakes seen in fresh water lakes, those in Sundifjord and Uland are famous for these creatures; so that the inhabitants of the adjacent counties dare not venture to cross them in boats".

The historian Olaus Magnus had already written about these in 1555, in his comprehensive account of the Scandinavian peoples:

There is also another serpent of incredible magnitude in a town, called Moos (that is Lake Mjosa), of the Diocess of *Hammer*: which, as a comet portends a change in all the World, so, that portends a change in the Kingdom of *Norway*, as it was seen, Anno 1522, that lifts himself high above the waters, and rolls himself round like a sphere. This serpent was thought to be fifty Cubits long by conjecture, by sight afar off; there followed this the banishment of King Christiernus, and a great persecution of the Bishops, and it showed also the destruction of the Countrey.

Olaus also remarks of the sea serpent that "it comes out of its caverns only on summer nights in fine weather to devour calves, lambs and hogs". Shades of Arthur Grant's goat-devouring monster, or so Oudemans seems to have quite seriously thought in 1934. In 1884 a Dutch journalist, back from a visit to Norway, told Oudemans that strange movements sometimes seen on the surface of Lake Mjosa were attributed by the local people to the movements of a "sea serpent" which was still seen from time to time.

From other early books on Scandinavia, and from many minor local chronicles, the Norwegian folklorist Elizabeth Skjelsvik has collected legends of other lake monsters. In the *Hammer Chronicle*, for instance, which dates from 1617 to 1624, there is another mention of the monster in Lake Mjosa, this time as one of the portents seen before the last Catholic Bishop in Norway was taken prisoner by the Lutherans. The same monster was also mentioned in Jacob Ziegler's *Schondia* (1532), where he again says its appearance portended changes in the kingdom of Norway, as it was seen just before the death of King Christian II. "Its body", writes Miss Skjelsvik, "was of many colours, and it had eyes the size of hoops". Another monster in the deep Lake Lunda in Dalane on the borders of Rogoland was also said to appear when the kings of Norway died; but it seems to have been of a conservative temper, as it failed to appear under the Bernadottes.

So much for the legends. Moving to Iceland we find more material monsters. Dr Johnson, so Boswell recounts, could repeat an entire chapter of Harrblow's *Natural History of Iceland*, the whole of which was "There are no snakes in Iceland". This omission of nature is made up for by the skrimsl.

The early Norse settlers certainly knew of it, for it is mentioned in *The Landanamabok*, a history of early Iceland, and is referred to in several sagas. The *Icelandic Chronicle* notes the appearance during the summer of 1345 "of a wonderful thing in the Lagarflot which is believed to have been a living animal. At times it seems like a great island, and at others, there appeared humps . . . with water between them. No-one knows the dimensions of the creature, for none saw its head or tail, consequently there is no certainty as to what it was". The

Lagarflot is a long fresh water mountain lake in eastern Iceland.

In the *Thjoth Sogur* Jon Arnason quotes a description given him by eyewitnesses of the skrimsl seen in the Lagarflot between 1749 and 1750. The witnesses were educated people, a lawyer named Peter and two others.

They described it as having been the size of a large vessel, and to have been moving rapidly. These men, after watching it for some time, came at dusk to Arneither-sted, where they mentioned what they had seen. While they were speaking the monster rose to the surface in front of the farm. It appeared to be very long and showed one large hump. One of the men thought that he saw signs of a tail moving below the surface. All the farm people, without exception, at Arneither-stede, saw the creature. After this, the inhabitants of Hrafnagorthis saw three humps rise out of the water and remain above it all day.

Soon after this the animal was seen at the top of the Lagarflot, and again in 1819 at Arneither-stede.

We should remember that at this time Iceland was a remote island, with few people, mostly living on widely separated farms. Yet it was a community which highly valued learning, hence the availability of these reports.

During 1860 a student of the ancient sagas and a member of the Norse Literary Society, the Rev Sabine Baring-Gould, then only 29, toured the remoter parts of Iceland on a gothic version of the Grand Tour, painting watercolours of volcanoes, geysers and glaciers. Near the end of his travels he arrived one evening at a small provincial settlement.

To our great delight, we met at Skogkotr with Martin and the Yankee, who had just come from Skoradalsvatn, where they had been spending a week fishing. They were full of the appearance of a Skrimsl, a half-fabulous monster, which is said to inhabit some of the Icelandic lakes, but which has generally been considered the offspring of the imagination.

It so happened that my two friends had arrived at the lake only the day after the monster had been seen disporting itself on the surface, and they were able to obtain some curious information with regard to it. One morning, the farmer and his household had observed something unusual in the lake, and presently they were able to descry a large head like that of a seal rising out of the water. Behind this appeared a back or a hump, and after an interval of water, a second hump. The creature moved slowly and seemed to be enjoying the sun.

One of the two travellers who visited the Lagarflot sent on to Baring Gould the following description of the animal:

The Skrimsl measures 46 feet long, the head and neck are 6 feet, the body 22 feet and the tail 18 feet, according to the estimate of the farmers on the shore of the lake. The monster was seen the day before we arrived at Grudd, by the farmer of the place. His story and description of the fish were so remarkable that we instituted inquiries which resulted in our hunting out several individuals who had seen the monster.

On one occasion it was observed by three farmers who reside on the shores of the lake, two of whom I met and questioned on the subject. One of these men produced a sketch of the creature, which he made whilst it was floating and playing on the surface of the water for half-an-hour.

I should have been inclined to set the whole story down as a myth, were it not for the fact that the accounts of all the witnesses tallied with remarkable minuteness, and the monster is said to have been seen not in one portion of the lake only but at different points.

Baring-Gould reproduces in his book the farmer's sketch of the skrimsl. This naive drawing is a splendid piece of evidence,

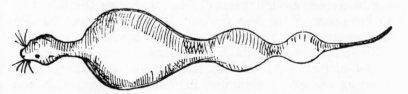

Fig. 23. The Skrimsl, from an Icelandic farmer's sketch 1860.

as it is one of the earliest we have of a lake monster, and is, moreover, the work of someone quite unaquainted with other descriptions of sea serpents. Though it shows the head and humps of the descriptions, the neck seems too short, nor do the proportions seem to fit the farmer's own report. All the same, the delightful pair of whiskers tell us that the animal is a mammal, and we might guess that it must be related to the seals or otters.

As a matter of fact, other evidence seems to show that off the Scandinavian coasts there are two kinds of sea serpents: the long-necked type now so familiar from Loch Ness, and another type which has a long pointed tail (as in the farmer's sketch) and a short neck, Heuvelman's super-otter. It is quite likely that some of the second type might have made their way into an Icelandic lake.

On his return to Rekjavik, Baring-Gould learnt more about the skrimsl from an Icelandic scholar, a Doctor Hjaltalin. He told Baring-Gould that for many years he had considered the skrimsl to be a legend, until he was shown a mass of flesh and bones which had been washed up on a beach of the Lagarflot. The bones were, he said, quite different from a whale's and he was unable to identify them as those of any marine animal known to exist in the northern seas.

Dr Hjaltalin, so far as I know, is the only scientist who has ever examined the remains, or rather the alleged remains, of a lake monster. It would be interesting to learn what became of the bones which he saw, and whether he ever published a description of them, as he seems to have been one of the leading intellectuals of his day in Iceland. More than likely he wrote nothing at all, and the remains themselves have been lost long since.

The skrimsl was also known to the fishermen along Iceland's northern coast, around the small island of Grimsy. One was often to been seen in the Thorskafjord "like a large boat floating keel uppermost". A skrimsl was said to have come ashore in 1819 leaving tracks behind it in the sand.

One of Pontopiddann's successors in the See of Bergen, Dr Neuman was also a naturalist. Periodically between 1820 and 1845 he inquired among his clergy about sightings of sea serpents. According to J. D. Morries Stirling, writing in the

Illustrated London News soon after the *Daedulus* affair, "the amount of proof thus collected was sufficient to convince anyone, however sceptical, as it was not merely hearsay evidence, but the testimony of known and respected persons in various walks of life".

The Norwegians even went so far as to hold judicial enquiries into reports of sea serpents, and the eye-witnesses were summoned to give an exact account of the incidents. Such a court was held at Mandel, for example, in 1867. A sea serpent had been seen by several people in Mannesfjord close to the town in July of that year. Eight witnesses were called, but nothing definite was proved.

Once established this habit of enquiry persisted, so that for many lakes in Norway we have not just hearsay evidence, but the "testimony of known and respected people in various walks of life". Soon the scientific spirit of the century found even scientists making their own investigations, but more of that later.

One such enquiry was held into reports of a monster in Lake Suldal, a long narrow mountain lake in the Rogoland district of Norway. The creature was said to be about the size of a small island. The colour was grey-brown, and seemed to be slimey or shiney. Others said it was shining black with some white, about the size of a four oared boat, with a head pointed like a bellows and large eyes. The reports were a mixture of the likely and unlikely: one man said he had been rowing across the lake when a dark head with large eyes appeared about 100 yards away, which followed him, disappearing when he approached land: another said his arm had been grabbed by the creature which only let go when he recited the Lord's Prayer – leaving his arm covered in slime. Exaggerations such as this naturally spread alarm in the neighbourhood.

In the summer of 1892 the local school inspector A. J. Olsen (who was also President of the Directors of the Stavanger Museum) visited the lake to look into the affair after hearing about the monster from reliable friends. Thinking it might prove to be an illusion of some sort, he set about discovering the cause of the reports. Those he heard were in general agreement: usually in warm weather, when the lake was still, the water would begin to boil and seethe, and a large dark body appear, shaped like a capsized boat. After splashing up and down for some minutes, the object would sink.

He visited the upper end of the lake where the monster was usually seen, near the Roalkvam farms where two rivers entered the lake. On both these rivers there were sawmills. He found to his own satisfaction that the "monster" seemed to be caused by sawdust carried down from the mills. On the lake beds the dust, covered by slime, would ferment and burst up onto the surface.

This was his theory, but none of the local people believed it. The chairman of the local council and other influential men arranged an inquiry. At the autumn assizes the Board of Directors of the Stavanger Museum summoned some of the witnesses. But their sworn evidence did nothing to change the minds of either the doubters or the believers. A suggestion was made that the monster should be captured somehow, and the Museum was approached to pay the expenses of an expedition, in return for which they could have the stuffed monster for their exhibition. The incredulous directors declined the offer.

The next year there was a sequel to the affair. One day in the spring of 1893 the local teacher Mr Roalkvam and his brother were watching the lake when they noticed a strange movement in the water about 20 metres from the shore. The water was disturbed and muddy with a lot of white foam, and what seemed to be a large log appeared on the surface.

Could it be the monster? They rowed out to the place at once only to find a small patch of foam was left. But they were in luck, for just then the water started to seethe in another place and at last an object like a capsized boat came to the surface. It swayed backwards and forwards and then slowly sank till only a small part was visible. Then the water became calm and the object was still. The men again rowed out into the lake after the object. They were greatly surprised to find that it was actually "a complete mass of saw-dust, semi-rotten plants, pine-needles, pieces of wood and mud from the bottom of the lake. They tried to float it ashore but had to give up the attempt".

This remarkable account (retrieved from a report on the Suldal monster which A. J. Olsen wrote for the annual of the Stavanger Museum in 1897) has provided Maurice Burton with

Kenneth Wilson's first photograph of the monster, the classic pose of a real animal

Wilson's second photograph, **showing the** head about to submerge

THE SEA SERPENT IN THE HIGHLANDS.—The

village of Leurbost, parish of Lochs, Lewis, is at present the scene of an unusual occurrence. This is no less than the appearance in one of the inland fresh water lakes of an animal which from its great size and dimensions has not a little puzzled our island naturalists. Some suppose him to be a description of the hitherto mythological water-kelpie; while others refer it to the minute descriptions of the "sea serpent," which are revived from time to time in newspaper columns. It has been repeatedly seen within the last fortnight by crowds of people, many of whom have come from the remotest parts of the parish to witness the uncommon spectacle. The animal is described by some as being in appearance and size like a "huge peat stack," while others affirm that a "six-oared boat" could pass between the huge fins, which are occasionally visible. All, however, agree, in describing its form as that of the eel; and we have heard one, whose evidence we can rely upon, state that in length he supposed it to be about 40 feet. It is probable that it is no more than a conger eel after all, animals of this description having been caught in Highland lakes which have attained a huge size. He is currently reported to have swallowed a blanket inadvertently left on the bank of the lake by a girl herding cattle. A sportsman ensconced himself with a rifle in the vicinity of the loch during a whole day, hoping to get a shot, but did no execution.—*Inverness Courier.*

The first with the news—from *The Times,* March 1856

Painting by George Cooper of a hump that appeared in Loch Morar

Loch Morar S

Above, photograph taken in August 1934 by F. C. Adams, showing a blunted head sometimes mentioned in reports. *Below,* controversial photograph by Peter O' Connor, April 1960—the real thing?

Daily Exp

Two famous photographs from the Fifties: the first by Lachlan Stuart, which may not be an animal at all...

...and another by P. A. MacNab taken in 1955, showing two animals together

North American monsters: **the** fictional monster of Lake **La** Metrie meets its end...

...and the real one of Lake Manitoba photographed in 1962

Associated Press

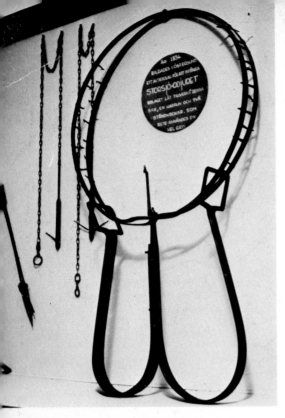

Harpoons and trap made to catch the Storsjö animal in 1895

Hallings Foto Ostersund

A modern mock-up of the Storsjö monster outside Ostersund today

Hallings Foto Osters

The Daedalus sea serpent, the great sensation of 1848

The Secret of the Loch: the monster (based on Gould's theories) in an early starring role

Marie Hunt

Victorian vignette of prehistory; a plesiosaur at Sydenham
made by Waterhouse Hawkins in 1853

the type specimen of his "vegetable mats" as an explanation for the Loch Ness reports. Though it seems true – though how the animal-like details of the earlier reports were derived from such a load of old rubbish I cannot see – that the first published accounts of monsters in Norwegian lakes appear with the advent of saw mills on the mountain streams, this could merely be coincidence. But were there, in fact, saw mills at Mjosa in 1553?

Miss Skjelsvik has put us in her debt by collecting from the archives of the Oslo folklore institutes details of other lakes in Norway said to be haunted by monsters. But here we are back with mere hearsay evidence, with vague traditions for the most part devoid of any details. Others do have some detail. The animal in Lake Bullare, in Sweden, had a body the size of a year old calf, with a 12 foot long neck. The Rommen lake animal had a head like a calf, and a body like a log. The Odegardskilen monster was also the size of a log, but could move in curves and had a long pointed tongue. Sorsasjoen had an animal the size of a brownish 12 inch wide log. In the Ringsjoen an animal seen in 1868 had the head of a horse which had white teeth and "was large enough for a cat to walk into".

A J. A. Saumuelson is recorded as describing the Bergso animal as having a neck 1 metre long, 7 or 8 iron grey links about a metre each in length and as thick as a man's thigh. Saumuelson also says the Oyvanna animal had a calf-like head with eyes "the size of a hollow hand".

The Krodern animal was said to have had a head the size of a small house, which is ridiculous, but also to have had large eyes and to have bellowed like a cow which sounds more likely. Here the reports have suffered by being written up by a journalist. Ivar Wiel however, writing in a Norwegian geographical journal tells us more calmly that the Tyrifjorden animal was 2 to 8 metres long.

A folklorist again reduces the material to the ridiculous when he recorded that the Stuvsfjordhylen animal had a body 18 feet long, a tail "like a barn door and eyes like the blade of the spade" which means the tail was divided and that the eyes were no more than slits.

The animals in a small lake in Deblemyren near Mandal, the

Repstadvanet, Tinnkjodnet, and Sogne all had manes like horses on their necks. While the animal in Lundevatnet had 8 or 9 humps and swam faster than a motor boat. The one in Mosvatnet was brownish black with a seal's head with a white collar and a body like an uneven aspen log. The one in Ormsjoen (Monster's Lake) was said to also be brown but with the baroque additions of spikes and water plants.

However the creatures in Krovatnet were grey with large and small yellow spots. That in Storevatn was 9 or 10 metres long, shining black and shaped like a capsized boat. The Torfinns-vatnet monster had a dragon's head, a large mouth, and limbs like a crocodile. According to a writer in 1872 the Skodje monster was as thick as a man's waist, with a horse's head, a mane and eyes like plates. Someone said it was 20 feet long. But one in Sandsavatnet was supposed to be 200 feet long, while that in Jolstravatnet reached to half a mile.

Odd details in this fantastic farago will sound familiar, but for the most part the reports are too over-coloured to be of real use. Clearly these Norwegian reports are more than mere vegetable mats, but must be more closely investigated before we can be certain about most of them. Miss Skjelsvik notes that the Kro monster in Orekram is mostly seen in summer; another in Sor Somna lake about midsummer, and a third in Lake Snasa during calm weather, usually about sunrise. She comments that "the appearance of the monster are very often accompanied by 'boiling' or some movements in the water". All of which she feels supports the vegetable-mat theory. But as we shall see these details could just as easily be used to support an animal theory. For there can be little doubt that something more than vegetable mats are seen in Lake Storsjo in central Sweden.

8

The Storsjö Animal:
Dr. Olsson Investigates

One of those animals forced to swim in the icy
currents of abominable lakes.

Beowulf

LAKE STORSJÖ IS a large deep lake in the mountains of central
Sweden; the deepest in Scandinavia, as a matter of fact. Until
about 1880 Ostersund, on the east shore of the lake, was only
a small remote village. With the opening up of the timber
industry in Jamtlands province and the arrival of the railway,
the place grew and prospered. Several newspapers were published in the town, and it was a series of reports in these during
the 1890's that brought news of the mysterious monster of Lake
Storsjö to the outside world, and to the attention of Dr Peter
Olsson.

Olsson was a zoologist who taught science at the Ostersund
State High School. He was the author of several studies in the
field of marine biology and a description of the fauna of Jamtlands province. He was more than merely interested in the
reports of a mysterious animal in the lake below his house.
Stimulated by a series of reports in the summer of 1898, he set
about collecting and collating earlier ones to build up a detailed
picture of the monster.

Here at least there was little doubt that this was an *animal*.
Between 1820 and 1898 he found some 22 reports from quite
trustworthy witnesses. Some of the reports he copied from the
local papers, but many were obtained by personal enquiry.

The first reports dated from 1820 when a farmer had claimed
that the animal had followed his boat near Funas at the south
end of the lake. In the 1830's a housepainter who saw it was
impressed enough to call it "the Storsjö leviathan". The

Lutheran Swedes were stern Bible readers, and in these reports from the 19th century there is an odd contrast between farmers using cubits to describe the animal's size, and the newly educated engineers using metric measures.

About 1839 or so, one Aron Andersson from Hackas, with some others, saw the animal swimming out from the shore into the open lake. It appeared similar to a sort of red-grey horse with a white mane, which disappeared suddenly when in deep water. His son often heard him relate this story later, and thought his father generally a reliable man. Olsson in his reports goes to some pains to assure us of the honesty and reliability of his witnesses: we can take their character references for granted at this date, I think.

In 1855 on the 25 July, the local administrator reported that Deputy Paul Andersson had told him that with four farmers on 19 July at 10.30 in the morning, outside Sanne from a distance of 500 cubits, he had seen the animal – about 25 feet long about the width of a rowboat – moving in the same direction as they towards the south but going much faster than their boat. He claimed that the monster was seen later in the year in another part of the lake but was harmless to men: it might well have been merely a large pike.

One day in 1858 (according to a local paper) another farmer, Erik Isaksson, was outside Ostersund and was followed in his boat by a big animal whose shape reminded him of an upturned boat. No other details are given, but that description is now quite familiar from other places.

In 1863, on one bright sunny summer day, J. Bromee and some of his family were coming from Billsta in Hackas across the lake, when they saw a large animal close to the land near the beach below the farm. His mother-in-law had thought the splashing was children swimming, but on coming closer they saw that it was not children. In the turbulent water they saw some big animal with short thick feet. Bromee decided to close up on it. With some men he set out after it in a boat. They likened the animal to 10 or 12 ducks scooting along the water one after the other. These "ducks" were shiny black humps. The animal got away from them after a short chase. No-one could say for certain how big the animal was, though the part above the water line was 10 cubits long.

On another clear summer afternoon in 1868, a man saw the animal in Assjoen, an area of the lake to the north of Ostersund. He remembered that the water was mirror-calm. He saw it about 100 metres from the shore. There was a strong swell on the water, as if a boat had just passed. Then he saw something which he thought was a smooth barkless balk of timber, which moved at "arrow speed" (a Swedish expression which defies translation) for about 200 metres and then disappeared.

In 1870 the animal was seen, for a change, in the late autumn, when the lake was disturbed by a storm. J. Bromee, again with some of his family, saw an animal pass in the distance, about 12 cubits long and looking again like a balk of wood. However it was moving with more speed than a row boat could manage, from Billssa in the direction of Hoverberget. The wake was very large, and they thought the animal must have been quite strong to swim so fast.

In the midsummer of 1873, Erik Olsson from Ostersund who was going from Kjalsmarsundet to Hallen, saw something in the distance ahead of him. They thought it was a log of wood, but then when they got closer they saw it was an animal moving with great speed. It followed the boat out of curiosity until some of the oarsmen became scared. They made for the small island near Gaje and the animal turned away. It had a dog-like head, which they saw clearly even though this was just before sunset.

In 1889 on a fine August day a church warden named Östman saw a "monster" in Assjön, at a time when no one locally talked yet of the animal, though of course sea serpents were well known. About 150 to 200 metres out in the lake, he saw something moving through the water which he thought was a waterspout and so made back towards the shore. But the "wind" also increased its speed behind him. He heard noises behind him and looked back to see what was making them. About 70 metres from the shore, and about three metres high was a long neck which so scared him he fled at once; though not without noting that it was about 10 metres long and 1 metre wide and grey in colour. About a quarter of an hour later he came back the same way and it made the same noises, moving with much greater speed before vanishing in the lake.

During the autumn of 1892, according to a local paper, Lars

Larsson and his son saw a large animal in the lake at the mouth of Assjon. It was like an upturned boat and moved with great speed. The animal seemed to have a pair of short paddles or back fins. Also it was said to make a noise that could be heard a great way off. The length from his position seemed to be about 12 metres.

What brought the monster to everyone's attention however was an incident in October 1893. Two girls of Sorbyn were washing clothes on the shore below Ås. They were Marta Olsson (18 years) and her older sister Karin (21 years), whom neighbours described as truthful girls. The two girls had gone down to the beach at 9 o'clock to wash clothes. Suddenly they saw something in the lake making in towards the shore at great speed which stopped in front of them. They saw not much more than the head which was rising and falling in the water for an hour and half. The head was large and round, with good-sized eyes, shining skin, with short fins, larger at the rear than at the shoulders. They were uncertain about any tail; or about the ears, for on the head there were things laid back which looked as if they had been clipped. The colour was grey with big black spots. Karin picked up a pile of stones in the hem of her dress, and started to shy them at the animal, at which it turned toward the shore sending Karin racing up the bank to the safety of the railway. Marta climbed a nearby tree, from which she could still see the animal. The animal churned up the water, diving under and up again before finally disappearing.

Karin gave quite a detailed description of the animal to the editor of the *Ostersund Post*, who specially interviewed the two girls. The animal's head was round like a dog's. The eyes were as large as saucers, and dark in colour. They stared without blinking. The mouth was wide and open, the interior dark red like a fish's, with a tongue which flickered in and out. The eyes were set about 6 to 8 centimetres apart. The head was 3 feet wide and equally long. The neck was about 8 or 9 feet long, with the back being 14 feet long. There were no forefeet, more likely fins. On the head two big ears which were laid back along the neck. Also two objects on the neck which could be extended – one is reminded of the "kippered herrings" someone saw on the Loch Ness animal's neck. When the animal turned away from the shore and dived out of sight, it seemed funny to have been so afraid of it. As the animal swam away from them, they saw the back and rear end clearly, behind which there was now a long wake. They saw the forefeet stroking through the water, as every time it would rise in the water at every stroke. None of these details were changed by the girls under close questioning later on.

Remarkable though it was, theirs was not the only curious report that year. On Christmas morning 1893, a workman named A. M. Johannsson and his wife were crossing the bridge to Froso island from Ostersund when they heard a strange noise, the sound of the new ice on the water breaking up. From a hole in the ice below them an animal's head shot up to about $2\frac{1}{2}$ feet for a moment and then sank back at once. The movement was quick and darting like a snake's. It disappeared so quickly that they thought it must have been frightened by the sight of them. Two other men also saw, then, and later it appeared at other places during the day. It's total length was said to be about 12 or 13 cubits, about 24 or 25 feet.

It was as a result of these reports that an effort to catch the animal was organised in 1894. A wealthy Ostersund widow set up a limited company to capture the monster. King Oscar II is said to have been persuaded to contribute some of the firm's capital. An experienced Norwegian whaler was hired but in a whole year spent on the lake he never saw the monster even once. Today in the local museum in Ostersund the interested visitor can inspect the harpoons which were specially made for him. Other equipment includes large barbed hooks, and an immense trap with spring jaws which was to have been baited with a live piglet. Despite these elaborate preparations the company failed in its purpose, and went bankrupt. The whaler was fired and the search called off. But if the whaler failed to kill his quarry, it was not because it had disappeared. Far from it, as the continuing reports showed.

In 1896 Nils Ling saw what he called "two sails" on the surface of the water about 12 or 15 cubits from his boat. They were about one cubit long and $1\frac{1}{2}$ high. They were moving with some speed *against* the wind, certainly faster than the boat though parallel to it. This animal also made a loud noise before sinking suddenly out of sight. They saw no more details.

On December 31, 1897 a party on their way to Odensala saw

the animal out among the broken ice floes in the clear afternoon light. It was seen first by J. Franzen from Ope and resembled once again an upturned boat about 40 feet long. They shouted out and the animal changed direction, sinking down in the water and moving this way and that. So they observed from several sides for about half an hour before it disappeared. All the while it was churning up the surface of the water.

In 1898 on June 2, the animal was seen outside Hacknas for half an hour going towards the north. Some half a dozen people watched it from a distance of about quarter of a mile. This time it resembled two boats moving up and down in the water; that is, there were two humps about 30 to 40 feet in overall length. It was moving in the same direction as the witnesses' boat. In the sunlight the skin seemed glittery and slimey. The front was dark green to brown, the back lighter grey and yellowish. On each side they could see something like a propeller moving in the water. The animal's speed was enough to put the wind up the oarsmen. Then the animal lay still for a short time on the water then, swimming against the wind, it did a couple of turns to the north before disappearing.

On July 10 the same year the animal was seen by a newspaper researcher along with five other people. P. E. Asen observed it about 1 kilometre from his house on the shore of the lake. At first he thought it was a capsized boat and put out to investigate. But on coming closer he saw that it was really a floating body, though it did look like a raft. The size and the movement of the fins soon dispelled any idea that it was inanimate however. It swam off towards the north against the wind, which was picking up. Asen rowed around the floating animal which was making a great many waves. Then it suddenly turned and he glimpsed the belly and two fins. The body was about 4 feet high and $1\frac{1}{2}$ feet wide, narrowing to an inch at the top. He was uncertain about the length, which might have been about 4 to 5 metres along the water line. The head and neck were $1\frac{1}{2}$ metres long, though the head was not raised clear of the water. The ears, as he called them, were set about two feet apart above the water. The body was smooth with small warts over it in places. It was a sort of cinnamon colour, and he thought slimey and scaley.

The "ears" were white and lay back along the neck. Along the back, dark protuberances – clearly the vertebra – stood out.

Also there were green things hanging off it, whether a mane or water weed is not clear. At the front something was moving in the water, but what it was, whether a paddle or a foot, he could not see.

The animal moved off quietly and slowly towards Vallniken, after he had watched it for about half an hour. Then somewhere on the lake a steamer whistled. The animal cocked its ears out of the water, seemed distressed or frightened, turned off to the south and sank out of sight.

A week later, on July 17, two small boys saw the animal near the home of Olof Peterssons in Valla. They brought it to his attention and some dozen other people also saw. The animal, like an upturned boat yet again, was moving against the wind. The weather was clear so everyone could see it perfectly. The animal had ears or fins in a shining white colour, though the body was a reddish colour. A boat approached from Nordero, and when the animal heard it, it turned around and sank in a mess of seething water.

On August 1, 1898 – being the nearest to his investigation naturally enough produced the most reports – a mechanic A. Johansson was standing on the shore at Ostersund, when he saw the animal about 7 or 8 metres away. It was the size of an upturned boat, dark in colour. On the back near the neck he could see a pair of light coloured fins, about 4 decimetres high and 2 decimetres long. These were, clearly, the ears cocked up. Suddenly it moved away at great speed into the lake and sank. In all he saw it for about a minute.

On August 18 Olof Johansson of Sunne was out on the lake in his boat. He saw an object like a log moving west slowly in the opposite direction. Then it rose up in the water a couple of cubits. When he got closer the animal became scared and sank out of sight. It was 12 to 14 metres long, and some sort of dark colour.

At the end of September or the beginning of October 1898, the animal was seen at 8 in the morning opposite Optland by a farmer named Ward, a hunter and a servant girl. Ward was 400 metres from the shore, and the animal itself was about 600 metres out in the lake. At that great distance he estimated its length at about 10 metres. The body stuck up as small humps. The head was silvery white. The animal was staring at the land.

Ward fired two shots at it, though how he hoped to hit it at a range of a thousand metres I don't know. At the second shot it dived down out of sight.

On October 4 near Funas three men saw the animal move quickly towards the south, turn and disappear. They saw this for about 4 minutes. Though the wind was light, there were strong waves where the animal was seen. They estimated it was about 8 metres long.

Finally on November 20 a group of people saw the animal off Sunne. The lake was mirror calm. The animal was "two stones throw" from the shore. Because it was so close they were able to guess its length to be about 20 or 30 feet. At first they saw the head only, then the rear. The hump was one foot over the water, though one of the witnesses thought there were really four humps. There was movement in the water like a boat's propeller. Suddenly the animal went off very fast. Two of the group tried to give chase in their boat, but the animal swam so quickly that it disappeared before they could catch up with it.

Varied though they are, on the basis of these reports Olsson was able to arrive at some idea of the animal's shape and appearance. In length it varied from report to report (inevitably as the witnesses only saw parts of the animal). The estimates varied from $3\frac{1}{2}$ to 14 metres, about 11 to 45 feet. Only two witnesses made any mention of the breadth, which was about a metre (probably at the thick part of the neck). The shape was generally described as long, sometimes as an upturned boat, a large log of wood, a string of birds, two or three barrels or boats, a long coalboat or a skein of ducks.

The skin was smooth, glossy, shining or slimey and scaled. The colour was given as greenish-grey with large black spots, dark, foreparts brown or dark green and behind light grey or yellowish, cinnamon with dark stripes, or, finally, reddish grey.

The head was described in four reports. It was said to be round like a dog's and smooth, with large eyes, 6 to 8 centimetres apart, with a white mane (really the ears?). The animal swims with its head over the water only on occasion, dipping it down when stones were thrown at it.

The animal's "organs of motion" are described as short stumpy feet, possibly big clumsy fins, or long webbed hind feet.

On the back of the head are two floppy "ears" or "fins" which can be laid back along the neck.

Fig. 24. Profile of the Storsjö animal, based on reports.

The animal swims sometimes with the head over the water, sometimes with only the "fins" showing over the surface. There seems to be some confusion in the reports between the humps, fins and sails, as not all the witnesses were very good at putting into words what they had really seen. Nevertheless the general picture is clear.

The animal's speed was generally agreed to be very fast, perhaps about 45 m.p.h.

In one report the animal is said to have come partly ashore, but for the most part it was seen out in deep water. The depth of Lake Storsjö is well over 294 metres. The animal sinks rapidly or slowly as it pleases, though it often churns up the water violently.

The animal is usually seen during quiet summery weather, or when the surface of the lake is calm, though it was once seen in the middle of a storm. It has been reported at all seasons of the year, including icebound winter. Sightings have taken place all around the lake, so that the concentration off Ostersund is due entirely to the larger number of people living there.

Olsson, on the basis of one report where the animal was seen in a shoal of fish, assumed that it lived on a diet of fish. It was harmless, though it showed some curiosity by its habit of following boats. It was sensitive to noise and easily frightened, especially when young girls threw stones at it. It had a loud cry, and a mobile tongue in a wide mouth.

Such was the evidence. How did Olsson interpret it? After very briefly considering various theories, that it was a giant ray, a plesiosaur or basilosaurus, he settled for the giant seal theory which Oudemans had outlined in *The Great Sea Serpent* a few years before. The evidence undoubtedly did support the contention that the Storsjö animal was a mammal of a kind related to the seals. Dr Olsson wrote up the evidence and the results of his investigation in a small pamphlet published in Ostersund. His scientific conclusions, which are those of a trained zoologist, were reached, we should note well, some thirty-four years before the Loch Ness monster created an international sensation.

Oddly enough, though papers in Stockholm and Oslo gave a great deal of space to the Loch Ness monster, they printed little enough about their own lake monsters. The Oslo *Tidens Tegn* reproduced a report from Denmark of a monster seen back in the 1840's in the Farrisvannet, a small lake in the south of the country; no more was heard of this. In another issue they also ran a photo of an alleged lake monster said to have been taken in a lake on Bear Island near the Arctic Circle. The photographers name is given as G. Horn, but I have been unable to find out more about him. If the photograph were genuine we should surely have heard a great deal more about it, especially at that time.

As for the Storsjö monster, that is still around. Its history has been pushed back a little further. On the island of Forso there is a memorial stone carved with a runic inscription and a picture which may well be the Storsjo animal. The long neck can be clearly seen, as well as the divided tail or rear flippers.

The animal made a further show in the summer of 1907, after which it seems to have lain low for several years. At the end of the Second World War, however, the *New York Times* under the headline "Normalcy?", reported the animal's reappearance as a comforting portent of the new peace in Europe: there couldn't be all that much amiss if people were back to seeing monsters in the land of aquavit. The Stockholm paper *Der Tidningen*, quoting three eyewitnesses, reported that "the lake's calm shining surface was broken by a giant snake-like thing with three prickly dark humps. The animal swam at a good parallel to the shore, on which the waves caused by the animal were breaking". We were also back it seemed, after the carefulness of Dr Olsson, to the careless sensationalism of bad journalism.

Since then the animal has been seen quite regularly. In 1959 an Ostersund journalist brought Olsson up to date. He managed to discover several older witnesses, as well as some new ones. The pattern of their evidence remained the same however, so there is not much point in going into any more detail. As recently as the summer of 1965 the *Scandinavian Times* reported a new outbreak of sightings. After giving details of some recent incidents, the magazine said that tourists were flocking to the lake in the hope of seeing the animal. The Jamtlands tourist board makes use of the monster in its brightly coloured brochures, pointing out once again the resemblance to the Loch Ness monster. Outside Ostersund a mock-up of the monster welcomes the visitor to the town: again the ears and divided tail are not too large a departure from reality.

Swedish zoologists however have not followed up the pioneering research of Dr Peter Olsson. They put the reports down to the effects of aquavit, which is a gross libel on the honesty of the local witnesses. An interested layman who inquired recently at the zoological department of Stockholm University was told that there was no scientific value in the subject. One hopes that with all the attention now being given to Loch Ness, some Swedish scientist may be inspired to look into their own monsters.

Our own investigations, however, must now take us out of Europe to the Americas in search of more monsters.

9

Slimey Slim and Others:
United States of America

"Monsters? Why, of course, there are Monsters.
Don't be so silly".

An American child, in conversation

IN THE EARLY decades of the last century, the Sea-Serpent was
a frequent summer visitor along the shores of the New England
coast. The usually hard-headed Yankees were seeing them in
nearly every little bay, it seemed. Or so their fellow Americans
thought, laughing over the latest sensation from the bays of
Massachusetts. When monsters started to be reported from
fresh water lakes all the way across the continent, these stories
were in turn received with derision. Yet, like the evidence for
the American sea-serpent, the evidence for the lake monsters
is large, varied and well-documented.

There were, of course, many traditions about such animals.
The Crees, Algonquins, Onondaga and Ojibway all believed
in them. The Huron had their angoub, and the Chinook of
British Columbia their hiachuckaluck, though both of these
were said also to live in the sea.

This connection between the sea-serpent and the fresh water
animals was grasped by one of the first scientists seriously to
consider the matter at all. The brilliant Samuel Rafinesque, in
an article in 1819 about sea snakes, drew attention to reports of
a monster in Lake Erie, which had been seen in July 1817, was
about 35 feet long, one foot round and dark mahogany in
colour. A later report said it was nearer 60 feet, with bright
eyes. Rafinesque believed the reports and thought it might be
a giant eel.

In some quarters these reports were taken quite seriously. A

German science journal even published an account of a Lake Ontario monster in 1835. But on the whole the topic was treated less ponderously.

For instance, in 1835, the local paper in Logansport, Indiana, then on the western frontier, had great fun with a "monster" in nearby Lake Manitou. So much fun indeed that it is now hard to discover whether it was not a hoax invented by an imaginative editor of the *Telegraph*, John Brown Dillon. A few names, an unlikely description, and a bad sketch was all the real evidence, and not much of it stands up to scrutiny. The real purpose of the exercise seems to have been a creditable effort on the part of Dillon to set down some of the traditions of the Potawatomi Indians, who even as he wrote his articles were being driven out of Indiana by the U.S. Army. The frontier was moving slowly westward, and with its advance more stories of monsters emerged to eclipse the Indian traditions.

These reports fall into three groups: those from the Wisconsin lake land, those from the Nebraska plains, and finally those from the mountain states.

The Wisconsin lakes seem to teem with the animals. Among the lakes with recorded sightings are the Madison Four Lakes, Lake Waubeau, Red Cedar Lake, Lake Pewaukee and Elkhart Lake.

An article in the *Lake Mills Spike* (August 31, 1882) described the Rock Lake monster. The paper claimed that "the saurian" was first seen lurking in a clump of reeds by a Mr Hassam in 1867, and that other lakeside residents had seen it frequently since. During August 1882, some men rowing on the lake saw what appeared to be a floating log, which then reared up a huge head out of the water. One witness said the air around was heavy with "a most sickening odour", so this monster may well have been one of those vegetable mats of Dr Burton, exploding on the surface.

The Red Cedar Lake Monster was seen in 1891: an undulating form like a huge snake or fish, with a huge head and a row of protuberances like a saw-tooth along its back. But it has been unkindly suggested that this monster was connected with efforts to sell lakeshore sites.

The "sea-serpent" in Lake Monona, near East Madison, was

not (I think) a hoax, and seems to have been more than a bubble
of gas. The *Wisconsin State Journal* (June 12, 1897) reported
the reappearance of the animal, which had lately been seen by
several people.

> They say it was at least 20 feet long, and travelled east on
> the surface of the lake until Eugene Heath, agent of the
> Garr-Scott Company, fired several shots into it, when it
> turned and disappeared.
>   Mr Schott and others who saw the 'thing', whatever it may
> be, insist that it is a reality and not a joke or a creature of
> their combined imaginations. Its appearance is not that of a
> serpent. Mr Schott says, however, that he saw it plainly in
> the bright moonlight, and its shape was like the bottom of a
> boat, but it was twice as long. (That is, 30 feet or so.) Mr
> Schott's two sons saw it, and were so firmly convinced that
> it was a dangerous animal that neither of the Schotts, who
> had spent a large part of their lives on the lake, would
> venture out on it.

Not everyone was quite so timorous. A hunter named
Christopher Egstein was brave enough to loose off a shot at a
monster that reared out of the Great Sandy Lake in Minnesota
in 1886.

The difficulty with these American reports is that however
they start, as mild editorial facetiousness or serious reports
from actual witnesses, sooner or later they are turned into
"American folklore". So that what might have been acceptable
as just credible becomes quite incredible. The Alkalie Lake in
Nebraska in an instance.

This lake is a few miles south of Hay Springs. In 1939 the
indigent scholars and writers employed on the Federal Writers
Project, which was collecting "American folklore", summarised
the history of the monster there, which they facetiously call
Giganticus Brutervious. When the monster appears the earth
trembles and the skies cloud over. When he comes ashore, to
devour calves it is said, a thick mist covers the shore around him.
His gnashing teeth rumble like claps of thunder. (How reminiscent this is of the Chinese dragons, originally gods controlling
the rain and thunder. Did the Chinese coolies working on the

American railroads in the 1870's leave one of their deities behind them in Nebraska?) The writers archly describe the horror of the monster, how his appearance made men mad or turned their hair white. He was said to be over 300 feet long and to have swallowed a small island in the lake. By 1939 the monster was seen so infrequently that some thought it was gone away, others that it was hibernating.

This is an example of folklorists at their worst. Rather than treat popular stories as topics of serious interest, the writers feel that to justify their spending time collecting and rehashing them, the stories have to be given a facetious treatment, and the bourgeois prejudice of the reader pandered to by making what his grandfather believed an object of ridicule. This is not literature, nor is it social science. It is rubbish. They would have been better employed exploring the coincidence of their local folklore with Chinese mythology.

Curiously, straight fiction provides more interesting material than what is supposed to be folklore.

> Years and years ago, I heard vague accounts of a strange lake up in an almost inaccessible part of Wyoming. Various incredible tales were related of it, such that it was inhabited by creatures which elsewhere on the globe are found only as fossils of a long vanished era.

That sentence is from a short story, a piece of early science fiction called "The Monster of Lake La Metrie", which appeared in *Pearson's Magazine* in September 1899. The story itself is pretty silly. Two scientists travel up to Lake La Metrie to explore it. After a volcanic disturbance what appears to be a large log comes to the surface. This turns out to be an elasmosaurus, an American type of plesiosaur, "exactly twenty-eight feet long with a black hide and a swan-like neck". When his friend cuts his throat, one of the scientists slices off the top of the animals skull, removes its brain, and transplants his friend's brain into it. The personality of Framlingham is absorbed into that of the reptile and he turns on his friend. But just at this moment an army patrol chasing some run-away Indians (this is still the Wild West) arrives at the lake. The captain orders his men to unlimber their field gun and fire on the monster. The poor beast tears out into the lake in its death agony and sinks. The captain concludes his report: "I think some attempt should be made to rescue the body of the elasmosaurus. It would be a priceless addition to any museum".

The interesting thing about this story is that the author, Wardon Allen Curtis (about whom almost nothing is known) seems to have based it on rumours he had himself heard of monsters in lakes in the western mountain states. Stories of animals in "a wild and unknown part of the mountains" are still current and have been since the middle of the nineteenth century.

In the 1840's to escape the embarrassment and persecution which Americans customarily inflict on their minorities, the Mormons trekked west into the desert of Utah, where they laid out a new city at Salt Lake and set up a Mormon state. Travellers such as Sir Richard Burton and numerous journalists went out to see these notable polygamists. Some visitors brought back stories of strange animals in the Utah lakes.

The Indians had respected several lakes as sacred places. Panguitch Lake was believed by them to be haunted by the ghosts of the dead Navajo chiefs, while the Salt Lake itself was the abode of storm spirits. "Nor", wrote a journalist in 1883,

> are the other lakes of Utah exempt from the same superstitious associations. The Utah Lake (a freshwater lake south of Salt Lake city) has a legendary monster. But Bear Lake is pre-eminent for its mysterious reputation, inasmuch as there is abundant testimony on record of the actual existence at the present day of an immense aquatic animal of some species as yet unknown to science.

And this is all of fifty years before the appearance of the Loch Ness monster.

The Shosone Indians had believed there was such a creature in the lake; but they told the first settlers that it had vanished after the extinction of the buffalo in Utah during the snowstorms of 1830. According to the historian Austin Fife:

> They represented it as being of the serpent kind, but having legs about eighteen inches long on which they sometimes

crawl out of the water a short distance on the shore. They also say it spouts water upwards out of its mouth.

Yet in 1860, *The Deseret News*, a Mormon paper published in Salt Lake City, reported (July 27) that according to "reliable white testimony" the Bear Lake monster was still alive. Three weeks before, a resident of South Eden, a hamlet on the east shore of the lake, Mr S. M. Johnson, was driving along the shore road to Round Valley:

> when about half-way he saw something in the lake which, at the time, he thought to be a drowned person. The road being some distance from the water's edge he rode to the beach and the waves were running pretty high. He thought it would soon wash into shore. In a few minutes two or three feet of some kind of an animal that he had never seen before were raised out of the water. He did not see the body, only the head and what he supposed to be part of the neck. It had ears or bunches on the side of its head nearly as big as a pint cup. The waves at times would dash over its head, when it would throw water from its mouth or nose. It did not drift landward, but appeared stationary, with the exception of turning its head. Mr Johnson thought a portion of the body must lie on the bottom of the lake or it would have drifted with the action of the water.

This was Mr Johnson's own version as told to the reporter from the paper.

The next day the monster was seen again at the same place by an unnamed man and three women. The said it was "very large" and "it swam much faster than a horse could run on land".

On the Sunday prior to July 27, there had been another sighting. The Reporter also interviewed these witnesses: N. C. Davis and Allen Davis (of St Charles), Thomas Slight and J. Collins (of Paris, Paris Utah, that is) and six women. They had been driving from Fish Haven to St Charles and were about midway when:

> their attention was suddenly attracted to a peculiar motion or wave in the water, about three miles distant. The lake was

not rough, only a little disturbed by a light wind. Mr Slight says he distinctly saw the side of a very large animal that he supposed to be not less than 90 feet in length. Mr Davis doesn't think he saw any part of the body, but is positive it must have been not less than 40 feet in length, judging by the wake it left in the rear. It was going south, and all agreed that it swam with a speed almost incredible to their senses. Mr Davis says he never saw a locomotive travel faster, and thinks it made a mile a minute easily. In a few minutes after the discovery of the first, a second one followed in its wake; but it appeared to be much smaller, appearing to Mr Slight about the size of a house. A large one, in all, and 6 small ones hied southward out of sight.

One of the large ones, before disappearing made a sudden turn to the west, a short distance; then back to its former track. At this turn Mr Slight says he could distinctly see it was a brownish colour. They could judge somewhat their speed by observing known distances on the other side of the lake, and all agree that the velocity with which they propelled themselves through the water was astonishing. They represent the waves that rolled up in front and on each side of them as being three feet high from where they stood. This is substantially their statement as they told me. Messrs David and Slight are prominent men, well known in this country [i.e. Utah], and all of them are reliable persons whose veracity is undoubted. I have no doubt they would be willing to make affidavits to their statement.

This account is not as clear as it might have been. But the large wakes, the great speed, colour and sharp changes of direction which the witnesses mention are already familiar from Loch Ness. We can be fairly certain that we are dealing with the same phenomenon in both places. The Bear Lake Monster did not remain, luckily, merely one of distantly observed wakes.

Later that same year (1860), *The Deseret News* claimed that Marion Thomas and three brothers named Cook had seen one of the Bear Lake monsters while they were fishing opposite Swan Creek.

Its head resembled that of a serpent and the 20 feet of its

body which they saw was covered with light brown fur like that of an otter. Two flippers extended upwards from the body which were compared to the fishermen's oars, and they affirmed that they came so near it that they might have shot it with a rifle.

Again, preconceptions about what monsters must be has influenced them to speak of a serpent's head, when from the exactness of the rest of the account we can see it must have been a mammal. The light brown fur, like an otters', is a detail worth noting. Clearly this is no otter, though.

In 1871 there was more news of the monsters. The *Semi-Weekly Herald* carried two reports and another appeared in *The Deseret News*.

On July 19, Milando Pratt and Thomas Rich saw, north of Fish Haven, an unusual commotion in the water. The head and part of the body of an animal emerged – "a body in diameter like that of a man and a head which suggested a walrus without tusks". When they fired several shots at it, the animal swam off towards the east shore with "a wavy serpentine motion". A walrus without tusks would obviously be a member of the seal family.

One of the other reports claimed that a young monster had actually been captured at Fish Haven. It was "a creature some 20 feet long which propelled itself through the water by the action of its tail and legs", and which had a large mouth. This perhaps was a hoax, as such a capture ought to have made more of a stir. Yet again we find that the actual description, far from being sensational as suits a hoax, is rather dull and commonplace. How else would a seal-like monster propel itself through the water except by using its rear flippers which have often been mistaken for a tail. What became of this animal, I do not know.

In 1883 Phil Robinson, writing about his wanderings in Utah for *Harper's New Monthly Magazine*, mentions the monster again, but says nothing of this capture. Professor Richard Owen (he of the Daedulus sea-serpent affair) had told Robinson that the sea-serpent might indeed exist. But if it did it would be a cuttle-fish, or a seal, and not an animal entirely new to science. Owen had in mind the giant squid which had become for some a complete explanation of sea-monsters. By seal, can he have meant perhaps some as yet undescribed type? Mr Robinson thought such credulity as Owen's was a virtue, arising as it did from the intelligent recognition of possibilities. Fortified by this learned counsel, Robinson was prepared to defend the Bear-Lake monster on the evidence he had gathered, and thought it was a fresh water seal or manatee. Unfortunately the evidence he actually gives us is quite sketchy.

Driving along the shore of the lake one day, a party surprised the monster basking on the bank. They saw it go into the water with a great splash, and pursued it, one of the party firing at it with a revolver as it swam swiftly out towards the middle of the lake. The trail on the beach was afterwards carefully examined, and the evidence of the party placed on record at once.

Nothing is quoted from those accounts, yet Robinson claims that the evidence of this one party "substantiates the Indian legends, and established the existence of this aquatic non-pareil. Let the Smithsonian see to it".

Needless to say, the Smithsonian did nothing. "The aquatic non-pareil" of Bear Lake joined the New England sea-serpent in the realm of dubious folklore. Many folklorists have been content to list it as a hoax. Yet the details of the evidence are too plausible for that (compare them with the lurid account of the Alkali Lake). The report of the capture of the young one may be a hoax, but I have no doubt that the other reports are true. Nor, despite the edge of fear to the description, do I doubt this report from the Salt Lake itself which was reported by the *Semi-Weekly Herald* on July 14, 1877.

J. H. McNeil, who claimed to have seen it when the animal blundered out of the lake into his camp, said "it was a great animal like a crocodile, or alligator, approaching the bank, but much larger than I had heard of one being. It must have been 75 feet long; but the head was not like an alligator's, it was more like a horse's". When it came within a few yards of the shore the animal made a loud noise and he and his companion fled up the mountain side where they stayed the night. When they came down the next morning they saw tracks on the shore, but nothing else.

Though I have been able to find nothing more about the Utah monsters, rumours of others in "a wild and unknown part of the mountains" still exist. Though nowadays the mountains are better known and visited by more people.

Lake Payette in Idaho is a seven mile stretch of water, into which flows a mountain river. The ridges circling the lake are pine-covered, the slopes below them dotted with weekend cottages around the lakeshore. During the 1930's there were occasional reports of a sea-serpent-like animal in the lake, but these were never more than rumours. But in the summer of 1941 there was a sudden spate of sightings. I should explain that Americans and Canadians are keen boaters, and often the smallest of lakes will be crowded with boats and water-skiers at the weekends, and in the summer weeks overcrowded.

The animal was first seen on July 2, and during the following two months over 30 people saw it. At first it was discussed only in private, for no conservative middle-westerner wished to admit to having seen "a sea-serpent". But this silence was broken by Thomas L. Rogers, the auditor of a respectable Boise firm. After encountering the animal close to, he described it for a local reporter:

> The serpent was about 50 feet long and going five miles an hour with a sort of undulating movement . . . His head, which resembles that of a snub-nosed crocodile, was 8 inches above the water. I'd say he was about 35 feet long (on consideration).

After this report was published, the shores of the lake were crowded with eager tourists and hopeful photographers, anxious to catch sight of the three humps or the long periscope-like neck which other witnesses hastened to describe. The *Idaho Sunday Statesman*, however, soon introduced the inevitable note of levity with its suggestion that Slimey Slim – as the monster was now nicknamed – was really a giant sturgeon that had got away from the legendary woodsman Paul Bunyan. Though jokes were made about Slimey Slim in the United States Senate, and *Time* magazine carried an article about the sensation in August, no real effort was made to investigate and little has been heard of the animal since.

But there has been news of another animal in Flathead Lake, Montana. Though many reports have appeared in the papers no scientific efforts have been made here, either. However, Paul Fugleburg, the editor of the *Flathead Courier*, maintains a dossier of reports and had offered a reward for the first photograph of the monster. So far no-one has claimed it. Mr Fugleburg also thinks the monster could be a giant sturgeon, though such a theory is not supported by the evidence in his file.

Most of the incidents are not revealing. A Californian motorist drew up outside Poulson and watched in silent amazement as a black object moved with an undulating movement through the water. Suddenly its speed increased and it swam northward out of his sight.

In 1963, Ronald Nixon, an employee of the Northern Pacific Railway, who lives near the lake saw:

something at least 25 feet long and with enough substance to it that as it moved near the surface, it threw up a two-foot head wave. It was perfectly black, and it didn't have any sign of a fin on the back. It couldn't have been a fish, and I'm sure it wasn't man-made.

Mr and Mrs Dean Powell of Poulson City watched the monster swimming for several minutes between Birs Island and the eastern shore of the lake. "It was huge and black", said Mr Powell, "but it couldn't have been a boat, as it went up and down in the water, splashed around and circled".

And lastly Mrs A. B. Bartlett and her sister Mrs Harry Peterson, from Missoula Montana, were out in a boat off the old Poulson City dock when they saw the monster. "Neither of us spoke", Mrs Bartlett recalls. "I concentrated on thinking it was a peak wave. But it wasn't: it was jet black". Her more romantic sister thought "it looked graceful". The animal had no fins that she could see. There was no sound. The animal moved through the almost calm lake leaving a long smooth wake.

Attempts have been made to capture the monster. In July 1964 a fisherman tried unsuccessfully to hook it using whole chickens and lumps of liver as bait. A skin diver, Fuller Laugher of Malta Montana, searched the lake systematically for four days without result. A company called Big Fish Unlimited has offered a reward of $1,400 for the capture of the monster or any fish over 14 feet long which might be taken for a monster. In 1964 the president of the group offered another $100 of his own money to the reward. As yet no one has come forward to claim it.

Another lake in the mountains which is said to be monster-haunted is Lake Walker in Nevada. Here again there are Indian legends of a man-eating monster in the lake, though it was said to eat only white men by agreement with the Indians. The basketball team at the High School in nearby Hawthorne call themselves "The Serpents" to keep up the tradition.

There are, however, some recent reports as well. A couple from Babbitt, Nevada, wrote to the magazine *Old West* in the fall of 1969, claiming to have seen the monster back in late April 1956. It had the speed of a high-powered motor-boat and outdistanced their car as they drove along the shore, going at about 35 miles an hour.

> It started straight for us at a great speed for about a hundred yards, and there it whipped to the left and submerged. We watched this happen three times, then it disappeared around the point into deeper water. We are sure we watched it for all of ten or fifteen minutes. It must have been 45 to 50 feet long and its back stuck up above the water at least four or five feet when it was swimming fast. We think in our own minds that it was feeding on the mud hens which were plentiful on the lake at that time . . .

I have notes on other reports from Hollow Block Lake, Portland, Oregon; Lake Folsom, California; and Lake Champlain in Vermont: but not with enough details to write about them here.

However convincing this long tradition of lake monsters in the United States may be, stretching as it does all the way across the continent for a century and a half, the reports lack any physical evidence to support them. There is nothing we can consider apart from the reports; no photographs, no drawings, no alleged remains. For these we have to turn north to the lake of Canada, and we start where we finished in the United States, in the high hills of the Rocky Mountains on the Pacific Coast.

10

Ogopogo and Others: Canada

"Monsters? Why, of course, there are monsters.
Don't be so silly".

A Canadian child in conversation

AFTER THE RETREAT of the last Ice Age, which spread far down into what is now the United States, Canada was left sprinkled with hundreds of thousands of lakes, like puddles drying in the sun between the Arctic and the Great Lakes.

Lake Okanagan is one such lake in British Columbia, in the far west on the Pacific slopes of the Rockies, in an area only recently cut off from the sea in geological time. The lake is 69 miles long and varies in width from three-quarters of a mile to 2½ miles – in area it is about 127 square miles.

About a third of the way up, the lake bends and there, 22 miles from the town of Penticton at the foot, is a small island. Barren and rocky, this place now seems unremarkable. Yet only a century ago, and for a long time before that, the local Indians – a branch of the Shushwap tribe – went in awe of the waters round it. For there lived Naitaka, the monster spirit of the lake, whom it was necessary to appease with ritual offerings. Whenever the Indians ventured out on the lake, they carried a chicken or a pup to drop into the dark forbidding depths for the monster.

Once a visiting chief named Timbasket, though he had been warned about the monster and told to keep a certain distance from the island, ignored the advice. The canoe carrying him and his family was upset in a sudden unpheaval of water, and all disappeared in the swirling foam.

The Indians have left crude drawings on stone of what is thought to be Naitaka, in which we can see the now familiar long neck, flippers and even the two "ears" on the crown of the head.

Fig. 25. Petroglyph of Naitaka.

The superstituous dread with which the Indians regarded Naitaka did not vanish with the advent of the first white settlers in the Okanagan Valley. They still spoke with dread of the *soore-appos*, of the water-demon. The beaches of Monster's Island, so they claimed, had often in the past been scattered with the bloody remnants of its meals.

Not all the stories, however, came from the Indians alone. In 1854 a halfbreed swimming a team of horses across the lake drowned them. He claimed they had been pulled down into the water by some strong force, and he had to cut them loose from the canoe for fear of drowning himself.

The early settlers are said to have continued the custom of carrying a small offering, partly because they themselves had seen a strange animal in the lake. Among these pioneers of the Okanagan Valley were the Allisons. Mrs Allison, who died in 1928, made an intensive study of Indian folklore, contributing articles on the subject to London journals. She was not the sort of person to be superstitious. Once when her husband was across the lake getting supplies in the store at Okanagan Mission, stormy weather came down. His wife was worried for his safety. She went out on the cliffs by their cabin overlooking the lake to see if she could see his boat returning. All she could see across the rainswept water was what appeared to be a large log. But then as she watched it began to move against the waves, with, so she thought, a slight undulating motion. It left a distinct wake behind it despite the rough water. After a while it vanished. When her husband landed, she told him what she had seen, but he only laughed and made light of it. But she was to have the last laugh.

On a later occasion, a friend of theirs named John McDougal was bringing his own team of horses across the lake, towed behind his boat. Though a believer in appeasing the monster, this time he had forgotten to bring his usual offering. In the middle of the lake his horses were pulled under, and if he had not cut them loose, his boat would have overturned. Had the horses merely panicked and drowned themselves? Or had the half-breed been right about the Monster?

The old Indian name for the animal was Naitaka, or Nha'a'itk; the settlers name for it is now Ogopogo, which is far more recent in origin. It is not, as some seem to have thought, an Indian word. Back in 1924 the following music hall hit from London was sung one night in Vernon:

> His mother was an earwig,
> His father was a whale.
> A little bit of head,
> and hardly any tail,
> And Ogopogo was his name.

Whatever about the animals strange parentage, the anatomical details are actually accurate enough. Ogopogo has a small head and hardly any tail. The name stuck, as such names will.

Vernon may have named the monster, but further down the lake, Kelowna disputes their complete right to him. To back their claim, the citizens have immortalised him (or is it her) with a statue, the first ever erected to an animal which "doesn't exist".

On and off since the beginning of this century the animal has been seen: sometimes just a black hump, sometimes a series of humps speeding up the lake. At other times the head and neck are seen. There is general agreement that the creature has a goat-like head, a long neck, the ability to change the shape of its back, and some say is covered in scales. A young girl out riding frightened the Ogopogo which was lying on a beach: it plunged back into the lake. It was a big snake-like creature, she said. Another witness said it was "an apparent prehistoric monster, at least 20 feet long, a heavy snake-like body, a horse's head and well-bearded".

The lake contains other things besides hypothetical plesiosaurs. In 1914 (a portentous year indeed) the rotting carcase of a strange animal was found washed up on one of the beaches. It was 5 to 6 feet long, weighed 400 lbs., with a round head stuck on its shoulders. Bluey-grey in colour, with flippers and a broad tail, it was completely unlike anything in the known fauna of Canada. Some local amateur naturalist casting through his books seems to have identified it as a manatee, or a sea-cow. The habitat of these creatures is in the West Indies, South America and possibly the Aleutians. How such an animal got into the lake no-one seems to have discovered. It is my guess that the animal was actually an ogopogo, as the details of this mammal with flippers and a broad tail and dark colour are all that we would expect. But that the carcase was mangled so much that the long neck was already gone.

When the Loch Ness monster became news, some stories of the ogopogo were trotted out in the press. Ian Hassal recalled that when he was in British Columbia in 1926 he had heard many stories of the alleged monster in Lake Okanagan. Miners told him it was "about 60 feet long, and swam with great speed" and that "its goat-like head, with two 'horns' at the sides, towered about 5 feet to 8 feet above the water on a slim neck". They said his suggestion that it was a strangely shaped log was impossible as it had been seen swimming against the current. A doctor, for instance, saw it so and tried to keep up with it in his car, but it outpaced him. Hassal was told by another miner that he had seen the animal breaking through the ice which covers the lake in winter. In 1934 Captain House of the Canadian Fishery Patrol described Ogopogo in *The Morning Post* as being like a telegraph pole with a sheep's head. An American visitor described him "as a mighty serpent with the face of a sheep and the head of a bulldog. He struck me dumb with horror".

It was not until after the war that reports of the animal appeared with any frequency. On July 2, 1949, ogopogo was seen by a Mr Kray and a Montreal family named Watson, who were crusing off Kelowna, when they noticed a dark shape drifting north. Kray described it:

What the party saw was a long sinuous body, 30 feet in length, consisting of about five undulations, apparently separated from each other by about a two-foot space, in which that part of the undulations would have been underwater. The length of each of the undulations that could be seen would have been about five feet. There appeared to be a forked tail, of which only one-half came above the water. From time to time the whole thing submerged and came up again.

This party were one of the few who have actually seen the animal's tail in the water and described it. Actually it is probably not a tail but a bilobate pair of flippers. At last it moved off across the lake, apparently chasing a shoal of fish, leaving a large wake behind it. When they saw it first it was swimming in six feet of water, feeding, so they thought, on the weed that grows to the surface of the lake near the shore.

In contrast is the description of the animal given by the Rev W. S. Bean, the Rector of the Anglican Church in Penticton, who saw it on August 12, 1950, in the lake before his cottage at Naramanta. About 4.30 on a calm lake, he saw a terrific disturbance in the water, after which several humps appeared, leaving a great wake, which slowly settled.

The same year, on the lake shore road near Naramata, Mr Bruce Miller and his wife saw ogopogo from their car and pulled up to watch it. They saw "a lithe, sinewy monster, 75 feet in length with a coiled back and dignified demeanour. Periodically his progress would be halted as he lay quietly on the water, head well raised, as he surveyed the lake with calm dignity".

Such archness on the part of reporters hides the real feeling of many witnesses, which is surely surprise and fear. One Sunday in July 1952, Mrs E. A. Campbell was entertaining her sister-in-law and a Scottish visitor on the lawn of her Kelowna house. Mrs E. W. Campbell from Vancouver described her reaction when the animal appeared a few hundred feet from them:

I am a stranger here. I did not even know such things existed. But I saw it so plainly, A head like a cow or horse that reared right out of the water. It was a wonderful sight. The coils glistened like two huge wheels ... There were ragged edges like a saw (along its back). It was so beautiful, with the sun shining on it. It was all so clear, so extraordinary. It came up three times, then submerged and disappeared.

The ragged edge along the back seem to be some kind of ridge such as is often reported on the Loch Ness animal.

The following account of Ogopogo was written by the owner-publisher of *The Vernon Advertiser* (where it appeared on July 20, 1959). Mr R. H. Millar does not disguise his excitement at seeing "this fabulous sea-serpent".

Returning from a cruise down Okanagan Lake, travelling at 10 miles an hour, I noticed, about 250 feet in our wake, what appeared to be the serpent. On picking up the field glasses my thoughts was verified. It was ogopogo and it was travelling a great deal faster that we were. I would judge around 15 to 17 miles an hour.

The head was about nine inches above the water. The head is definitely snake-like with a blunt nose ... Our excitement was short-lived. We watched for about three minutes, as

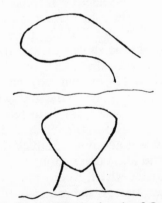

Fig. 26. Dick Miller's sketch of Ogopogo.

Ogie did not appear to like the boat coming on him broadside, very gracefully reduced the five humps which were so plainly visible, lowered his head and gradually submerged. At no time was the tail visible. The family's version of the colour is very dark greenish . . . This sea-serpent glides gracefully in a smooth motion (without snake-like undulations sideways). This would lead one to believe that in between the humps it possibly has some type of fin which it works together or possibly individually to control direction.

Mr Miller's suggestion of fins was conjectural, but such an animal must have some such method of propelling itself. As at Loch Ness, some witness have claimed to have seen fins or paddles. On July 22, 1949, the owner of a caravan site at Sunny Beach, a Mr Faulkner, with his small son, found what he claimed were ogopogo's tracks on the shore there. They were six inches across. Were these genuine, or another hoax like the "Monster's Tracks" found at Loch Ness?

Here are three of the more recent reports. On July 17, 1963, a 72-year-old fisherman named Sy Jenkins was fishing at Naramanta Bay, when he noticed a disturbance in a weed-choked corner. Then a 20-foot black object, showing three humps, travelled past his boat out into the lake. The next summer, off Kelowna, a Mr Leslie Kerry and his wife saw a large object moving 300 yards off-shore. They distinctly saw a head and part of the shoulders. "It looked very much like a seal's head, although I thought I could make out two horns. It was travelling very fast and making quite a commotion". It is good to have the horns shown on the Indian drawing and those rumoured by Hassal's miner friends confirmed. On September 3, 1964, a 15-year-old boy named Kenny Unser was playing with his dog near the old wharf in Kelowna, throwing sticks into the water for it to fetch. He saw a wave first. Then about 75 yards out, three feet of dark green tail rose out of the water. "It was about a foot thick, with big scales, and rounded off at the end like a dog's chopped-off tail". This hit the water hard splashing the wharf. Kenny ran for his life. I think we can ignore the scales, though the rounded off end is a nice description of the animal's rear, which, as we know, is not a tail.

This last report reminds us of the Indian legends of Naitaka's ferocity. Despite the apparent shyness of these creatures, to judge by them submerging at sounds or the approach of a boat, like most animals they can be dangerous when annoyed.

Four years earlier this report of ogopogo was published. The monster had been seen by Hans Gerade, the German vice-consul in Vancouver and by Philip Daum from Bacon Beach. Herr Gerade saw "a spoil of waves with white foam in the middle of the lake very strange to see. It looked like the wash of a boat moving swiftly from north to south, but there was no boat". Mr Daum said he saw "a creature about 25 feet long, with humps", which rose up and down in a mass of white foam. "I never did believe in ogopogo," he said later, "but after this I certainly do".

Even those of us who have not been lucky enough to see ogopogo can be persuaded of its existence by the evidence of these witnesses. Lake Okanagan, however, is the Canadian Loch Ness: it has got all the attention, and reports from other places have usually been ignored until recently; even though some are quite as interesting.

The Canadian Indians have legends of other lake monsters besides Naitaka. Still in British Columbia, in Lake Sushwap, there is a monster which the Indians call the Ta-Zam-A; and in nearby Lake Cowichan another called the Tsinquaw; and yet another in Lake Pohengamok. In the far north the Alaskan Eskimos have also legends. The oilman Sam Slick investigated with the help of Commander Stanley Lee, the reports by U.S. Navy airmen of animals seen in Lake Iliamna in Alaska. In 1966 a New York photographer, Leonard Rue, tried again to find if there was anything to the legends. The Crees claim that a fish-like serpent exists in Lake Meminisha on the Albany River in Ontario; and in 1947 a journalist was told of some recent encounters.

Early settlers, as we have seen, picked up these Indian legends. Sailors on the Great Lakes told stories of the "sea-serpents" they had seen. And though a couple of reports made their way into scientific literature, for the most part these were dismissed as mere legends. There were hoaxes as well, such as a series of reports from Silver Lake in New York State, intended to boost the summer trade.

Yet sometimes quite circumstantial reports were published in the newspapers, such as this from the Toronto *Globe* of July 8, 1880. The year before, a French Canadian fisherman out at night on Lake Duchene (actually an enlargement of the

Ottowa River) was startled by a dark object rushing past him. Then, on July 6, 1880, two men on the north shore of the lake near a phosphate mine saw the creature again.

> Mr Williams, the foreman of the mine, and a French Canadian named Blanchette, noticed the water of the lake was agitated about one-eighth of a mile out, between Little Island Lighthouse and the shore. After watching a moment, the Canadian cried out, 'Le serpent!' Mr Williams says that the creature in the water was a serpent of some kind, and a very large one at that. It wriggled along in the water quite fast. They could see about four feet of its back from the head, but it appeared to be more than three times that length from the motion of the water, while in thickness its body seemed to be about the size of a small telegraph pole. It was dark green in colour.

The two men, who had clearly seen the long neck of the animal rather than its body, rushed back to the mine for guns, but when they returned there were only ripples on the surface. The monster had been seen at the same place once before by a farmer, Mr Bradley, and his sons.

Coming on nearly a century, reports of a monster in Mocking Lake, also in Quebec, have been seriously investigated by a scientist. There had been occasional sightings over many years. In 1958 the Director of the Quebec Department of Game and Fisheries, Dr Vadim Vladikov went out to the lake to make a personal investigation.

> I have questioned a great many people in Saint Eleuthre (the local village), and they all tell me the same thing – an animal between 12 and 18 feet long, brown or black in colour, with a round back two or three feet wide, and a sawtooth fin down the centre. Any time anyone approaches close, the animal slithers away and sinks below the lake's surface.

A few descriptions were forthcoming from the local people. Donat Lavaseur said he saw a grey-coloured animal, at least 35 feet long, with a head like a hornless deer. Mrs Philip Gage and her husband were fishing when the animal surfaced near them; nine feet of the back were visible, and the head was as big as a rugby ball. Philip Forrest claimed that several years before he and his father-in-law had tried to shoot one of the animals with a .303 but the bullets had been ineffective. Doubtless they passed harmlessly through the thick layer of body fat on the animal.

During the 19th century there were persistent reports of a "sea-serpent" in Lake Simcoe in Ontario, as well as earlier Indian legends of a monster. In 1952 the report of an Indian trapper gave some credence to these stories. And according to the *Oakville Journal Record* on July 27, 1963:

A Presbyterian minister, a funeral director (anglice, an undertaker) and their families are the latest to claim to have seen *Igopogo*, the lake Simcoe sea-serpent. The Rev L. B. Williams of Mount Albert, and Neil Lathangue of Bradford, their wives and children were boating in the lake on Monday when something came towards them; Mr Lathangue said it was charcoal coloured, 30–70 feet long and had dorsal fins.

The paper quoted another witness as saying it was "a dog-faced animal with a neck the diameter of a stove-pipe".

But these reports are small beer compared with the reports that have come recently from the group of connected lakes around Winnipeg: Lake Winnipegosis – Manitoba – Dauphin lakes; from Lake Manitoba in particular, a great sheet of water covering 124 square miles. The landscape, in its tree-lined loneliness, is reminiscent of Scandinavia; the scene suits a monster. In the 19th century, Icelandic settlers were attracted to the lake. The monster was soon part of their folklore: had they brought the Skrimsl with them from the old country?

The animal was first credibly reported in 1908, but the first account I have is from a trapper Valentine McKay of the Hudson Bay Company in 1909. He saw a huge creature swimming at a speed of about two miles an hour. It had a dark upper surface which glistened, he said, and part of the body projected about four feet into the air.

After this there were only rumours – such as the ice heaving up mysteriously in midwinter – till 1935 when C. F. Ross, a timber inspector, and Tom Spence saw a strange animal at the

north end of Lake Winnipegosis. It had "a single horn protruding from the back of its head like a periscope". The head
itself was small and flat, the body resembling a dinosaur with
a dull grey hide "like an elephant". Had they been reading in
their papers about the Loch Ness monster? Certainly there is
an echo here of the plesiosaur of the Scottish loch in their
mention of a "dinosaur" despite the obvious fact that what
they saw must have been a mammal.

Near St Rose du Lac on Lake Manitoba in 1948, C. P.
Alric heard an unearthly cry. Then, 400 yards away in the
marshes, a "brownish-black thing about 6 feet long" reared up
for a moment. This cry will be heard again in another part of
the world. This is one of the very few times anyone has heard
it, and again it suggests strongly we are chasing a mammal of
some sort.

During August 1955 near Graves Point (where McKay the
trapper saw his animal in 1909) Joseph Parker, Albert Gott and
two of Gott's sons saw an object rise "about four feet out of
the water" which was about 2½ feet thick. They rowed within
400 yards of it before it disappeared. The same year, only a
month later, Charles Burrell and three Americans, saw three
or four feet of an animal's back break the surface near Overflowing River on Lake Winnipegosis.

In 1957, on Lake Manitoba, Louis Betcher and Eddie
Nipanik, who were working on the shore, saw a serpent-like
animal. This and other reports that same year – one witness
spoke of hearing "a bellow like a goods train whistle" – caused
such concern that the government sent a team to search the
lake. The State Minister of Industry and Commerce, Mr Jobin,
was quoted as saying that "the safety and prosperity of many
Manitobans are tied up with this expedition, and we hope it
will prosper". The economic threat foreseen by the minister
failed to appear and the party had to return.

But the reports continued. In July 1960, Mr A. R. Adams of
St Rose saw "a creature resembling a large snake" with a
diamond-shaped head eight inches wide. Swimming at 15 miles
per hour, as he estimated, it threw up a wake eight feet behind
the head. Later, 14 miles away, Mr Christopher Stople, his
wife and her sister saw "a reptile-like beast" surface 30 feet
away from their boat. For fear of it the women waded ashore

through a marsh. At Manipogo Beach on July 22, twenty people, among them a government land inspector Mr Thomas Locke, saw a large "reptile". Three weeks later, on August 12, 17 people on the same beach saw three monsters, two large ones and a smaller.

After this spate of sightings, Professor Dr James A. Mac-Leod, chairman of the Zoology Department of the University of Manitoba, organised an expedition which he led to the northern end of Lake Manitoba in search of the animal. Like most of those who believe in the existence of nondescript animals, Dr MacLeod makes much of the recovery of the coelecanth off the South African coast in 1938. He suggests that other primitive animals, long thought to be extinct, might still exist in places like Lake Manitoba and Loch Ness.

The next year (1961), early in August, Dr MacLeod announced that he hoped to return to the search if he could obtain the equipment and skilled help he needed, especially skin-divers. The divers were to search the lake for the remains of the monster.

Sometime in the 1930's (my sources are vague) a Mr Oscar Fredrickson dredged up a strange bone of great size from the bed of Lake Winnipegosis. The original has been destroyed in a fire long since; but a wooden replica of it exists. The bone was apparently a spinal vertebra, about six inches long and three inches wide. Dr MacLeod commented cautiously that the replica was a good copy of a bone from an animal long extinct or thought to be. Or it might have been a model made by someone who had studied palaeontology. Or, I suggest, with access to a large museum. As evidence the replica is of no value, considering its obscure and dubious provenance.

A photograph of the replica was published on August 5, 1961, by the *Winnipeg Free Press*, and August 12 by *MacLean's Magazine* (the Canadian news-magazine) illustrating articles on Dr MacLeod's scientific search for the monster.

On Saturday, August 19 of that year, seven people were watching about 8.30 over Lake Manitoba from Twin Beaches. Mrs Blanche Konecki asked, "Isn't that a boat sinking?" "No", another of the party replied. "It's the monster!" Patrick Rakowski described the monster, which they watched for four or five minutes. "It was over 40 feet long, with one large hump –

232 of Lake Monsters_

about 35 feet long – and a short hump at the end. It was yellowy-brown, and looked slimey". They estimated it was swimming at five to seven miles per hour. They were encouraged to report what they had seen by the recent articles and by Dr MacLeod's serious interest in the problem.

Early in August 1962, fishermen on Lake Manitoba again reported sightings of Manipogo, as the newspapers were now calling the monster, in imitation of the Okanagan animal. Then, on August 12, two fishermen, Richard Vincent and John Konefell, with the aid of an American television commentator, managed to photograph the monster for the first time.

"We first spotted the object to the left of our boat about 300 yards away", said Mr Vincent. "After swinging into the direction it was heading we saw what we believed to be a large black snake or eel . . . which was swimming with a ripple action . . . it was about a foot in girth, and about 12 feet of the monster was above water. No head was visible".

They estimated that the hump visible in the photograph was about two feet long. As the gunwale of their boat appears in the photograph, their estimate that the object was 50 to 75 yards away seems accurate enough. Though their boat had a ten-horse power outboard engine, they had to give up trying to catch up with it and so the animal escaped.

Dr MacLeod was asked his opinion of the photograph. He thought it was genuine. "If that isn't the monster, I'd like to know what the deuce it is". Certainly it bears an uncanny resemblance to the animal seen on Lough Ree in 1960, and to some reports from Loch Ness, such as Mrs Christie's in 1962. It is quite unlike the sort of animal a faker would be likely to produce, as it is hardly monstrous at all. I take it that the rounded section is a hump, and that the white crescent is a wave. Altogether a very interesting conclusion to the search for North American monsters.

I suggested that the Icelandic settlers might have brought the monster with them in their legends, and that some early reports might have been influenced by those from Loch Ness. But something more than a legendary skrimsl haunts these lakes. Though the evidence is not extensive, it is consistent with what we already know, and the photograph confirms the existence of some curious animal in the lakes.

11

The Patagonian Plesiosaur: South America

"The plesiosaurus! A fresh-water plesiosaurus!"
cried Summerlee. "That I should have lived to see
such a sight! We are blessed, my dear Challenger,
above all zoologists since the world began".

Arthur Conan Doyle: *The Lost World*

THE LOCH NESS monster was not the first of its kind to be reported, as we have seen. Nor was it the first to get world-wide attention. Eleven years before, in 1922, newspapers around the world – including even the august *Times* – were carrying stories of the search for the Patagonian Plesiosaur. But because it was a plesiosaur, and because it was in Patagonia, no-one took it seriously.

Patagonia already had a reputation as the haunt of bizarre beasts. The most southerly region of South America, it is wild, desolate and mountainous. Very few people live there, and even today parts of it are not well known. Just the sort of place, like some others in South America, from which odd rumours come from time to time. But in the case of Patagonia, scientists are wary of believing them and all because of the Giant Sloth, the Megatherium.

The sloth is a well-known animal, which spends its life hanging upside down from tree limbs, leading an unexhausting life. The giant sloth, however, was a prehistoric animal which lived on the ground. It stood 15 feet high, and under its long hairy skin were embedded small plates of bone which armoured it. The first remains of it were discovered in 1789, and described by Baron George Cuvier, the famous French anatomist. "It would be hard to find the cause of its destruction alone", he wrote, "but if it lived, where could it have hidden from the searches of hunters and naturalists?"

Cuvier hardly wanted an answer to that rhetorical question. Clearly, such an animal no longer existed. Yet something very like it was known in the legends of the local Tehuelche Indians: an immense monster immune to arrows, which would fit in with the armoured megatherium or mylodon as it was now called. Even if he had heard of these legends, I doubt if Cuvier would have believed them. Science was not a matter of native legends, but of physical evidence.

Gradually it was realised that early man was a contemporary of this giant. Then, in 1898, a mylodon skin which had been discovered in a cave at a place called Last Hope Inlet, was brought over to London. The cave had also contained human remains, a hearth, hay and droppings. The skin itself was rolled up inside out. Dr Moreno, the South American who brought it to London, was of the opinion that it was several hundred years old and exceptionally well preserved by the dry air of the cave. But the scientists who saw it at the London Zoological Society were not so sure. Sir Arthur Smith-Woodward thought it must be relatively new because the skin was still supple. The question now arose, if the skin were that fresh, could the giant sloth still exist somewhere in the forests of Patagonia.

There was some evidence that it did. Several years earlier, Ramon Lista, an eminent politician and exployer, had reported an encounter with an animal very like the mylodon. He had shot at it, but it had escaped his bullets unharmed. An account of such a hairy animal, called the *succareth*, was found in an early description of South America written by André Thevet. This, judging by the legends he repeats about it and the use the Indians made of its skin for cloaks, could well have been a surviving mylodon. Encouraged by these hints, several expeditions, including one sponsored by the *Daily Express*, set out hopefully around the turn of the century to try and capture a living specimen. All failed. Gradually the thought that anyone even imagined a mylodon still existed became a joke among scientists. It became a sort of zoological credo that no large animals remained to be discovered in South America.

Thus scientists were prepared to reject any stories of strange creatures seen in that continent. Their assumption was that the place was by now too well-known for any large animal to have escaped attention. Yet, though the mountain forests of Patagonia, the jungles of the Matto Grosso and the Amazon basin are mapped in some sort of way, they are still largely unexplored. The modern technique of making maps from aerial photographs gives the impression that large areas are well-known, when in fact no-one may ever have gone through them on the ground. On a continent where whole towns are hard to find, and ancient cities are completely lost, anything may be hiding unknown in the surrounding jungle. Are we foolish to dismiss all the rumours as nonsense?

Some people believed them completely, as did the extraordinary British explorer Colonel Percy Fawcett. His dream of a mysterious white race and their splendid city lost somewhere in the Brazilian jungle led eventually to his unexplained death. But he was an accurate and truthful observer, and not given to exaggerating his own experiences. In his memoirs, edited after his death by his son, he writes of rumours about monsters.

In the Madidi, in Bolivia, enormous tracks have been found, and the Indians there talk of a huge creature described at times half-submerged in the swamps . . . Certainly tracks have been found belonging to no known animal – huge tracks far greater than could have been made by any species we know.

Rumours are never very definite. Fawcett says elsewhere in his book that "in the forests of the Madidi some mysterious and enormous beast has been frequently disturbed in the swamps – possibly a primeval monster like those reported in other parts of the continent".

Fawcett was the inspirer of one of the great romances about South America. On the banks of the River Verde, on the border between Brazil and Bolivia, tower the immense Ricardo Franco Hills, which Fawcett travelled round in 1909.

Time and the foot of man [he says] had not touched those summits. They stood like a lost world, forested to their tops, and imagination could picture the last vestiges there of an age long vanished. Isolated from the battle with unchanging conditions, monsters from the dawn of man's existence might still roam those heights unchallenged, imprisoned by unscalable cliffs.

On his return to London, Fawcett was introduced to the writer Arthur Conan Doyle. The explorer talked excitedly of the Ricardo Franco Hills and their suggestive isolation, and he showed Doyle the photographs he had taken of them. Doyle, who was already turning over the idea of a new novel in his mind, asked Fawcett for more information, which was willingly supplied. The result of this meeting was, in due time, *The Lost World* which was serialised in *The Strand* in 1912.

This conversation with Colonel Fawcett was the catalyst for several ideas floating around in Doyle's imagination. While on a cruise he had actually seen a sea-serpent off the Greek island of Aegina, "a curious creature around four feet long with a long neck and large flippers". It was he thought a young plesiosaurus. An Australian friend sent him a description of another "baby plesiosaur" netted on Madgee Beach, which was exactly like what he and his wife had seen.

In 1909 Doyle had gone to live in a new house at Crowborough. Near his home was an open quarry where he discovered some fossil tracks. He got very excited about this find and wrote to the British Museum about them. An expert geologist was sent down, and he and Doyle examined them together. Doyle's interest in geology continued after this and he accumulated a large collection of fossils. It was around these, the baby plesiosaur, Fawcett's mountains, and the then current controversy about the Ape-Man, the so-called Missing Link, that the first of his scientific romances wove itself.

The Lost World, drawn from the Ricardo Franco Hills, is inhabited by ape-men who pose a grim threat to the explorers. There are also all kinds of other creatures, including a dinosaur. Also, you will recall, Malone the Irish reporter, says of Lake Gladys on Maple White Land:

> Once upon a yellow sandbank I saw a creature like a huge swan, with clumsy body and a high flexible neck, shuffling about upon the margin. Presently it plunged in, and for some time I could see the arched neck and darting head undulating on the water. Then it dived and I saw it no more.

This animal was, of course, a plesiosaur. The words "huge swan" suggest that Doyle imagined the creature as being white for some reason. Perhaps he recalled the dead sea-serpent in Kipling's short story *A Matter of Fact*, which was also white. Curiously, only one witness has ever described the Loch Ness monster as white. Wild life imitating art? Maybe, for *The Lost World* was a great success, and inevitably coloured popular ideas. Thus the stage was set for the appearance of the Patagonian Plesiosaur.

Early in 1922, the Director of the Buenos Aires Zoo, Dr Clementi Onelli, received a letter from an American prospector named Sheffield, who at that time was looking for gold in the Andean foothills of the Chebut Territory down in Patagonia. Near a mountain lake in the Esquel region, he had come across huge tracks, smashed through the scrub. Bushes and undergrowth were crushed by deep marks which could only have been made by a very heavy animal. Sheffield followed them until they disappeared by the lake shore.

But that was not all. "I saw in the middle of the lake an animal with a huge neck like a swan, and the movements made me suppose the beast to have a body like that of a crocodile".

In announcing this splendid news to the local papers, Dr Onelli said that Martin Sheffield was an old friend whom he trusted. "He is not scientific, but I have not the least doubt that he has seen a large and strange animal with a swan-like neck swimming in the lake as he asserts". Sheffield's description was, for a layman, a good outline of the plesiosaur, which though unknown today was familiar to palaeontologists from fossil remains.

Nor was his the only report. In 1897 Onelli himself had been travelling in Patagonia. From a Chilean farmer living on the shores of White Lake, he learnt that at night strange noises could be heard, as though a heavy cart were being dragged over the pebble beach. On other nights, when the moon was shining, a huge animal could be seen swimming in the lake, its long reptile-like neck rising high over the water. At the slightest sound it would dive down and disappear into the depths.

Dr Onelli had heard of another monster in 1907. A Norwegian engineer named Vaag (who had been a member of the Boundary Demarcation Commission which had settled the border between Chile and Argentina in 1902) was exploring a stream he had called the River Tamango, when he found the remains of a huge animal. And also the tracks of another, which Onelli now thought might have been a plesiosaur.

After his initial announcement, Onelli received yet another report that a similar beast had been seen by an Englishman in 1913 in a lake in the territory of Santa Cruz further south.

In view of all these stories, Dr Onelli believed Sheffield's report. He had the patriotic support of a few colleagues in Argentina. The public was thrilled at the prospect of discovering some prehistoric creature like those in Conan Doyle's novel: a popular café in Buenos Aires was even renamed *El Plesiosaurio*.

Scientists everywhere else, commented the *Scientific American*, had only "scornful scepticism" for the whole notion of "an antediluvian monster" alive and hiding in Argentina. They remembered the megatherium affair only too well and were going to have no truck with any of this "lost world" nonsense. Dr F. A. Lucas, Director of the New York Museum of Natural History, thought the whole affair was a ridiculous rumour. "The nearer one goes to the source of such reports the less people seem to know about them. Nobody seems to know how these wild rumours start".

Onelli was determined to find out. On March 16 The *New York Times* reported that he considered the animal at the source of the rumours was a glyptodon, a sort of giant version of the armadillo. However, the newspapers at this time were bandying monsters about with a fine disregard for their identity ("Andean 'Plesiosaur' May Be An Armadillo A Modern Megatherium, Onelli Thinks" was one typical headline), so just what Dr Onelli actually thought is not very clear, as no doubt it was not to the witless reporters.

The failure of the earlier expeditions to discover the megatherium did not discourage Onelli. He proposed to set up his own expedition to search for Sheffield's monster. Having refused complete financing from a film company, he hoped to raise the money for the expedition by public subscription. Already he had had letters from 100 volunteers. He needed 2,000 pesos, and some 3,000 were soon sent in.

The expedition left Buenos Aires on March 23, 1922. It was

led by José Cihagi, the Superintendant of the Zoo, and Emillio Frey, an Argentine engineer who had been a member of the Chile-Argentine Boundary Commission 20 tears before. Frey had explored the territory of Chebut at that time.

The expedition was not, obviously, looking for one immortal plesiosaur, but for a descendant of that species about 4 metres long, of which there was likely to be a small colony in the lake. They had among their equipment elephant rifles, lassoos and dynamite to mine the lake. The party sailed to Mauquen, travelled by lorry to Barliloche, and went on from there by horse into the Chebut. If after six weeks they had had no success, they planned to go on to other, remoter, parts of the territory.

The expedition had angered some Argentinians. The President of the Society for the Protection of Animals, Dr Albarrin, demanded that under State Law Number 2786, which governed the hunting of rare animals, the Minister of the Interior should refuse permits to the expedition. If the plesiosaur really did exist, he thought it should have protection under the law, which forbade the killing of rare animals. How much more creditable to their country if the plesiosaur were left alone to reproduce itself. This earnest effort provided yet more amusement for foreign scientists.

When the expedition was already far up country, some confusion arose about their permits. The Governor of Chebut said he had not issued any edict forbidding the hunting of the animal. But Cariga in the interior was under the impression he had. The expedition halted while the question was settled. So while the permits were straightened out, according to an exclusive dispatch in the *Chicago Tribune* on April 14, "the expedition of scientists and near scientists is enjoying a holiday, encamped in the beautiful lake region known as the Argentine Switzerland at the expense of the schoolteachers, lettercarriers and other workers who donated funds which made the expedition possible".

After that tart radical note nothing was heard of the expedition for ten days. Then, on April 26, it was announced that the project had failed and the party was returning.

They had reached the lake† where Sheffield had seen the

† This was not Lago Epuyen, as was said in some papers at the time. The real lake seems to have had no name.

animal, which was 50 miles from the nearest settlement on October 18. The Welsh colonists there had lent them a boat which they had powered with an outboard engine. The lake was carefully searched and watched. Finally Frey exploded 11 cartridges of dynamite in the lake, hoping to force the supposed prehistoric animal to the surface. Nothing appeared.

Back in Buenos Aires Dr Onelli confirmed that the expedition was returning but the reason was not failure but the approaching winter. He still had hopes of finding a plesiosaur in some Andean Lake, so another expedition would be sent out the next summer. And that seemed to be that. The Patagonian Plesiosaur, concluded The *Scientific American,* "if it ever existed, appears to have fled to parts unknown".

The search for the Patagonian Plesiosaur was mounted in great confusion. I think we can now try and straighten out what was seen, where and by whom.

Sheffield reported his sighting from a mountain lake near Esquel, and this was where the 1922 expedition went. But this was not the only lake involved.

Onelli himself announced that he had received a report of a similar animal from further south in Santa Cruz by an Englishman in 1913. He may or may not have been referring to the following report.

In April, George Garrett, then living in Toronto, recounted an experience he and his son had on Lake Najuel Huapi in 1910. He told a reporter from *The Globe*:

So far as I know, my son and I are the only white men who have ever caught sight of one of these antediluvian monsters. It was about the year 1910. Having pioneered a penninsula on that most beautiful lake, Najuel Huapi, I was appointed manager of a newly-formed company.

At that time I speak of the government engineer was surveying the property, and my son and I were navigating him and his staff of assistants around the wild, rugged coasts of the penninsula. We had put the engineer, his men and instruments ashore, and were sailing about for pleasure, with about half a gale of wind. We were beating windward up an inlet called 'Pass Coytrué', which bounded the penninsula. This inlet was about five miles in length, a mile or so in width, and of an unfathomable depth. Just as we were near the rocky shore of the penninsula, before tacking, I happened to look astern towards the centre of the inlet, and, to my great surprise, I saw about a quarter of a mile to leeward, an object which appeared to be 15 or 20 feet in diameter, and perhaps six feet above the water.

Having time only for a glimpse, as the boat was now racing within a few yards of the rocks, I told my son to keep his eyes on the curiosity while I tacked our somewhat cumbersome craft. This was accomplished with all speed, and in the twinkling of an eye we were tearing towards the spot – when the thing disappeared. Only a very few minutes could have elapsed ere we were tearing towards the spot where the object had been, but there was not the slightest trace of it in the clear waters of the lake. On mentioning my experience to my neighbours they said the Indians often spoke of immense water animals they had seen from time to time.

Mr Garret has made the most of a brief encounter, but it is worth having his account down on the record.

When the Onelli expedition reached Bariloche on the shores of Nahuel Huapi, they heard rumours of yet another monster from San Martin de los Andes on the shores of Lago Lacar, 150 miles to the north.† They turned south to Epuyen, however, so it was not for many years that this other monster was heard of again.

Lago Lacar lies in the north-eastern section of the southern Andes, inside what is now the National Park of Lanin. At the eastern end of the lake, standing 800 feet above the water and looking right out over the lake, is the house of Mr Barney Dickinson. He has lived there since the late 1940's. Prompted by a series of articles on the Loch Ness monster, Mr Dickinson wrote in 1959 to the *Illustrated London News* to describe his own experiences.

In the evenings he often sat and watched the lake, through which very few boats pass. Over the years he noticed more

---

† This place was confused by hasty journalists with Lago San Martin, far to the south. A Catralan writer Fabia Vidal claimed there were monsters in both San Martin and Lago Viedma close by, but this seems to be a mistake.

times than he can remember "strange water formations" which he cannot readily explain. They seem too large for any known animal such as an otter, even though the South American otter grows to great size. Could it be that they are made by a monster?

Local legend explains them so. The Auracanians, the local Indians, have always believed in the existence of a monster in the lake. They call it by the Spanish name *Cuero*, meaning cowhide, because of the animal's resemblance to a cowhide; that is, round, dark and rough in appearance. It is also called El Bien Peinado, the smooth-headed one, from the similarity of the back to a bald pate. There are the usual stories of strange tracks found on the shore, and the remains of the monster's meals; skin, fur and feathers. Mr Dickinson says the Gauchos have reported seeing the creature, but always towards evening, just floating on the water surface, a large single hump with the texture of a cowhide. This is the shape so familiar already from Loch Ness reports, the monster as an up-turned boat.

In 1922 a Catalan journalist produced rumours of other monsters in Lago San Martin (though personally I think he has got confused between San Martin delos Andes and the southern lake) and in Lake Viedma. But I have not found any actual reports from these places.

Finally what is perhaps strictly a sea-serpent report. Lieutenant Commander Bevilaqua, the commander of the Argentine ship *Keweah*, then visiting Philadelphia, told the *New York Times* (March 17, 1922) that he too had seen "a strange and monstrous animal" on the Patagonian coast. This was during 1906, while his ship was in the straits of Magellan, about 500 yards off-shore, while he was on afternoon watch.

The visibility was high and I do not believe I could have been mistaken. I was scanning the skyline toward the shore and I heard a sound and saw a huge ice-covered boulder splash into the sea from the high rocky shore. A moment later a large animal appeared at the point from which the boulder had dropped and looked out towards me. The head was like that of a hound and the neck was a full 30 feet long. It was not a turtle, because turtles do not have necks of that length. I am equally sure that it was not a snake as snakes don't live in the ice and snow.

Nor, indeed, would a plesiosaur. Whatever about the exaggerated length of the neck, we can be sure that the officer saw a mammal.

In April 1905, the captain of the *Rhone*, while he was preparing to round the Horn, saw off the coast of Chile "the head of an animal which I cannot compare to anything but those which used to decorate the prow of Viking ships and the big junks of the Niger". The neck reached only 5 feet out of the water, and it followed "the undulating movements of the body, which seemed to me to be long". This is the only other report known of a sea-serpent off the south cape of America. Is this, I wonder, the same animal that Commander Bevilaqua was to see a year later?

These sea-serpents are leading us away from our real quarry, the lake monsters of Patagonia. Charles Fort, the American eccentric who collected reports of such curiosities, wrote to Professor Onelli after reading about the Patagonian Plesiosaur in the *Scientific American*. Onelli replied (August 15, 1924) saying that he had heard again of the monster but giving no details. Bernard Heuvelmans wrote to Onelli some years ago to find out exactly what was known about the animal, but was told that Onelli had been dead for many years. In 1956 another expedition, organised by Dr Marinesco of the Universidad de Corboba, investigated the Chebut monsters; but with what result I do not know.

Patagonia, with its forested uplands, recalls the climatic environment of Scotland. We have become used to the fact that monsters are most often reported from alpine mountain lakes. In 1922, if any other scientist had been bold enough, the mystery of the Patagonian plesiosaur might well have been solved by a thorough investigation. But disillusioned by the more promising affair of the living mylodon, and wary of becoming involved in anything that smacked of the adventures in Conan Doyle's lost world, no-one was prepared to do so. So that aside from Onelli's original expedition, there has been only one more attempt.

As I said at the beginning, South America is not as well

known as it might seem. There are still blanks on the map, white spaces where unknown animals might well lurk. As Professor Challenger remarked to Malone and the others before the start of their expedition into the lost world:

"Now down here in the Matto Grosso" – he swept his cigar over a part of the map – "or up here in this corner where three countries meet, nothing would surprise . . .".

12

The Dragon of the Ishtar Gate: Western Asia

And in the same place was a dragon which they
of Babylon worshipped'
The Book of Bel and the Dragon

IN 1902 ONE of the most remarkable Mesopotamian monu-
ments, the Great east gate of Babylon, was uncovered after
four years of work by the German archaeologist Robert
Koldewey. In itself this discovery was important enough, but
it also revealed a mystery which has yet to be solved: what is
the Dragon of the Ishtar Gate?

Even ruined, the Ishtar Gate is impressive. Approached by a
walled-in causeway, which passes under a tall arch flanked by
watchtowers, the gate is built of glazed bricks, coloured yellow,
blue and black. The causeway walls are decorated in alternating
rows of bas-reliefs of stalking lions; while the towers are covered
in alternating rows of other animals. And this is where the
mystery begins. The gate was reconstructed by Nebuchadnezzar
about 600 B.C. A cuneiform inscription proudly announces the
king's intentions:

Fierce *rimi* and grim *sirrushi* I put onto the gateways and
thus supplied the gates with such overflowing rich splendour
that all humanity may view it with wonder.

The fierce rimi were easily identified by Koldewey. Though th
pictures of them are stylised and a little inaccurate, there is
doubt that they are Aurochs, the fierce wild cattle of Eura
the last of which died in Lithuania in 1627. The reliefs sho
rim in profile, as if it had only one horn, and this may

given rise to the legend of the unicorn. (The unicorn of the Bible, which could not be tamed to pull a plough, is a mistranslation of the Hebrew word from rim; the Septuagint had never seen an auroch, and confused that animal with an Arabian gazelle.) The rim was as real an animal as the ferocious lions on the causeway walls. Both had been chosen for their terrible reputations, to stand guard over the city gate, and overawe the visiting peasants.

The sirrush is more of a problem. On the Ishtar Gate it is represented as a monstrous quadruped. The rear legs have large claws, while the front have lion's paws. The creature has a long tail and a neck with a small snakeish head crowned by a horn, and a forked tongue darts from the closed mouth. As it is covered in scales, we can suppose it is intended to be some sort of reptile. Yet, Koldwey wrote, "it is remarkable that in spite of the scales, the animal possesses hair. Three corkscrew ringlets fall over the head near the ears; and on the neck, where a lizard's comb would be, is a long row of curls".

What can this creature be? Robert Graves suggests that, like the Chimera, it is intended to be symbolic: a composite calendar beast of lion, eagle and serpent, presenting the three traditional seasons of the year.

Or is it, like the lions and bulls, intended to be a real animal? In the first report of his excavations at Babylon, Koldeway hinted that this might be so. "If only the forelegs were not so emphatically and characteristically feline, such a creature might actually have existed".

If Henry Layard had discovered the Ishtar Gate a century before, the *Sirrush* would have been considered just another of those fantastic monsters so common in Mesopotamian art. The creature's name, after all, meant "Splendour Serpent", and its odd mixture of animal features would have been thought impossible. But in that hundred years the science of palaeontology had come into existence. Cuvier and others had reconstructed from fossil remains monsters quite as improbable as anything an artist could imagine. "No twentieth-century nightmare", remarks Jacquette Hawkes, "no poetic imagination however macabre, could produce anything so magnificently fantastic as the reptiles of the Jurassic and Cretaceous worlds".

Fossil dinosaurs had been discovered which had long necks and tails, small heads with horns, similar features to the sirrush.

Some years later, in *Das Ishchtar Tor in Babylon*, the sumptuous reports of his excavations, Koldeway threw all his previous scholarly caution to the wind:

> If such a creature like the *sirrush* existed in nature it would belong to the order of Dinosauria and the sub-order ornithopods. The iguanadon of the cretaceous layers of Belgium is the closest relative of the Dragon of Babylon.

But the sirrush cannot be a reconstruction such as a modern scientist would make of an iguanadon: the Babylonians were not palaeontologists. The sirrush is either a fantastic creature which by sheer chance actually approaches the description of a dinosaur. Or it is a real animal, but like the aurochs, known only by rumours from some remote district. An Assyrian obelisk describes Tiglath-Pilser I (1175–1093 B.C.) as a "destroyer of the wild rimi at the foot of the Lebanon". Was the sirrush also to be found in some equally remote part of the Babylonian empire?

The American writer, Willy Ley, thinks not. He believes the sirrush is based on rumours of aquatic monsters in Central Africa, partly because a traveller there picked up glazed bricks similar to those used to build the Ishtar Gate. Some of these bricks were brought back to Europe by the hunter Hans Schomburgh, who had found them while he was capturing animals for Carl Hagenback, the director of the Hamburg Zoo. This was several years before Robert Koldwey published the account of his discovery at Babylon.

Schomburgh also brought back rumours of some mysterious animal which was known throughout Central Africa. Exploring around Lake Bangweolo, he was surprised to find there were no hippos in the lake. The Africans told him that there was an animal living in the lake, which though smaller than the hippos, hunted them down. The animal never came ashore and its tracks were never found. Schomburgh thought this story was a fairy tale, and did not bother to investigate further. When he told Hagenback about it, he learnt that his employer had also received reports from other sources which confirmed the story in detail. Hagenback sent an expedition out to Lake Bangweolo, but the party failed even to find the lake.

The Africans around Lake Banguweolo called the mystery creature the Chipekwe. Stories from other parts of Africa show it is not the only one of its kind, sometimes known as the Congo Dragon. Bernard Heuvelmans discusses these stories at great length in *On the Track of Unknown Animals*. He quotes the substantial evidence of more than 30 people, from places around the basins of the Congo, the Nile and the Zambezi. The animals are all amphibious and roughly the same size as a hippo. Yet in many points of detail and habit they are very different. Heuvelmans concludes that "the various descriptions of African 'dragons' obviously refer to at least three different types of animals – so it is not surprising that a mixture of these creatures has produced an absurd and fantastic beast, which is difficult to believe in, let alone identify".

The three types he distinguishes as a short-nosed crocodile, a giant catfish and a "water-elephant" (perhaps the supposedly extinct Dinotherium). Nevertheless, there is a residual amount of evidence for the existence of a large reptile with a small tri-angular head, a short stubby-horn, and a long thin flexible neck, which including its powerful tail would measure about 30 feet.

The Dragon of the Ishtar Gate, near enough. Or maybe a giant iguanadon. For, of course, everyone was eager to make it a dinosaur. Writing in an East African scientific journal, about various unknown animals, the anthropologist C. W. Hobley said that "a survival of some extinct race of saurians is a thing to thrill the imagination of the scientific mind". And the not-so-scientific mind: after World War I, there were several expeditions by ex-army officers to hunt "the Brontosaurus in Katanga".

But little is clear about this creature from the reports, and their vagueness calls for caution. Heuvelmans gives only tentative support to the "dinosaur theory":

> All that we can really say is that there seems to be a large and unknown reptile in Central Africa. Its identity remains to be determined, and in view of its size it is probably, like the crocodiles, the Komodo dragon and the giant tortoise, a relic of the great reptile empire that flourished in the

Jurassic period. I have already mentioned the remarkable geological and climatic stability in Africa, which could hardly be better for preserving such an ancient type.

Loch Ness-type monsters are rare in Africa, though the *lau* of Lake Victoria, mentioned by Constance Whyte, which seems to have a long neck and humps, calls up the familiar form. The lau was known only from native reports at first, but was then seen by steamer officers and travellers. Scottish soldiers returning from African service after World War I, brought reports to the attention of the Reverend William Graham of Ardersier. "The lau is said to have a humped body up to 100 feet in length, coloured brownish above and light yellow below". writes Mrs Whyte. "The neck is long, snake-like and described as having tentacles".

There is some confusion here about the lau. Constance Whyte claims, on hearsay, that the lau belongs to Lake Victoria, and is the same type of animal as the Loch Ness monster. But H. C. Jackson, in a study of the Nuer people published in 1923, says the lau haunts the swamps around the source of the White Nile. Lake Victoria has another mystery animal. Sir Harry Johnson, the discoverer of the okapi, brought attention to it in his book on Uganda in 1902:

There are also persistent rumours among the natives that the waters of the Victoria Nyanza are inhabited by a monster (known to the Baganda as *lukwata*). This creature, from native accounts, might be a small cetacean or a large form of manatee, or, more probably, a gigantic fish.

Later Arnold Drummond Hay claimed to have seen a "sea-serpent" on Lake Nyasa, but it may well have been only a large python swimming with erected head. Heuvelmans considers both the lau and the lukwata to be the same species, probably a large catfish, which would explain those tentacles mentioned by Mrs Whyte: around their heads catfish have long barbels.

The confusion clears when we move on to South Africa, for here we are definitely dealing with a more familiar monster, which makes a change from dinosaurs.

But first, there are a series of reports from the Orange River. In 1922 Mr Fred C. Cornell claimed to have seen a monster back in 1910 near Great Falls on the Orange River, at the junction of the Oub and the Orange. With him were W. H. Brown and N. B. Way of Capetown and three Bantu.

At the cries of the natives I saw something black, huge and sinuous swimming rapidly against the current in the swirling rapids. The monster kept its enormous body under the water, but the neck was plainly visible. The monster may well have been a very gigantic python, but it was of incredible size. This reptile may have lived for hundreds of years. Pythons approaching it in size have been said to have lived that long.

The animal had a huge head and a neck 10 feet long like a bending tree. The Bantu claimed it attacked their cattle and dragged them under the water.

A similar animal had been seen on the same river near Upington in 1899, by a Mr G. A. Kinnear. And in 1929 a prospector named Hayes reported a sighting at the junction of the Orange and Gooinet Rivers. In 1950 a fourth sighting by a man named Atherstone on the Ingruenfisi River attracted a certain amount of attention in the South African press.

A few years later the continued appearances of a monster in the Vaaldam caught the interest of Professor J. B. L. Smith, the scientist who first described the coelacanth. The idea that other presumably extinct animals might still survive from past ages was one that he of all people had most right to hold. He told the press that personally he had no doubts that there was such an animal behind these reports of monsters. The Vaaldam monster was popular enough to have a song composed about it in Afrikaans!

Could any of these monsters have been the original of the Dragon on the Ishtar Gate?

The *sirrush* [writes Bernard Heuvelmans] could have lived in Central Africa, where it has been proved the Chaldeans went, and where they could have seen a giant lizard. When Hans Schomburgh came back from Africa with native tales of the Chipekwe, he also brought back several glazed bricks of the same type as those on the Ishtar Gate. Naturally he had no idea that the beasts and the bricks could have any connection. It is therefore possible that one of the amphibious species of the Congo 'Dragons' was known to the Chaldeans 5,000 years ago from travellers tales, and that this was the *sirrush* of the Ishtar Gate.

Well anything is possible, but this argument is, I feel, improbable. The bricks brought back by Schomburgh are strangely elusive. Either they were Babylonian or they were not. Bernard Heuvelmans tells me that "they certainly looked Chaldean". But that is hardly good enough to support his theory. Willy Ley, who had mentioned them in the first place, realised this, for the "glazed bricks" have been dropped from the most recent revision of the book in which he discusses the mystery. The east African coast was probably known vaguely to the Mesopotamians (and we must not forget that the Phoenicians had circumnavigated Africa before the time of Herodotus), but we have no idea of how extensive their explorations were. Africa seems too remote and unlikely a place to look for the Babylonian sirrush. But before tracking it to its more likely lair, there is other evidence to consider.

The sirrush plays a part in the great Babylonian creation myth, the Enuma Elish. In this religious hymn, sung at high festivals, the supreme god Marduk slays a monstrous emanation of the rebellious goddess Tiamat, or, it may be, the goddess herself. The Enuma Elish formed the dramatic part of the Babylonian new year ceremonies, during which the king took the part of the god in enacting the slaughter of the dragon and the binding of the goddess. (This is the ultimate origin of the icon of St George slaying the dragon; originally the princess had been tied up by the hero himself.)

We know from a curious passage in the apocrapha that the priests of Marduk kept a "dragon" in the god's temple at Babylon. This remarkable animal is referred to in *The Book of Bel and the Dragon*:

And in the same place was a dragon which they of Babylon worshipped.

And the king said unto Daniel, Wilt thou also say this is of
brass? lo, he liveth, he eateth and drinketh. Thou cans't not
say that he is no living god: therefore worship him.

Then Daniel said unto the king . . . Give me leave and I
shall slay this dragon without sword or staff. The king said
I give thee leave. Then Daniel took pitch, and fat, and hair,
and did seethe them together, and made lumps thereof; this
he put in the dragon's mouth, and so burst in sunder.

This animal was probably a large monitor lizard from India
or Egypt, used to overawe the people during the annual drama.
It was certainly no dinosaur, and does not seem to have been
the model for the dragons on the Ishtar Gate and elsewhere.

Babylonian mythical monsters, such as the winged bulls and
bird-headed men, had a comparatively short life in Mesopotamian art. The sirrush, the lions and the aurochs appear
continually over 2,000 years until the reign of Nebuchadnezzar,
who rebuilt the Ishtar Gate. The sirrush on the Ishtar Gate are
the most magnificent, but not the only examples of this beast
in art. Similar animals appear, usually as attributes of Marduk,
on land boundary posts, a couple of which can be seen in the
British Museum.

Marduk and the sirrush also appear on cylinder seals
illustrating scenes from the Enuma Elish, where Tiamat is
pursued by the God. One of these seals is quite extraordinary.

Accompanied by an attendant, Marduk is shown in pursuit
of the serpentine ally of Tiamat. The monster has a conven-
tionally scaled skin (to show it is a reptile), with a long neck
and a small horn on the crown of its head. Reading Professor
Hook's book *Middle Eastern Mythology* soon after I had
finished Constance Whyte's on the Loch Ness monster, the real
significance of the seal was clear to me. For the animal on the
4,000 year old seal is the same animal as that in Kenneth
Wilson's photograph of the Loch Ness monster.

The resemblance is remarkable: both have the same long,
gracefully curving neck, the same small head with the same
small "horn". The crudely cut seal, like the relief on the Ishtar
Gate, is only an artist's impression, suggesting that both were
done from traditional designs and not from life. The picture
of the aurochs was not drawn from life either, and for that

reason there are mistakes in the representation. Nevertheless the aurochs existed, though only in remote areas. So there seem to have been two kinds of "splendour serpents". One was a large reptile of some kind as seen on the Ishtar Gate; the other may have been an amphibious animal of some kind, as seen on the cylinder seal. I take it that the small paws on the seal animal are intended as flippers, and that the rest of the body was not quite clear to the artist. Where were these monsters found?

As we have seen, monsters have most often been reported from mountain lakes, such as Loch Ness or Okanagan, or lakes on high plateaus, such as Lake Labynkr. The lakes of the Anatolian highlands, though outside the usual climatic band, resemble these other environments. There may be some lakes, such as Lake Van, which have monsters, but I have found no recent references. The Armenians had the usual legends about dragons, usually imagined as great serpents and as sea-monsters. But these may only have been a personification of the whirlwind or sea-spout.

More interesting are the Nhangs. "These monster spirits, at least in Armenian mythology, stand close to the dragons", writes Mardiros Ananikian. The word is Persian for crocodile, although in one Persian tale "the Nhangs appear in the semi-mythical character of a sea-monster, which is extremely large". The Armenian translators of the Bible use the word for the crocodile and hippopotamus, so it is equivalent to leviathan. A medieval geography says that they can be seen in the River Aracani (the Murad Chay) and in the Euphrates, so they must be something other than crocodiles or hippos, for these are not found in those rivers. Though some writers claim the creature is a devil, the same writer says others believe it to be an animal. The Armenians then, seem to have some unfamiliar river animal behind their traditions of monsters.

Another obvious place to look for the Babylonian dragon would be the marshes at the mouth of the Tigris, yet another "lost world". One of the very few travellers who know the marshes well is Wilfred Thesiger, the English explorer. In *The Marsh Arabs*, his account of several journeys among the Mandan, he mentions in passing some of the venomous reptiles to be encountered there.

As if there were not enough real snakes, the Mandan firmly believe in two monsters, the Anfish and the Afa. The first was reported to have a hairy skin and the other to have legs. Both are said to inhabit the heart of the Marshes and to be very deadly.

Here surely is the origin of the Babylonian dragons. Perhaps this, indeed, was how they heard about them: a traveller's few words in his account of the impenetrable wilderness to the south of their fertile plain.

The Babylonians had the advantage of discovering more about them than we have even heard about the anfish, which I take to be the long-necked mammal we are so familiar with, and the afa whose legs relate it to the sirrush. These thick, reedy and unexplored, almost unmapped, marshes are an ideal retreat for threatened species. Gavin Maxwell, who accompanied Thesiger on one journey, brought back to England with him an otter which was later classified by the British Museum as a new species, *Lutrogale Maxwelli*, Maxwell's Otter.

If large unknown animals survive anywhere, the Tigris marshes are a likely place to find them. Other travellers in the Marshes may yet reveal to us the Dragon of the Ishtar Gate.

13

Dragons and Dinosaurs: Eastern Asia

"Just the place for a Snark", the Bellman cried.
Lewis Carroll: *The Hunting of the Snark*

THE DICTIONARY DEFINES a dragon as merely "a huge serpent or snake", and tells us that the word derives from the Greek for a snake. The original dragons, it seems, were snakes kept at shrines and heroes' tombs for oracular purposes – they represented the spirits of the Underworld. In the Middle Ages, due to Oriental influences, the dragon took on its now more familiar shape of a monstrous reptile, the one familiar from paintings of St George.

Charles Kingsley realised – as did Norman Douglas later – that the dragon was not a completely fabulous animal. He wondered if they might have been merely great snakes and nothing really extraordinary. But are all dragons just snakes, or could they be something more ancient? Even dinosaurs, some have suggested daringly. The last dragon in England, by the way, "a strange monstrous serpent" nine feet long, haunted St Leonard's Forest in Sussex, if we are to believe a contemporary broadsheet, until the year of Shakespeare's death.

The Oriental dragon is something quite different. Perhaps it were better not called a dragon at all. Landor writes in *Corea and Its People* that the dragon "In shape, as the natives picture it, is not unlike a huge lizard with long-nailed claws and a flat long head . . . possessed of horns and a long mane". The Oriental dragon is usually a benign creature. Traditionally it is described as having the head of a camel, the scales of a carp, the eyes of a rabbit, deer's horns, cows ears, the neck of a snake, the claws of a hawk with the footpads of a tiger: all of which, in its complexity, suggests that it evolved from cults of those animals. The dragon was the rain god to which the Chinese prayed for water in time of drought: swallows, to which it was thought to be particularly partial, were thrown into lakes and rivers as offerings.

But what was the Lung, as the Chinese called it? Chinese mythology associates the dragon with rain and water, so it has been suggested that the final form of the dragon is based on one well-known animal, the Chinese alligator of the Yellow River. But Chinese tradition distinguishes between the alligator and the lung. Now merely a heraldic beast, what was its obscure origin? A French naval officer in 1895 suggested that sea-serpents, two of which he had just seen in the Gulf of Tonkin, "known and feared by the Annamites, have furnished them with their conception of the dragon, which, changed and amplified by legend, became the heraldic beast of their national emblem".

But even now the dragon, long dead in Europe, is something more than a heraldic beast in the Orient. In some places, as the following story from Laos during 1966 showed, it is still a god. There the delicate balance of power between the Royalists, Neutralists and Communists was threatened by a dragon's anger.

The dragon lives in the Mekong River in front of the Lan Xang Hotel in Vietiane, the Laotian capital. During the summer of 1966 a peasant farmer dug up three eggs which, by tradition, the dragon's daughter was said to have laid. Though these had hard white shells, rather than the traditional soft mottled shells, there was no doubt that they were dragon's eggs, for the dragon himself appeared to the peasant in a dream and demanded their return. If he did not get them back he threatened to flood Vientiane to a depth of six feet. General Kong Le, the commander of the Neutralist army, was to lead the citizens of Vientiane in ceremonies of atonement. The terrified peasant took the eggs off to Kong Le, who warned the Premier Prince Souvana Phouma of the impending danger. The more sophisticated prince ignored the warning. But after the monsoon, the Mekong continued to rise above the high-water mark, flooding into parts of the city. The right-wing generals, on whose support the Prince depended, would not allow General Kong Le near the city, so the ceremonies demanded by the dragon were not performed. The flood duly receeded. Angered by the attitude of his enemies, Kong Le refused to give up the eggs, so that Vientiane remained threatened by the dragon's wrath. But despite the hold that the dragon's warning might have had over the superstitious peasants, Prince Souvana Phouma was returned at the next election. The balance of power was restored – for the moment.

I can't help wondering if there is not more to this story, that the dragon might not be more than a local demiurge. The Loatians would tend to see a dragon where we would see a monster or a dinosaur. What a pity no naturalist looked into the affair. Some of the plesiosaurs were oviparous. Were their eggs soft shelled – as crocodile eggs are – and mottled? The eggs the peasants found may have been, of course, those of some common animal. The Chinese used to collect fossilised ostrich eggs in the Mongolian desert, which they believed were dragon's eggs, and their shells do have a brown mottled colour.

There are lost worlds everywhere but, of these, central Malaya, is surely one of the remotest. At its heart the Tasek Bera, a swampy lake surrounded by thick jungle, is accessible only by boat down weed-choked rivers, or by a long helicopter flight.

Mervyn Sheppard, one-time advisor to the native ruler of Negri Sebilan State, and an expert on the area and its peoples, said that "the whole area is the same as it was thousands of years ago, you might almost say since time began". He had been asked by a journalist if rumours of a monster in the Tasek Bera could be true. "If anything of that nature could survive". he replied, "then the Tasek Bera would be the place to look for it".

The people of the Tasek Bera are the Semelai, a shy retiring forest tribe, who believe completely in the existence of the monsters, which they call nagas. The nagas are legendary creatures related to the Chinese dragon. Dragons and mountains are usually associated in Oriental myth – because rain clouds gather round them, I suppose. The Semelai believe the nagas were born on Gunong Chini, a nearby mountain, and then made their way into the lake. They hold the nagas in great awe and have a special dance to propitiate them. The Semelai are, however, reluctant to talk about these ceremonies to strangers.

But there is nothing legendary about the monsters. In the

early 1950's a senior officer in the Malayan police force reported
that he had seen a strange animal in the Tasek Bera. Late one
afternoon he had moored his boat beside a small headland
called Tanjong Keruing, near which was a stretch of water
clear of weeds, where he dived in to cool off. Glancing over his
shoulder, he saw rising over a clump of rassau weed 40 yards
away, the long neck of some huge creature. The head stood some
15 feet above the weeds. Behind it he could see the contours of
two silver-grey curves above the surface. Swimming back to
his boat, he paddled himself swiftly away, looking back only
once: the creature was still there, watching him.

The policeman's commander told Stewart Wavell, a producer
for Malayan Radio who was looking into the reports, that the
man was utterly reliable and had a fine record. "He doesn't
exaggerate and normally I should accept his word every time.
But as for this monster, I must say it seems a bit of a queer
story".

Stewart Wavell first heard of the monster from the Semelai
themselves while he was recording songs and stories at the
Tasek Bera in 1952. He went back in 1957, spending much of
his nine day holiday getting into the lake along the almost
impassable Sungei Bera River. He stayed at a village called
Ba'Apa. Around the fire at night he heard stories of the "giant
snakes". These were folktales, of course, like one about a
Semelai Jonah who was swallowed by a naga while asleep in
his boat. Waking up, he cut his way out, and picked off some
of the dead monster's golden scales. Later the Semelai said that
it was grey all over, admitting that the golden scales were only
legendary.

In fact, when not telling stories, the Semelai were quite
matter of fact about the creatures. The monsters, for there
were several, were quite often seen swimming around, feeding
on water-plants. They never attacked people, which they
thought was strange behaviour for a snake. Another strange
feature was that the monsters had two horns on the top of the
head, very small and soft horns. No-one had ever seen the entire
length of one because they never came completely out of the
water; perhaps, the Semelai suggested, the monsters were not
able to support the weight of their bodies on land. Wavell
asked if the monsters had legs, then. The Semelai thought they

had for the body swelled out near the water and into a wide underbelly. When he sketched a dinosaur for them, with its long neck, small head and large body, they were amazed that a stranger could draw so well a creature he had never seen.

Wavell asked about its call, which had previously been described to him as "half like the trumpet of an elephant but louder". The Semelai did imitations of it for him. Two of them said it was "like a barking deer, but short and strong; a great echoing boom".

The morning after his arrival, Wavell set out north along the lake shore to Tanjong Keruing. On the headland he and his two guides camped and made a fire for tea. While he was preparing his camera and wire recorder, a cry shivered the air. "A single staccato cry from the middle of the lake . . . It was a kind of snorting bellow, shrill, strident like a ship's horn, an elephant trumpet and a sea-lion's bark all in one". After a moment he flipped the *record* switch on his machine to capture the next cry. It never came.

Wavell left the Tasek Bera with the hope of returning, but other duties prevented him. He had however collected on his short visit enough information – including the vital details of those two small horns and the animal's strange cry – to warrant a far fuller investigation by scientists. In 1962 an RAF expedition of enthusiastic amateurs went into the Tasek Bera to investigate, but so far as I know, they learnt nothing new.

These animals in the Tasek Bera are clearly related to our old friends in the other areas of the world we have already looked at. But Malaya is not our only source of rumours, nor are they the only kind of mysterious animals. Travellers in other parts of Asia have heard of monsters, and some have seen them. A Victorian journalist, W. H. Marshall, described in 1860 how he had seen an enormous crocodile swimming in the Irrawaddy, over 45 feet long, with nearly half its body out of the water. This is nearly three times larger than the Gavial crocodile usually seen in that area. Philip Gosse thought this animal was, once again, a plesiosaurus; but Bernard Heuvelmans more plausibly suggests that it was an example of what he has called the Marine Saurians. He thinks they may be a form of Thalattosuchia, the sea-crocodiles with fish tails from the Cretaceous.

And it seems that in some remote parts of Asia other primitive crocodilians survive. In 1951, following a fantastic report in an Indian newspaper of a prehistoric monster rampaging through Assam, a *Daily Mail* expedition led by Charles Stoner went out to investigate the rumour at its source among the Api Thani tribesmen of the Dafla Hills. Needless to say, the original report had been completely inaccurate. There was indeed some non-descript animal, but it had been extinct for several generations. The Burru, as it was called, seems from the traditional descriptions obtained by Stoner to have been a type of alligator or crocodile. The tribesmen said it was about 14 feet long, with a short neck, a roundish body and a long tail. Dark in colour, with a white belly, it had three rows of small spines or lobes along the back and short legs with claws. A German anthropologist, who wrote the standard work on the Api Thani, recently revisited the tribes but heard nothing about any monsters.

Ralph Izzard, in his book about their adventures in Assam, recounts some of the rumours he and Stoner heard at Rillo, several hundred miles from Api Thani where the Burru were said to exist. There the people said the animals had been seen up to the year before, but aside from that added nothing to what had already been discovered. Two tea planters described an experience they had while duck hunting in a swamp near Sadiya. One evening they heard sounds of some large animal wallowing around, and on investigating were astonished to see a reptilian head raise itself on a long neck over the reeds. They shot at the animal but it escaped into the swamp.

As in South America, these sort of rumours yield neither names nor exact details of places. Yet their existence is a fact that has to be considered. Sir Walter Raleigh's remark on the stories current in Elizabethan days of strange creatures in South America is apposite. "For my own part, I saw them not, but I am resolved that so many did not all combine or forethink to make report".

We pass now from the wilderness of Assam to the wilderness of Siberia, from rumours, and rumours of rumours, to eyewitness reports.

Only quite recently have these virgin lands become of interest to the government of the Soviets. Russian scientists are now exploring this vast area and making some surprising discoveries. In 1955 the map makers were surprised to discover that whole ranges of mountains, which were thought to be well-known, actually spread in quite different directions. "Where mountains can so long remain· unknown", Bernard Heuvlemans observed in 1958, "there is hope for the naturalist".

Not long after he wrote, the *New York Times* (July 18, 1964) reported that Soviet scientists were actually on their way to eastern Siberia to investigate rumours and reports of monsters in the lakes there.

> The scientists are going to Lake Labynkr on the frozen Sordongnokh plateau, where a geologist reported seeing a strange creature ten years ago. Another geologist who saw a huge creature in nearby Lake Voronta told the English language weekly *Moscow News* that it was 'an ominous looking dark grey shape. Its body resembled an oversized, glistening, tin-barrel with a slanted horn rudder on its back'.

The comment of one sceptical Scot, a shepherd at Drumna-drochit on Loch Ness – "I see that even Khrushchev says there is a monster in a loch in Siberia; everyone is getting in on the act now" – was typical of Western reaction.

These news reports were innaccurate and sensational. Because of some fantastic incidents involving claims by Soviet scientists, they were disregarded. These Soviet notions were not obscurantist, as had been the case with Lysenko, but verged almost on science-fiction. There was the photograph taken from a submarine in the Pacific, which was said to show the track of a sea-serpent: it turned out that they had been looking at the picture upside down. In 1963 there was a claim to have brought to life a lizard frozen for several thousand years: Western scientists said it was merely a dormant newt. And more recently, a Soviet astronomer said he had received signals from an advanced civilisation in cosmic space; even his own colleagues doubted that one. So despite the great achievement of Soviet scientists in many fields, there was a perhaps justifiable distrust in the Western world of their more extravagant claims. The lake monsters got short shift, even though they were reported by trained scientists, the ideal witnesses according to critics of the Loch Ness monster.

The reports came from four lakes: three in north-eastern Siberia, and another in Tien-Shan to the South.

The earliest report, given in an article by Dr S. K. Klumov in *Prioda* (Moscow) in August 1963, was from Lake Vorota. In July 1953, a geologist, V. A. Tverdokhlebov, was leading a prospecting party on a geological survey of the Sordongnakh Plateau. They arrived at Lake Vorota, which is 120 kilometres from the nearest village, on a bright sunny day, with scarcely any wind. Out on the smooth surface of the lake, Tverdokhlebov and his assistant Boris Bashkator, saw, about 300 metres away from the shore, what they took to be a floating petrol drum. Then they noticed, to their surprise, that the object was alive and moving in towards the shore. They climbed further up the cliff face for a better view.

The animal came closer, and it was possible to see those parts of it which emerged from the water. The breadth of the fore parts of the animal's body, evidently the head, was as much as 2 metres. The eyes were set wide apart. The body was approximately 10 metres. It was enormous and of a dark grey colour. On the sides of its head could be seen two light-coloured patches. On its back was sticking up, to a height of half a metre or so, what seemed to be a kind of dorsal fin, which was narrow and bent backwards. The animal was moving itself forward in leaps, its upper part at times appearing above the water and then disappearing. When at a distance of 100 metres from the shore it stopped; then it began to beat the water vigorously, raising a cascade of spray; then it plunged out of sight.

Though they kept watch for half an hour, the animal did not surface again.

This report illustrates a danger in dealing with reports of unknown aquatic animals. The Lake Vorota animal, like the Assam burru, is clearly different from the humped monsters with long necks that we have met so often. The width of the animal, the wide space between the eyes and especially the single curved-back dorsal fin suggest at once a large fish or a dolphin. In 1918 a freshwater dolphin, all-white however, was discovered in land-locked Lake Tung-Ting in Northern China. The Lake Vorota animal could well be some similar creature.

Lake Labynkr, mentioned in the *New York Times* article, is

another of the lakes on the Sordongnakh Plateau. The natives, who are mostly fishermen and hunters, believe the lake is haunted by a demon which carries off hunting dogs. A fisherman said he had been attacked on his raft by it; he claimed it had an enormous mouth and was dark grey in colour. These details again suggested some large fish or whale.

During 1964 two journalists from the Italian magazine *Epoca* visited Lake Labynkr during their journey through Siberia. According to Brunello Vardano, they were told that a party of hunters saw a deer swim out into the lake followed by a dog. Both disappeared below the surface. Then a black monster emerged through the mist, snorted and plunged back. One of the party, "a scholar" according to the journalist, assured his friends that they had seen a dinosaur. It is hard to share the "scholar's" certainty.

But there are more recent reports from the lake, for in 1963 a Soviet expedition visited both lakes. Four members of the expedition watched an object for several minutes from a distance of 800 metres. It rose out of the water several times before finally submerging. As it was nearly sunset there was not enough light to photograph it.

In July 1964 yet another expedition set out for Siberia to solve the mystery of Lake Labynkr. This time they were equipped with aqualungs for diving. The expedition was divided into three parties which could relieve each other on watch in turn. The first group, despite diving to a depth of 30 metres, found nothing. The second group was also unsucessful.

The last and smallest group arrived towards the end of August. At Lake Labynkr they saw three rather large round objects moving 300 metres from the shore. They ran along the shore trying to photograph them, but failed to do so. They observed that the objects submerged and re-emerged simultaneously, but whether it was one animal with three humps, or three separate animals they were uncertain.

There is no mention from either of these lakes of the long neck characteristic of the animals seen elsewhere. The three humps recall, of course, the Loch Ness monster, but on the whole the animals in these reports are most probably large fish or dolphins. As Soviet scientists will doubtless pursue their researches on the Sordongnakh Plateau, we may soon know.

In 1963 Moscow Radio, reporting the news from the lakes on the Sordongnank Plateau, added that in the Tien-Shan mountains to the south in Turkestan, another monster had been reported in Lake Sary-Chalek. Dr Klumov, however, believes that this monster can be attributed to a string of cormorants swimming in line and giving the impression of a serpent-like creature. What evidence he based this on, I do not know. In any case, no further reports have come from there.

More conclusive is the evidence from the fourth lake, Lake Khaiyr in the Yanski Region of Yakutia. From June to October 1964 an expedition from Moscow University explored the mineral deposits of the Kular Range and the surrounding districts. They heard rumours from the local people about a monster in a lake three miles from the village of Khaiyr. As the group's plans included exploring this area also, it was decided to look into the rumours.

An engineer, A. Kharchenkov, a post-graduate scientist V. Gomoharov, and six other people made their way through the flooded swamps and marshes of the tundra to the remote village. The lake where the monster was supposed to lurk lay over a recent fault in the earth's crust. For that reason it was thermal and froze over later than other lakes in the district. They were told all the local legends about the place. Hunters never went there; there were no fish in it (though the other lakes were well stocked); wild ducks and geese never lighted there. The people often heard splashes and strange sounds which they took to be made by the monster. However, the scientists could not find anyone who actually claimed to have seen the monster.

But they themselves were luckier. G. Rukosuyer, the deputy leader of the expedition, in an article written for the communist youth paper *Komsomolskaya Pravda* (November 21, 1964), describes what happened:

N. Gladkika, a biologist and staff member of the Yakut Branch of the Academy of Sciences, literally ran into it quite unexpectedly. Here is how it happened. Gladkika went out to the lake to draw water and saw a creature that had crawled out onto the shore, apparently to eat the grass – a small head on a long gleaming neck, a huge body covered with a jet-black skin, a vertical fin along the spine.

Fig. 27. Gladkika's sketch of the Lake Khaiyr monster.

Badly frightened, Gladkika ran to wake the chief of the biological station. When the workers at the station ran to the lake with cameras and rifles, the 'monster' had already gone. Nothing remained by the trampled grass. They thoroughly examined the shore but failed to find any traces of grazed grass. Though the morning was very calm, there were waves on the surface, evidently caused by the creature as it dived in. Returning to his tent, Gladkika hastily sketched the animal as he remembered it.

The remarkable sketch drawn by Gladkika should be compared with both the Wilson photograph of the Loch Ness monster and with Arthur Grant's drawing of the same animal. The correspondence between the two drawings is particularly important, as the Russian scientist had it seems no knowledge of the Loch Ness evidence at all. The Russian sketch shows those needle-eyed eyes that some witnesses have referred to. What Gladkika takes to be a sort of dorsal fin is the ridge along the back which several Loch Ness witnesses have compared to a horse's spine. Though both show the front flippers clearly, the confusion over the back pair and the tail remains. Two final points about the Russian sketch: the hatching is an attempt to reproduce the rough appearance of the skin which is often referred to; and on the crown of the head, I take the rising stroke to represent a pair of small horns (even though these are not actually described in Gladkika's account).

Fortunately for Gladkika's credibility, the animal appeared again and was seen by several other people, including the leader of the expedition and two of his workers.

Suddenly a head appeared in the centre of the lake, then a dorsal fin. The creature beat the water with its long tail, producing waves on the lake. You can imagine our astonishment when we saw with our own eyes that the stories were true.

Rukosuyer, who is a geologist, ends by speculating about whether this is an animal known to science or not and wonders himself if it might not be "the last of the long-extinct ichthyosaurs?" Well whatever it is it certainly is not an ichthyosaur, which looked like a giant armour-plated fish. It could, of course, be a plesiosaur, but one regrets the hold that the long extinct dinosaurs have on people's imagination. If Gladkika himself had any ideas about what the animal was, we are not told them.

We have come a long way from the Laotian dragon and the Semelai nagas, yet what little contrast there is between these scientific reports and those stories. When Rukosyer invokes the image of a dinosaur to describe what he saw, the word becomes as mythical as the Laotian use of dragon. Both the scientist and the peasant are speaking mythically.

More seriously, though these are journalistic accounts, is there much intrinsic difference between the quality of the scientists hurried sighting and the peasant's story? I think not, but we are forced to give more weight to the scientist and in this case it is willingly done. For here is what critics of the evidence of Loch Ness have long demanded: a clear sighting of the animal, on land in good light, by a trained scientist. What more could one want?

The dragon with which we began this chapter occupies a natural place in Oriental belief; the dinosaur in ours. These reports come from the lost worlds of Asia: Malaya, Assam, Siberia, landscapes where monsters are to be expected. It is perhaps surprising that we have no reports of lake monsters from countries like China and Japan. Perhaps people there do not care nowadays to say they have seen a dragon. Recently there were reports of a snowman in northern Japan, and I have no doubt that there are lake monsters there as well.

"Lake Chuzenji in the mountains of mid-Japan is the reputed home of a monster", according to Miss Kathleen Conyngham in a letter to *The Times* (December 21, 1933). "The strange 'night-tides' that occasionally break in waves on the shores of the lake are said to be caused by the monster's movements". Lake Chuzenji, 50 miles up in the mountains north of Tokyo, is about 7 miles long and of considerable depth.

The King of Bhutan, His Highness Jigme Dorgi Wangchuk, (according to an article on his country in the *National Geographic*, in September 1961), has actually seen one of that country's semi-legendary animals, a Loch Ness-type monster which lives in one of the northern lakes – a great, white, fast-swimming shape. Native reports like these, even from kings, are usually ignored. Only when Europeans also see dragons is any attention given.

14

Waitoreke and Bunyip: Australasia

The professor sighed, and gave it up. "Do you know
what a Boojum is?"
"I know!" cried Bruno.

              Lewis Carroll: *Sylvie and Bruno – Concluded*

WHEN CAPTAIN COOK visited New Zealand in 1769, Chief
Taniwara told him about a strange man-eating lizard. As Cook
noted in his journal:

> Lizards of enormous size are also said to exist here, more
> than two and a half yards long and as thick as a man, which
> occasionally attack people and devour them. They are said
> to dwell in underground caves and to be killed by the people
> lighting fires at the mouth of the cave.

No-one paid much heed to this colourful tale. The first British
Governor of New Zealand, Sir George Grey, thought the whole
thing was a fairy story, though his version seems slightly
different. The Maori dragon "was in size a monstrous whale,
in shape like a hideous lizard". He contrasts a passage from
Spencer's *Faerie Queen* with the native story.

> Their strict verbal and poetical conformity are such that at
> first lead to the impression either that Spencer must have
> stolen his images or language from the New Zealand poets,
> or they must have acted unfairly by the British bard.

But soon it began to seem that there might be something behind
all these legends. J. S. Pollack, a Jewish merchant, in a book on

New Zealand published in 1839, reported the existence of giant lizards or guanas. They lived on Victoria Island, he wrote, though a few also occurred on the islands in the Bay of Plenty in the South Island. "The natives tell stories of its cannibal habits; but it is undoubtedly a harmless creature".

Though he was much abused by other naturalists (mainly because he was Jewish, scientists being open to the same low prejudices as everyone else), Pollack was nearly right. In 1839 another explorer, Ernst Dieffenback, obtained the first specimen of an odd lizard from the islands in the Bay of Plenty. It was called *tuatera*, and though once quite common, then seemed to be limited to the offshore islands.

The tuatera is certainly an odd little lizard. It is the only genuine relic of the age of the dinosaurs. On its forehead it has a pineal gland which functions as a sort of third eye. It lives in burrows in the sand which it shares with birds. But it is only two feet long, not two yards as Cook had been told. Was this little creature the great dragon of New Zealand legend? It hardly seems likely. Could there have once been on the islands a large monitor lizard, akin to those giants on Komodo, which has since become extinct. No-one knows.

This is not the only mystery animal in New Zealand: there is also the Waitoreke. This seems to be some kind of mammal, though not much more has been discovered about it.

In 1850 Walter Mantell (the son of Gideon Mantell, the man who discovered the Iguanadon) heard of a mammal the Maoris called kaurke, when he was camping not far from what is now the site of the town of Timaru on the South Island. He was told it was a rare noctural animal with light white fur, sometimes seen at drinking places. The natives said they would get him one, but failed to even after an intensive search.

Ferdinand von Hochstetter, writing about New Zealand in 1863, claimed that "from certain terms occurring in the Maori language, and from the most recent observations, we may infer beyond doubt that New Zealand still harbours some few sporadic mammalia, which have thus far escaped the searching eye". Among these terms

we find the name Waitoreke, which has been only lately clearly defined, having been hitherto applied sometimes to an otter-like, and sometimes to a seal-like animal. According to the reports of Dr J. Haast, the existence of this animal has been lately established beyond doubt; it lives in the rivers and lakes in the mountain ranges of the South Island, is of the size of a large cony ['badger' in the original German] with a glossy brown fur, and is probably to be classed with the otters.

This confident assessment was based on a letter from Julius Haast (June 6, 1861), reporting that he had frequently seen the animal's tracks on the banks of the Ashburton River in Canterbury Province, then a remote, little-known area. The tracks resembled those of a European otter, though they were smaller in size. A waitoreke had been seen by two sheep farmers on Lake Herreon, high in the mountains, who told him it was dark brown, the size of a cony (here a "rabbit" is meant). They whipped it and it disappeared, yelping, into the water.

And there the story seems to end. Haast was the first naturalist, and the last, to claim to have seen at least the tracks of the animal. In 1958 Bernard Heuvelmans, having run through the then available evidence, thought the possibilities were that it might be either a sea-otter, or a platypus. That the sea-otter, now confined to the North Pacific, could have got all the way to New Zealand seems most unlikely. Nor does such an odd and distinctive animal as a platypus cover the facts. He admits both are lean theories.

The difficulties against the waitoreke existing at all seemed to be conclusive to J. S. Watson, writing in 1960. He claimed to have gathered "all the available information", and concluded

> there is very little ground for any belief in the animal's existence; nevertheless a shadow of doubt remains and it would be unwise altogether to ignore the possibility however remote it may be".

However, like many naturalists trying to debunk unknown animals, Watson had not seen all the evidence.

In a pamphlet privately published in 1964, G. A. Pollack gathered up a great deal more, including many newspaper reports of sightings of an otter-like animal. Most of these came from a limited area of the South Island, mostly the mountain country around Lake Ellesmere.

Pollack, like everyone else, assumes that the Waitoreke is an otter, and he goes on to discuss how it might have got to an island where all the mammals were lately introduced by man. His theory, a most incredible one indeed, is that a Tamil ship from Ceylon visited New Zealand and left behind some fishing otters. This is too absurb even to consider.

Pollack, however, casts a little light on the meaning of the name Waitoreke. Though some philologists had found the name meaningless, he points out

the rather common practice, in South Island Maori dialect, of rendering 'ng' as 'k' – for instance, Waitangi – Waitaki; (Wh)angaroa–Akaroa. On this basis, the classical Maori equivalent of 'waitoreke' could be 'waitorengi', meaning 'disappearing under the water' – logical, surely, even if perhaps a little too pat.

The assumption that the waitoreke, "that which disappears under the water", is actually an otter seems to have been little considered. It seems most unlikely that it is an otter, or even a sea-otter. What then could it be?

Australasia is the land of the marsupials and the ratate birds. Mammals are the odd men out down here, recently introduced for the most part. The exception are seals. Around the New Zealand coast, the New Zealand Fur Seal and Hooker's Sea Lion are found, mainly along the shores of the South Island. Ferdinand von Hochstetter had originally reported that the name waitoreke was applied to a seal-like animal. His reference to an otter was the notion which everyone took up, on very little evidence, as being likely. Yet it is far more likely that the waitoreke is some sort of seal. What name could be more appropriate for a seal than "that which disappears under the water"?

Such is the meagre evidence of unknown aquatic animals in New Zealand. Though not in any way very monstrous, they are certainly very mysterious animals.

But even more mysterious are the Bunyips of Australia. The bunyip is a sort of Australian bogie, like the pooka. And like the pooka, there are some who claim to have seen it in the flesh. The word is derived from the Aboriginal, and is thought to mean something like "devil" or "spirit". To the whites it has come to mean any mysterious animal, any Boojum of the outback. Yet many accounts of these bunyips are surprisingly similar. Gilbert Whitely of the Australian Museum looked into the matter in 1939, and came up with a surprising collection of accounts, to which others have since added.

In June 1801 Charles Bailly and a party of French explorers from the Géographe, were moving up the bank of the Swan River (now above Perth). Suddenly they heard a terrible roar, louder than a bull's, coming from a bed of reeds. Thinking it was some terrible monster, they promptly fled.

Another explorer, Hamilton Hume, confirmed the existence of some such animal. He reported (in the minutes of a meeting of the Philosophical Society of Australia, in Sydney, on December 19, 1821) that in November 1821, he had seen an animal in Lake Bathurst, which was, from his account, presumed to be "the manatee or hippopotamus". The Society offered him his expenses if he would bring back a skull or skin.

He failed to do so, but reports similar to his continued to come in. E. S. Hall, who owned a farm at Bathurst, wrote in a letter to the *Sydney Gazette* (March 27, 1823), that in November 1821 he had heard and seen a strange monster, which made a noise like a porpoise and had a bulldog's head. Others had seen it as well, and he again in December 1822. The natives said it was a "devil-devil", wouldn't go near the lake and claimed the animal ate children.

A surveyor named MacBrien, it was reported in March 1823, had sighted "an animal of prodigious length" in the Fish River near Bathurst, and another had been seen elsewhere in the same river.

William Breton, an explorer, said of Lake George, "It is pretended that a species of seal, or as it is called, a devil, has been seen in it".

A newspaper in 1847 refers to the bunyip, which was called "Yaa-Loo" on the Hunter River, and also "Wowee-Wowee". It was said to have a human face, and its feet turned backwards. (This exotic detail is most revealing, as we shall see.) Reported from the Murrumbidgee River as having a head and neck like an emu, with a long flowing mane, the bunyip begins to sound more familiar. It also ate crayfish.

George Holder, of Lake Parker Station, said that some of his men had seen a bunyip in both Lake Paika and Lake Tarla.

W. H. Hovell said the Murrumbidgee natives also claimed they had seen an animal like a bullock in the lakes near the river. Natives on the Edward River called it "Tnata", though other names were also used.

By the middle of the century the bunyip was all the rage. T. Atholl Fletcher was told by natives on the Murrumbidgee that they had killed a "katenpai". He got hold of the skull and Hovell sent a drawing of it to the *Sydney Morning Herald* (February 9, 1847). The skull was examined by W. S. Macleay, who guessed that if it were a new animal, it must be placed between the horse and the llama. Then again, he added, covering his options, it might only be a deformed colt. But the English anatomist, Sir Richard Owen, to whom it was then sent, thought it was the skull of a calf. Which of them was right, or if it were a new animal, cannot now be settled: the skull has "softly and silently vanished away" in the cellar of the Australian Museum.

In 1847 Governor Latrobe obtained some native drawings of the bunyip from Victoria. But they too got lost when he sent them over to Tasmania.

A "real bunyip" turned up in the Port Fairy District of Victoria in 1848. Witnesses said it was brown in colour with a long neck and shaggy mane, and a head like a kangaroo. They also claimed it had strange powers of attracting its victims over the water.

Stocqueler, a naturalist who sailed down the Murray River in 1857 in a canvas boat, saw and drew "freshwater seals". They had two pairs of fins, or paddles, one attached to the shoulders, a long swan-like neck, a dog's head and a hairy body. They varied in length from 5 to 15 feet. When he showed his drawings to the natives, they said the animal was "the bunyip's brother".

A settler near Mount Gambier in South Australia in 1853 saw a strange animal 12 to 14 feet long in a lagoon near his station. In 1872 a shepherd saw another such aquatic animal at Midgion Lagoon near Narrandera in New South Wales.

Also in 1872 a strange animal was seen in Lake Corongamile, Victoria, where it so terrified one man he over-turned his punt. A Mr D'Arcy said it was "an animal like a big retriever dog, with a round head and hardly any ears". Another was seen by many people in Lake Burrumbert near Ballarat.

In a lagoon near Narrandera in 1873 a *wee-waa* which several people saw was also said to resemble a retriever, only it was much smaller and covered in black shiny hair. The same year an animal with a seal's head appeared near Dalby in Queensland; it also had a tail with two fins. Then in 1876 yet another hairy bunyip was seen in Crystal Brooke in South Australia. A reward was offered for it, £50 dead or alive, but no-one captured it. More reports from the reservoir at Malmesbury, Wagga Wagga, and other places in Victoria, all sound strangely like some sort of seal.

The moalgewanke of Lake Alexandria was described by the Reverend George Taplin in 1879 as some kind of weird merman with a red wig. The tunatapan of Port Philip, however, recalls the more familiar long-necked animals. "It was as big as a bullock, with an emu's head and neck, a horse's mane and tail, and seal's flippers, which laid turtles eggs in a platypus nest, and ate blackfellows when it tired of a crayfish diet".

A rider fording the River Monoglo in 1886 saw an animal "whitish in colour and about the size of a large dog". It's face recalled a child's, yet he threw stones at it to drive it away.

Until 1929 a truly fabulous bunyip with two heads which could swim two ways, haunted Tuckerbil swamp near Leeton.

But in 1890, more plausible reports brought a team from Melbourne Zoo to Eurora district in Victoria to hunt down a bunyip-like animal. And as late as May 1965, parties of local hunters at Mirramac Plains were searching the Nerang River, after local farmers had reported hearing strange blood-curdling roars, and seeing the water disturbed. Some thought it was a crocodile (supposedly extinct in the river), but old-timers said the bunyip had returned . . .

Reports of bunyips have also come from Tasmania. In 1852 one was seen in Lake Tiberias, which was 4 feet long, with a bulldog's head, and was covered with shaggy black hair. It was seen in shallow water so a glimpse was caught of its crooked feet.

Similar animals were reported from the Great Lake in 1863. Again they were between 3 and 4 feet long with a round bulldog head. They often splashed water 6 to 10 feet in the air, which reminds one of the antics of the Loch Ness Monster. They were also seen in Lake Echo. And shortly afterwards strange animals with round heads and dark flippers were seen in the Jordan River.

Between 1860 and 1870 there were numerous reports of them. In 1863 a witness observed one for a while and said it was a sort of sheepdog with two little fins, like small wings, moving at the fast speed of 30 miles an hour. Even the transformation of the Great Lake for a hydro-electric scheme did not drive them away, as they reappeared in 1932.

Gilbert Whitely concluded that "apart from the most extravagent fabrications, we must be struck with the comparative uniformity of bunyip descriptions over a long period". Usually it is said to be a furry animal, quite large, the size of a dog often and with a dog-like head. It has fins for swimming; and lives in rivers, marshes and inland lakes.

Could they be seals? Certainly they sound suspiciously like them. Seals and sea-lions are common enough around the Australian and Tasmanian sea-coasts, where they were heavily hunted in the last century. Thought of as sea-animals, the sight of one far inland might well give a farmer a surprise. There are freshwater seals in Central Asia, in the Caspian, the Aral Sea, Lake Baikal and Lake Oron. In Canada there are isolated colonies of Common Seals in some freshwater lakes. In Australia itself, the Australian sea lion has been found six miles inland, on rare occasions it has got even further. Fur-seals have been captured in the Shoalhaven, 70 miles from the sea, and in 1870 a sea-leopard was taken in the same river. At Congaro the skin of seal was kept for many years, where it had been killed in the Murrumbidgee, more than 900 miles from the sea.

So it is possible for the seals to get quite far inland. Moreover, many bunyip reports come from the drainage basins of the only really large rivers in Australia.

Some reports, however, come from places where it would be almost impossible to find a seal. So some scientists have put forward bolder theories.

The bunyip [writes Whitely again] has been thought to have been an extinct marsupial otter-like animal, rumours of whose existence have been handed down in aboriginal legends, the latter corrupted and confused with crocodiles in the north of Australia and seals in the south.

This sounds very like the waitoreke legends in New Zealand. But as Bernard Heuvelmans points out, the reports speak of the bunyip as a living animal not a ghost. In the weird world of the Australian marsupials, there are equivalents of most placentary mammals, except the truly aerial or truly aquatic. If it exists, the bunyip would fill the aquatic gap.

But does this explain all the bunyip reports? There is the bunyip reported in 1847 from the Murrumdidgee, with the head and neck of an emu and a long flowing mane. The real bunyip from the Port Fairy district was brown, with a shaggy mane, long neck and a head like a kangaroo. And then there are Stocqueler's "long-necked seals" seen on the Murray River in 1857. All of these sound more like our long-necked lake monsters than true seals or marsupial otters. However, where seals could go, doubtless long-necked sea-serpents – of which there are several reports from South Australian coasts – could also go. But the latest report is from 1857, so it would seem that this particular bunyip is no longer around.

The relevant point about all these reports from Australasia is that, whatever the animals may be, once again they are reported from the same climatic range as those in the Northern Hemisphere. South Australia, Tasmania and New Zealand are on the same band as the Mountains of Argentina from which other reports have come. Despite the Professor's despair, these Australian Boojum's may turn out to be Snarks.

15

More Mysterious Monsters

"I hope that some future Darwin, in a new *Beagle*,
will find the beast, or its remains; if he does, I know
he will confirm my drawing".
Henry Holiday: *on his drawing of the Snark*

ONE WOULD HAVE expected that such peculiar animals as those
in Loch Ness and their various relations around the world,
granted they actually exist, would have left some traces of
themselves in older art and literature.

And more than that, would have left at least one carcass
washed up somewhere for the benefit of science. I have found
one or two examples of their appearances in the art of ealier
times, but not much evidence of bodies for a coroner to sit in
judgement upon.

I have already mentioned in a previous chapter the remarkable animals found in Babylonian art. They bear a striking
resemblance to the Loch Ness animals, in some repects at
least. They are not, however, the only evidence.

Other curious animals, apparently water monsters, decorated
the great golden Menorah, the sacred candelabrum from the
Temple at Jerusalem, as carved on the Arch of Titus in Rome.
This monument commemorates the sacking of the city, and
shows Roman soldiers carrying away their loot, among which
is the Menorah. The monsters decorate in relief six small
panels around the base of the Menorah. Robert Graves and
Raphael Patai describe them as follows:

The symetrical and identical fishtailed creatures with somewhat feline heads shown in the top left and right panels are,
perhaps, the great dragons of Genesis I.21 . . . It may have

been a memory of these reliefs that a second-century Tan-
naitic rule explicitly forbids representations of dragons with
spikes protruding from their necks as being emblems of
idolatry; smooth-necked dragons, such as those shown on
the base of the Menorah, are permitted.

Fig. 28. Menorah and Loch Ness monsters.

On the end-papers of the American edition of their book, the
authors reproduce a drawing of one of the dragons with
spikes on the neck. Oddly enough, quite similar spikes were
once observed on the neck of the Loch Ness monster. They can
be seen in drawings made by Miss Janet Frazer, which appeared
originally in the *Illustrated London News* (January 19, 1934).
Are the monsters on the Menorah intended to be the long-
necked animals, or are they the smooth-necked ones? It is a
puzzle.

Nearer to the haunt of the Loch Ness animals are some
drawings from Britain itself. One of these is a curious creature
from an Urnfield Culture funerary pot, which is figured in
Pagan Celtic Britain by Anne Ross. The Urnfield Culture was
the one prior to the spread across Europe of the Celtic La

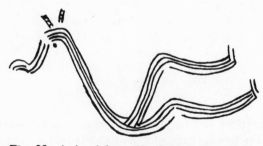

Fig. 29. Animal from Urnfield Culture pot.

Tene culture, which arrived about 500 B.C. No provenance is given by Miss Ross for the present drawing. She thinks it is a composite mythical animal, a cross between a swan and a stag – which would account for the two stubby horns. She admits, however, that there are no legends or traditions about such a remarkable animal. She is guessing in the dark. To my mind this odd creature is a drawing of one of our monsters. The two little uprights at the rear end are doubtless intended to represent the rear flippers, the central curves the two humps.

The schematic representation of the animal is typical of a more primitive art. There also exist more sophisticated examples. One is a mosaic floor of the cellar of the Romano-Celtic temple of Nodens "the cloud maker", a god of healing associated with a river cult, at Lydney Park on the banks of the Severn in Gloucestershire. This site was excavated and described by Mortimer Wheeler, who says that the animals on the mosaic are dolphins. Odd dolphins, indeed, with long necks and conspicuous flippers. These strike me as quite accurate representations of long-necks, even down to the smallest details. The flippers, like a seal's on land, point forward. But most importantly, it can be clearly seen that they have three digits at the end. This is revealing, because this is what Bright recalls seeing on the Loch Ness monster in 1890, and might help explain what Mrs MacLennan meant, in 1933, by the monster's "hooves". And it will be remembered also, that in 1969 Robert Duff said the Loch Morar animal that he glimpsed underwater had three digits on the front limbs. It is also striking that these animals should be associated in a way that is not quite clear to archaeologists with a river cult; I shall return to this point in the last chapter.

And finally, what may well be the earliest evidence we have of these animals. It comes from a prehistoric decorated cave discovered at La Baume-Latrone in France in 1940. The paintings in the cave are quite early and primitive in technique, and possibly date from 20,000 years ago. The drawing which concerns us is described by Sigfried Giedion:

Dominating the whole scene is a serpent over three metres in length. Attempts have been made to determine its zoological species, but it is better not strive for too great a scientific accuracy. Its astonishingly huge body ends unmistakeably in the head of a beast of prey equipped with gigantic fangs. The whole is a product of the imagination, one of the composite creatures so much favoured throughout primeval art. It arose from the same source of human fantasy that later gave birth to the dragon, and which here appeared at the very dawn of art.

Fig. 30. Cave drawing from La Baume-Latrone.

Not everyone agrees it is a product of the imagination. The German prehistorian Count Christopher Vojkffy von Klokock und Vojkovich has suggested that far from being fantasy, this is a crudely realistic drawing of a large otter-like animal, the explanation, he believes, of the Loch Ness monster.

Heuvelmans has identified among the seven types of sea-serpents one which he calls the Super-Otter. This is the animal with the long tail which I mentioned earlier, in the chapter on Scandinavia. It now seems to be restricted to northern seas, though as there has not been a single certain sighting of one since 1848, it may well be extinct by now. However, in the glacial periods of prehistory, during which man appeared in Europe, and the La Baume-Latrone cavern was painted, it may well have been driven further south along the sea-coast of the continent, and been known off the coast of Spain and France.

I offer this theory for what it is worth. Though the identification seems interesting to me, other prehistorians have different opinions about the drawing. Another French scholar, Leroi Gourhan, for instance, in his survey of prehistoric art, thinks the creature is feline, and that in any case, the whole site needs more careful study before any final conclusions can be drawn. The ever cautious scholar!

Whatever about prehistoric cave drawings, aquatic monsters are certainly a feature of early literature. Some examples have been quoted in the course of this book, but it is difficult, and not I think very worthwhile, to try and extract anything of value from such vague descriptions of the monsters slain by Finn, the "abominable lake creatures" of the *Beowulf* poet, or the dragons of the Orient. So we will turn instead to the more vexing question of what becomes of the bodies.

It is odd that in the whole long history of lake monster reports there are so few accounts of anyone finding the body of one. But perhaps this is not really so odd. If the monster is, as seems very likely, a large seal-like animal it would easily be able to get off the shore if it were stranded alive. As for dead monsters, it is unlikely that their bodies float, so we could not expect to find them often. Nevertheless, some have been found.

The first report of a dead monster is from Scotland. A Mrs Cameron of Corpach, near Fort William, in a letter to Captain Lionel Leslie quoted by Ted Holiday, claims that a small monster was found in Corpach lock by workmen clearing it out at the end of the last century. She says it resembled an eel, but was much larger and had a mane. Nothing more is known about this odd animal, nor about a similar one said to have been captured in a Lewis loch in the 18th century.

The next report is from Iceland, where Sabine Baring-Gould met a Dr Hjatlalin, who told him about a carcase washed up on the shore of the Lagarflot, which he himself had examined. Aside from the fact that it was of great size and completely unknown to him, we are told nothing more about this animal either.

Nor is much known about another carcase found at Lake Okanagan in 1914, except that it seems to have been a mammal related to the seals, as it was tentatively identified as a manatee, which it could not have been.

But the most tantalising report of all is one from Bear Lake in Utah, where it was claimed in 1876 that a living monster had been captured at Fish Haven. It was "a creature some twenty feet long which propelled itself through the water by the action of its tail and legs", and had a large mouth. This sounds so like what we would expect the animal to be that I doubt if it was a hoax. A joker would have made the monster more monstrous. Yet once again, after a brief appearance in the pages of *The Deseret News*, this monster also disappears for ever.

These seem to be the only reports of carcases, aside from a mention of a skeleton found in Ireland at Lough Mask, and a couple of dubious legends from Norway quoted by Pontoppiddan.

While this book was being completed, there came over the radio the surprising news that a large seal-like animal had been found dead on the shores of Loch Ness by the staff of an English zoo. The heart quavered. If it were the real thing, what then? But could it be? The radio said it had a large mouth and a short neck: that didn't sound like the familiar monster I had been chasing all these years. The story developed: the police had been alerted to detain the animal, as a local by-law forbade the molesting of animals in Loch Ness. At dawn a police patrol arrested the van which was carrying the monster into England at the Forth Bridge. Experts were summoned to the police station, and as one might have guessed by glancing at the date on the newspaper reporting these events – April 1 – it turned out to have been a hoax.

An elephant seal in transit to a small English zoo died en route. A couple of the junior staff hid it away in a freezer, and the day before had taken it up to Loch Ness where their boss was on the watch for the monster. They dumped it on the shore and reported it to him in a Scottish accent over the phone. He rushed down to the shore to find a green slimey mammal sans whiskers. And so began the wild goose chase that made it to the front pages of many papers.

It was a clever hoax because this time the jokers had used an animal close enough to the real thing to fool several people. I only hope that next time someone reports they have found a seal-like animal dead on the shores of Loch Ness, it is not dismissed as another April Fool joke.

It is also perhaps as well, seeing that we have no body for the scientists to dissect and discuss, that a conviction on eye-witness evidence alone can be obtained in courts of law without a body being produced by the prosecution.

16

The Long-Necked Seal: A Solution

"Come listen, my men, while I tell you again
The five unmistakable marks
By which you may know, wheresoever you go,
The warranted genuine Snarks".
Lewis Carroll: The Hunting of the Snark

HAVING SEARCHED OUT the monsters, the mystery of what they really are still has to be settled.

Though it has been clear from the beginning at Loch Ness that we have been searching out one particular type of animal, several others have got mixed into the matter. For the most part these have been clearly different. Many of the Bunyips of Australia are seals of ordinary kinds. Some of the Russian reports from Siberia refer to what must be large ceteceans. The buru of Assam, if that mystery beast still exists, is some kind of primitive crocodile. Only the sirrush comes close to being the archaetypical monstrous reptile of popular imagination – and what that might have been is still something of a mystery. When these are separated out – along with the odd Irish monsters such as the carabuncle – we are left with a large long-necked animal. It is this that we have now finally to identify.

The problem is best approached by going back to Loch Ness where we began and to its particular animals. By this time – if this were one of those old-fashioned detective novels – all the clues would be in the readers hand. As we went along I was careful to point them all out. It only remains to draw them together, filling out the details with the evidence from other places when necessary.

What have people imagined the Loch Ness animal to be? Well, back in the 1930's, they thought it was nearly everything under the sun. Gould, in his book, lists all the suggestions which he had been able to find, and which did not stand scrutiny: aquatic birds, salmon, otters, porpoises, plesiosaurs, tortoises, sunfish, rays, catfish, salamanders, turtles, sharks, eels, ribbon-fish, beluga (and other whales), sturgeon, squid, crocodiles, seals (including walrus, sea-lion, sea-elephant). A long and inclusive list, of which only the plesiosaur is still put forward. None of the others will fit the bill at all.

Today the main theories are fewer. There is the fish theory, that the monster is some species of giant eel. This seems to have been generally abandoned after having had something of a vogue in the 1950's. Though it might explain the humps so often seen, an eel of any size would not have a long neck.

That the monster might be an invertebrate, some sort of spineless giant sea-slug was suggested by F. W. Holiday. Inherently improbable in the first place, it does not seem to me to cover all the reports, or all the details of the evidence, such as the mane and fur so often mentioned.

Gould's theory that the Loch Ness monster could be a form of vastly enlarged newt attracted the support of only one well-known scientist at the time. While it had its attractions, again it explains too little of the evidence.

The plesiosaur theory, which appeared early on, still has many supporters. And indeed, with its long neck and flippers, the plesiosaur was a very attractive explanation. But again the difficulties, whether it could have survived for 60 million years undetected, whether it could live in a cold freshwater lake, are very great.

In fact the only theory that really seems to fit all the facts as we have them is that the monster is a warm-blooded mammal. Why this should ever have been a matter of doubt is difficult to understand. Perhaps because of pre-conceived ideas that the sea-serpent was a plesiosaur, some assumed, as many still do, that the monster was as well. Yet the details of the evidence never supported such an idea.

It is difficult to envisage a reptile surviving in the cold temperate conditions of Loch Ness, or most of the other lakes where sightings have been made. Only a mammal with a fur coat and warm blood is really suited to such an environment. Even in the earliest reports, such as those from the

1880's, witnesses mentioned that the animal had hair or a mane, which only a mammal would have.

These facts were clear enough to the anti-monster critics of the 1930's. But having reasoned thus far, many scientists concluded that the most suitable mammal to explain the reports would be a seal. But no known seal has the long neck which is the distinctive feature of the animal.

Only Oudemans, writing in Holland, took the next step of suggesting the monster was an unknown long-necked seal, an animal which would cover all the points of the evidence. True his animal has a long tail, but this notion was based on confusing reports of different types of sea-serpents. Having settled the question of the animal's basic nature, what else do we know about it?

The long-neck is a large animal, much larger than any of the seals to which it is related.

The head is small and flat, with a conical muzzle which lengthens with age. In some young animals it seems to be little wider than the neck, though in older specimens it is long enough to recall the shape of a horse's head. These differences can be seen in the photographs by Kenneth Wilson, showing the muzzle, and those by F. C. Adams where none is visible. The mouth, though seldom seen, is wide. The eyes are small, little more than narrow oval slits high on the head. The lighter colouring around the eye socket often gives the impression that the eyes are much larger than they actually are. Small "horns" have been noticed on the top of the head (again these

Fig. 31. The Long-Necked Lake Monster.

can be seen in the Wilson photograph): these are actually ears which the animal usually lays back flat on the neck, where they have been mistaken for a sort of frill.

The long neck is the animal's distinctive and identifying feature. Narrow behind the head, it widens to the shoulders and is strongly muscled. A mane or crest is mentioned on some animals, most probably the males: what could be more appropriate for a water-horse than a mane!

The body is large and heavy, much larger than that of most seals, thick and barrel-shaped. The animal is covered in fat, and shows two or three dorsal humps, caused by the rolling up of the fat under loose folds of skin. It has been suggested that these humps are inflatable air-sacs, functioning as hydrostatic tanks to aid diving, but on the present evidence they seem to be structural.

The humps have been the cause of much discussion, yet there should be no mystery about them at all, as one of Gould's witnesses actually observed how they change shape, and drew clearly for him the various aspects of the monster. On May

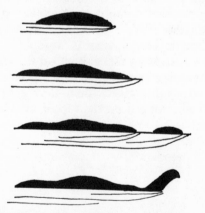

Fig. 32. The changing humps of the Loch Ness monster seen by Miss MacDonald.

Day 1934 Miss Kathleen MacDonald of Inverness saw the monster on the loch between Lochend and Abriachan; it was then a "brownish drab-coloured hump". This single hump then flattened out till there was a large central hump with a smaller one fore and aft. An even smaller hump then appeared in front of the main body, which proved to be the animal's head and neck when lifted clear of the water. Beside the smaller humps there was a continuous splashing and kicking. As the animal moved forward a short distance, there was a swirl of water at the rear end, which Miss MacDonald assumed was made by a powerful tail. What could be clearer or less mysterious. So much for the humps.

Along the animal's back, the spinal vertebra are emphasised by a crest of darker hair.

There is little or no tail, perhaps a mere stump. A careful examination of the 11 per cent of the reports that mention a "tail" show that the references are only in the most general terms. Observing movement in the water at the rear end, most witnesses, like Miss MacDonald above, assume the existence of a tail. No-one, except perhaps Arthur Grant, has even seen the monster's tail, and I believe he was mistaken about some of what he saw that dark night in January 1934. Against this we have the evidence of such witnesses as Mrs MacLennan at Loch Ness and Miss Carbury in Connemara that the animal's "tail resembled that of a fish", that it has "a divided, a V-shaped tail": which seem to describe rear flippers rather than an actual tail. So much for the powerful tail.

There are four webbed feet, on which the digits are large and clearly visible, sometimes giving the impression of three claws, or even of a cloven hoof. These details have been noted by Bright in 1880, Mrs MacLennan in 1933 and by Bob Duff in 1969. My conclusion is also based on the appearance of the long-necks shown on the mosaic at Lydney Hall and on Arthur Grant's version of his animal's flippers. The three-toed tracks found on the beach where that animal went down into the loch are consistent with this. And with the animal being a seal-like creature.

You will notice [writes Bernard Heuvelmans] that in all hind flippers of seals, digits I and V are the longest and best developed, and that the three inner digits are smaller and closely webbed, as if they were just one large wrinkled toe. This gives the whole flipper a three-toed aspect. Something like this:

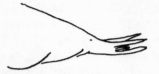

Fig. 33. The rear flipper closed.

When the flipper is broadly spread out like a fin it looks a little like this

Fig. 34. The rear flipper spread open.

and seen from a distance suggests a three-toed rather than a five-toed limb.

Hence the "cloven hoof" seen by Mrs MacLennan, and the three digits seen by Bob Duff and E. H. Bright.

The front pair of flippers are often seen. The rear pair, when pointing backwards, are frequently mistaken for a tail. When spread out, however, they have the appearance of a fishtail. Both sets of limbs are used in swimming, the front pair for balance, the rear for propulsion, as is the case with the walrus. The front pair are supported by a massive sternum which gives the animal a bulky appearance. As with the walrus and the sea-lions, the limbs are adapted for use on land, where the animal moves with considerable speed and agility.

The skin is covered with a very light fur which appears smooth and glossy when wet, but rough and wrinkled when dry or seen close to. The animal is a dark brown colour, and when wet often seems black or even olive green, with a lighter under-belly and a white slash down the throat. Some younger individuals are much lighter, an almost sandy camel colour.

The size of the animals seen in Loch Ness over the years has ranged from 18 to 30 feet, the pair photographed by P. A.

MacNab being representative of these sizes. The size of the animals has inevitably been exaggerated by witnesses assuming the animal has a long tail and extrapolating the real length from the visible parts. Most estimates of length ought perhaps to be reduced by a third. I doubt if most of them grow larger than 20 feet overall. The large animal in the MacNab photo is probably the old bull that has frightened several witnesses over the years.

As these animals are shy and retiring, few details of their behaviour are known. They are most often seen in bright calm summery weather, showing a preference for warm days. However, such weather is more likely to bring out people than monsters, for they have been reported not merely in the summer, but at all seasons of the year, even in the middle of winter snow storms.

Many witnesses are struck by their turn of speed, which is quite considerable, over 20 knots at times. The implication of this is that they feed on fast swimming fish, and what little is known of their movements about the loch confirms that they feed on the shoals of fish at river mouths and close to the banks. Their long flexible neck is well adapted to this existence.

Like seals, they use echo-location to trace their prey. This dependence on sonar may well be due to their being partially sighted, or even blind, from living in the dark gloom of the loch. As a consequence the animal's hearing is exceptionally sharp, and like the Snark it responds to "Hi, or any loud cry" by immediate flight.

The animal's breath has been observed once – from its mouth – and then by a naturalist. Its peculiar habit of lying motionless on the surface of the water suggests that it hyper-oxygenates its blood stream before lengthy dives. Seals do this as well: it has been found that Weddell's seal can dive to depths of 250 fathoms, remain down for half an hour and travel 20 miles under the ice without surfacing to breathe.

The animal dives swiftly, often straight down. Its other peculiar habit of rolling around on the surface may be to rid itself of parasites.

Though not reported from Loch Ness since 1923, these animals have a sharp staccato cry, much resembling a sea-lion's bark.

Nothing as yet is known about the reproduction, birth, growth or maturity of these animals. We can assume, however, that to maintain a population in Loch Ness, a herd of at least 15 to 20 animals must exist there.

These animals are found in many other steep-shored lakes in the cold temperate regions of the Northern and Southern Hemispheres, roughly in a band on either side of the 10°C isotherms. Often these are lakes in alpine mountain areas, but they are also found in rivers and marshes. Appropriately enough, in the Italian Alps Lake Maggiore is the reputed haunt of a monster. In 1934 fishermen reported they had seen it where the River Ticino runs into the lake. It was not however dreamed up just to cash in on the fashion for monsters, because this particular monster – said to have a horse's head and to live on fish – was mentioned at the beginning of the 19th century in one of his travel books by the novelist Stendhal.

The relation of the species with man is the subject of the final chapter of this book.

In summary: the Loch Ness animal (and its relations) is a large long-necked grassigrade pinniped, more specialised for a purely aquatic existence than any known seal. (It has reached the stage of giving birth in the water, which seals are only infrequently forced into doing.) The scientific name proposed for this animal is *Megalotaria longicollis*, "the big sea-lion with a long-neck", which was suggested by Bernard Heuvelmans in 1965. This name has not been generally adopted however, due partly to doubts still remaining with many zoologists about the existence of the animal, even though the evidence is so over-whelming.

Why this should be so is perhaps the only really mysterious feature of this whole affair. But as a minor prophet ought to have said at sometime or other: the mind of the scientist is exceedingly strange, who can know it?

17

Some Sea-Serpent Reports

NO BOOK ABOUT lake monsters would be complete without some account of their marine relatives, the long-necked sea-serpents. In some ways, reports of these help us fill out the detail of our impression of the animals.

Among the nearly 600 reports gathered for his book by Bernard Heuvelmans, there are some 82 reports of long-necks. Thirty-one of these are only probabilities, though some 48 are certain sightings. Among the uncertain sightings are, strangely enough, such classic affaires as the *Daedalus* sighting off Africa in 1948 – though that is one of those cases which are always mentioned in resumés of the sea-serpents history. The certain sightings provide much more interesting information about the long-necks, though most of the reports are not at all well-known.

Though there were several indefinite sightings off the New England coast in the 18th century, the first certain sighting of a long-neck was in 1846 when a Captain Christmas of the Danish Navy saw one between Iceland and the Faroes. While he was lying to in a storm, a herd of porpoises passed his ship pursued by a strange animal. The neck, which was as thick as a man's waist with a horse-like head, moved gracefully, like a swan's. As soon as it saw the ship, the animal dived head first out of sight like a duck.

This report was forgotten till recently, in contrast to the *Daedalus* affair. On August 6, 1848, while homeward bound in the South Atlantic, the officers of the ship saw a sea-serpent. The large animal swam past the ship at about 15 miles an hour, close enough for them to make out its features. It had a snake-like head, held about 4 feet above the water, with some 60 feet of the body breaking the surface. Dark brown, with a yellowish throat, the animal had "something like the mane of a horse" washing about its back.

On their arrival in England, their story appeared in the *Times* and the *Illustrated London News,* creating quite a sensation. Sir Richard Owen, one of the leading scientists of the day authoritatively pronounced the animal to have been a seal, which was roundly denied by the captain of the ship. Others enthusiastically accepted the report as evidence that the plesiosaur still survived.

An even more exact description of the sea-serpent was provided by the captain of an American whaler, *Hope On,* in 1883. The boats had been put out after what was thought to be a whale. A head like that of a horse rose from the water and dived again. The animal, which most of the crew saw, was almost 20 feet long, with a handsome horse-like head, with two horns protruding from it. The biownish hide was dappled black with four legs or fins, and a tail which was divided in two parts – actually the rear flippers thrown up as it dived.

In 1889 there was an even more remarkable sighting between Algeria and Gibraltar. The captain of a British ship reported seeing what at first he thought were two masts sticking out of the water from a wreck but when, examined through a telescope he saw two animals, one larger than the other, between 25 and 30 feet. The larger one raised its head for four or five feet over the water, the smaller about a foot. They were dark brown to grey in colour. Not only is this one of the few reports from the Mediterranean but also one of the few of two animals together.

Another British ship, the *Umfuli,* encountered a sea-serpent in December 1893 off the Mauritanian coast, an event which was, unusually, recorded in the log by the duty officer. The animal was about 80 feet long with a smooth dark brown skin and three shallow humps, looking like "a hundred-ton gun

Fig. 35. Captain Cringle's sea serpent.

partly submerged". Captain Cringle could see its eyes, and the jaws which occasionally appeared toothed. One passenger, a Mr Okell of Durban, had a camera with him but was too excited to use it. The neck was 15 feet long. The animal was swimming at a rate of 10 knots, as timed by the ship's speed in pursuit.

The coasts and islands of Scotland are a perennial haunt of sea-serpents of several kinds, especially the long-necks. In 1893 a London man, Dr Farquhar Matheson, and his wife were sailing in the Kyle of Loch Alsh, between Skye and the mainland.

Our sail was up and we were going gaily along, when suddenly I saw something rise out of the Loch in front of us – a long, straight, neck-like thing as tall as a mast. I could not think what it was at first. I fancied it might be something on land, and directed attention to it. I said, 'Do you see that?' My wife said she did, and asked what it could be, and was rather scared.

It was then 200 yards away, and was moving towards us. Then it began to draw its neck down, and I saw clearly that it was a large sea-monster – of the saurian type, I should think. It was brown in colour, shining, and with a sort of ruffle at the junction of the head and neck. I can think of nothing to which to compare it with so well as the head and

Fig. 36. Dr Matheson's sea serpent.

neck of the giraffe, only the neck was much longer, and the head was not set upon the neck like that of a giraffe; that is, it was not so much at right angles to it as a continuation of it in the same line. It moved its head from side to side, and I saw the reflection of the light from its wet skin.

The animal was swimming west towards the mouth of the loch and the Mathesons sailed after it, watching it sink and re-appear every few minutes.

I saw no body [Dr Matheson concluded] only a ripple of water where the line of the body should be. I should judge, however, that there must have been a large base of body to support such a neck. It was not a sea-serpent, but a much larger and more substantial beast – something in the nature of a gigantic lizard. An eel could not lift up its body like that, nor could a snake.

This is all very clear and precise, as one would expect from a trained observer. The angle of the head – seeming to be a continuation of the neck – we have seen at Loch Ness. The sort of ruffle is evidentally the "mane" mentioned by others.

These animals were familiar to the local people. Gavin Maxwell, whose island home Sandaig is only a few miles from the scene of the Mathesons' sighting, while shark fishing out of Soay, heard one or two stories of them. About 1900 a boy named Sandy Campbell fishing from a boat off Skye with two older men, saw a long neck rise 20 feet out of the water while the waves rippled against a dark mass below the surface. Campbell also said that the next summer two old men fishing off Rhum saw another neck rise 30 feet out of the sea. When it made towards them they fled.

We will come back to Scotland, but the deep bays of the Irish coast also harbour a few long-necks. Though there was a series of hoaxes along the Cork coast in the 1850's, there is no doubt about the truth of a report from 1907. In April of that year Arthur Rostron was bringing the *Campania* into Cobh Harbour when he warned his helmsman about a snag in the water ahead. The boat swung away slightly, but on drawing closer he and his junior officers saw the snag was actually an

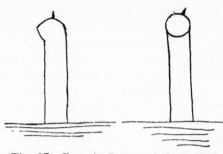

Fig. 37. Captain Rostron's long neck.

animal, a sea-monster. Rostron sketched the creature on the white doger board in front of him. "The thing was turning its head from side to side for all the world as a bird will on a lawn between its pecks". Rostron was unable to get a clear view of the animal's features, though the head rose 8 or 9 feet out of the water and the trunk of the neck was 12 inches thick.

In a newspaper interview Rostron added that he had seen two small protuberances where the eyes might have been and that the ears were small in comparison with its bulk. These "ears" appear in his sketch as two small "horns", reminiscent of those on the *Hope On* animal. (The animal of the woods, which Edith Somerville was told about, may well have been such a long-neck ashore.)

On the west coast of the country the deep bays of Connemara have also produced reports. In the autumn of 1910 Mr Howard St George and his son were coming in from the sea into Kilkerrin Bay when they saw "the beast" floating on the ebb tide about 80 yards away, a large brown animal as large as a small lorry, its head and neck moving from side to side observing. The two men were tired after a long day – they had just shot an old grey seal bull over 8 feet long – and did not stop to tackle this new and rather apalling animal.

In 1922, however, another sea-serpent was not quite so lucky. The large black humped animal with a 12 foot long neck, erect and shaped like a swan's, appeared off the quays in Limerick during the civil war. A small head moved from side to side, and one witness thought its bright eyes showed alarm. A Free State national soldier took a pot-shot at this irregular manifestation. The animal probably escaped harm, however, as it was later seen making down the Shannon river towards the sea.

In December 1933 another sea-serpent was seen at the mouth of the Shannon: one cannot help wondering if these animals have any close connection with the Lough Ree monsters?

On this last occasion the ship's captain, Hugh Shaw, says it surfaced to blow and take in air: any doubts that these are mammals should be dispelled by that remark.

Back at sea, in 1910 the first officer of the *Potsdam* saw an immense sea-serpent in the South Atlantic. It was at least 120 feet long, and was moving very fast, sometimes raising its head 8 or 10 feet above the water. It was black with white underneath. As it dived he saw that the tail was flat and wide in shape with a forked end. This last point is of some importance, as the tail of the Loch Ness monster has a disputed existence.

Actually the complete appearance of these animals ought to be settled by merely two reports, from different sides of the globe. The first is from Tasmania in 1913, and is important enough to be quoted at length.

The story was reported by a mining engineer to the Tasmanian Secretary of Mines who informed the press. Here is his account as it appeared in a London paper.

On April 20, 1913, Oscar Davies, a foreman prospector, and his mate were walking along the beach near Macquarie, a remote village, late one evening. Half a mile away they noticed a dark object under the dunes, which they made towards. As they came within gunshot, about 40 yards from it, the animal rose and rushed down to the sea. A short way out it paused, glanced round at them and then dived out of sight.

The characteristics are summarised as follows: it was 15 feet long. It had a very small head, only about the size of a kangaroo dog. It had a thick arched neck, passing gradually into the barrell of the body. It had no definite tail and fins. It was furred, the coat in appearance resembling that of a horse of chestnut colour, well groomed and shiny. It had four distinct legs. It travelled by bounding – that is, by arching its back and gathering up its body so that the footprints of the forefeet were level with those of the hind feet. It made definite footprints. These showed circular impressions with a diameter (measured) of 9 inches, and the marks of claws, about 7 inches long, extending outwards from the body. There was no evidence for or against webbing . . . The creature travelled very fast. A kangaroo dog followed it hard in its course to the water, and in that distance gained about 30 feet. When first disturbed it reared up and turned on its hind legs. Its height, standing on four legs, would be from 3 feet 6 inches to 4 feet.

Both the men were familiar with the seals along the coast and pictures of sea-lions, and knew of nothing that resembled the animal that they saw. Despite this, one is reminded of sea-lions and walrus which can point their rear flippers forwards and bound along on them as this animal did. That this was a "sea-serpent", and that this animal was actually a kind of long-necked sea-lion, struck no-one at the time. Nor was this made clear to many people by the next report.

In August 1919 a Scottish lawyer J. Mackintosh Bell was spending his holiday crewing on an Orkney fishing boat. On the way out the first morning, while the boat was making around Hoy, one of the sailors wondered if they would see the sea monster that day, and if they did would Mr Bell be able to tell them what it was. Shortly after one of them said, "There he is".

I looked up [Bell later recounted to Rupert Gould] and sure enough about 25 to 30 yards from the boat a long neck as thick as an elephant's foreleg, all rough looking like an elephant's hide, was sticking up. On top of this there was the head which was much smaller in proportion, but of the same colour. The head was like that of a dog, coming sharp to the nose. The eyes were black and small, and the whiskers were black. The neck, I should say, stuck about 5–6 feet, possibly more, out of the water.

The animal was very shy, and kept pushing its head up then pulling it down, but never going quite out of sight. The body I could not then see. Then it disappeared, and I said 'If it comes again I'll take a snapshot of it'. Sure enough it did come and I took as I thought a snap of it, but on looking at the camera shutter, I found it had not closed owing to its being swollen, so I did not get the photo. I then said 'I'll

Fig. 38. Mackintosh Bell's animal.

shoot it' (with my .303 rifle) but the skipper would not hear
of it in case I wounded it, and it might attack us.

It disappeared, and as was its custom swam closely along
side the boat about 10 feet down. We all saw it plainly, my
friends remarking that they had seen it many times swimming
just the same way after it had shown itself on the surface. My
friends told me that they had seen it the year before just about
the same place. It was a common occurrence, so they said.

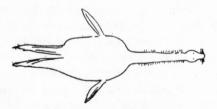

Fig. 39. Profile of animal.

As to its appearance, the body as seen below in the water,
was dark brown getting lighter as it got to the outer edge, where
it seemed almost grey. There were four fins or paddles, two to
the side, and two astern. The fishermen thought it might weigh
2 or 3 tons, others 4 to 6 tons (a sea-elephant of about the same
size would weigh nearly 4 tons.) In a letter to Rupert Gould in
1929, Mr Bell gave some more details about the animal:

Dimensions. *Neck*, or so far as seen, say 6 to 7 feet. *Body* never seen when neck straight up, but just covered by the water. You could detect the paddles causing the water to ripple. When under water, swimming, the body, I think, to the end of the tail flippers would be about 12 feet long – and, if the neck were stretched to say 8 feet, the neck and body 18–20 feet long. The skipper of the boat remarked that sometimes the top of the head, when seen from a boat vertically, was bright red. *Neck* thickness say about 1 foot diameter: *Head* very like a black retriever – say 6 by 4 inches broad. Whiskers black and short. *Circumference* of the body say 10–11 feet, but this I am not sure of, as I never saw all around it, but it would be 4–5 feet across the back.

From the remarkable drawings from memory done by Mr Bell for Rupert Gould we are left in no doubt about the shape of the animal He seems to have made the head more bird-like than his comparison with a retriever's head would have suggested, but the shape recalls the giant "bird" which a sportsman tried to kill on an Argyle lake before 1860. Nor can there be much doubt that this animal is a type of long-necked seal. (Indeed, an animal with a long neck seen in the Bristol Channel in 1883 left a greasy trail, which seals and sea-lions sometimes do.)

The details of these two reports are similar to many from Loch Ness. Unfortunately the only man who ever saw both types of animals never thought to leave us a comparison of the two. Captain F. E. B. Haslefoot who saw the monster in 1934 had seen the sea-serpent more than a decade before. In August

Fig. 40. Captain Haslefoot's sea serpent.

1923 HMS *Kellet*, under his command, was surveying Black Deep at the mouth of the Thames Estuary. This area had been closed to shipping during the war – and was then still closed – so "its waters were thus entirely secluded for the private activities of any sea-monster". His navigator twice saw a long serpentine neck rising some 6 or 7 feet out of the water, for 4 or 5 seconds. He could not positively make out a head. Captain Haslefoot, who saw the animal only once, sketched it showing a distinct head. He thought it rose 8 or 10 feet over the surface.

Peace and the resumption of ocean cruising brought several reports from liners. The *Mauritania*, on one voyage in 1934, saw no less than three sea-monsters, including a long-neck. A South African passenger on the *Dunbar Castle* in 1930 saw a long-necked sea-serpent whose movements he compared with a cormorant's as it swims away from a boat when frightened – that is with head held high and body low in the water. Like Haslefoot's navigator, he saw no pronounced head either. Another passenger on the liner *Chitral* in 1933 saw a small head on a long neck sticking out of the water, with a long black hump. Mrs Lilian Rawlings was surprised that no-one made any fuss – it was just a few months too early in that significant year for anyone to be monster conscious.

> When I *saw* the beast, and realised I was looking at a creature which was not very wonderful after all, and that, having once seen it, I might see it again and others would. Once assured of its existence, my mind accepted the fact and got rid of its astonishment immediately.

We might well end there with that most appropriate quote, on the eve of the Loch Ness sensation. But the sea-serpents continue to appear, and some recent reports are also of interest.

In July 1937, far south in the Atlantic, the officers of the French liner *Cuba* encountered a sea-serpent. Details of this interesting sighting were obtained many years afterwards by Bernard Heuvelmans through the good offices of a friend.

At about 5.20 in the evening the second captain's attention was called to "a steamer ahead". This turned out to be an enormous animal which he glimpsed momentarily in the act of leaping clear of the water. It dived, reappeared, and swam away at great speed, showing a long neck and two black humps. It was about 12 to 16 feet round, and 60 feet in length. His sketch shows an animal much like Bell's but completely clear of the water.

Nowadays most reports seem to come from individuals. In March 1934 Mr Wilkinson Herbert, a coastguard at Filey in Yorkshire, encountered another animal ashore. At this time the Loch Ness monster was all the rage, but Herbert's animal was not at all like the then popular conception of that beast. Walking along Filey Brig, a spit of low rocks running out into the sea, he heard a growling like a dozen dogs. Switching on his torch, he lit up a long neck, 8 feet high, only a dozen yards away.

> The head was a startling sight – huge, tortoise eyes, like saucers, glaring at me, the creature's mouth was a foot wide and its neck would be a yard round. The monster appeared as startled as I was. Shining my torch along the ground, I saw a body about 30 feet long. I thought 'this is no place for me' and from a distance I threw stones at the creature. It moved away growling fiercely, and I saw the huge black body had two humps on it and four short legs with huge flippers on them. I could not see any tail. It moved quickly, rolling from side to side, and went into the sea. From the cliff top I looked down and saw two eyes like torchlights shining out to sea 300 yards away. It was a most gruesome and thrilling experience.

The animal here is now quite familiar. The large bright eyes – an unusual feature – are doubtless due to the reflection of his torch on the retina. And though it recalls Malory's Questing Beast – which had the sound of 30 brachets baying from its stomach – one is glad to have confirmation that the animal is not dumb.

This was not the last monster to be seen ashore. In January 1962, Mr Jack Hay saw a 30 to 40 foot animal with a 3 foot long head and a long neck and body on the beach at Helensborough in Scotland. The animal slithered away into the water, frightening his dog but leaving behind a giant footprint in the sand.

And in the autumn of 1962, on Brisbie Island, Queensland, Robert Duncan had two sightings of what may well have been the same animal, or "horrible monster" as he is said to have called it. I suspect a reporter's hyperbole, as he says more simply that it was whitish-grey in colour, about 12 feet long and seemed to have a swan's neck, a whale's body and a fish's tail and fins. A fortnight after his first sighting he saw it again and noted that the long neck had a hairy crest and it was actually nearer 20 feet in length.

These are only a small selection of certain sightings of long-necks, but quite clearly they are the same type of animal as those in Loch Ness. As can be seen here some people mention hair and whiskers – Duncan above and MacKintosh Bell for example – and manes as well as large eyes. These features according to Bernard Heuvelmans are proper to the Merhorses rather than the long-necks. But as I suggested earlier I myself think that the two types may well be the same, and that the differences are due to sexual diamorphism.

Heuvelmans clarification of this whole problem has allowed us to see the sea-serpents for the first time in all their world-wide variety. Some are wide ranging, others are very limited in their distribution.

The lesser known types are the more restricted, perhaps because they are by now species in decline. The many-finned, for instance, is commonest off the coasts of Vietnam in the Bay of Along. The many-humped is found off the coasts of New England and the coast of Scotland for the most part. The super-otter used to be seen along the Norwegian coast, but as there has not been a certain sighting of one since 1848, it may well be extinct by now. It is an odd thought that such a strange animal should vanish without anyone ever really believing it existed, except a few dedicated zoologists. There are only nine scattered reports of the marine saurian. (Though to the reports collected by Bernard Heuvelmans I would add a sighting off the New Jersey coast reported in the *Scientific American* (October 5, 1895) where a party of Spring Lake residents saw an animal with a peculiar head shaped like an alligator's.) The super-eel is among the wide ranging animals, but not much is known about it.

The merhorse and the long-neck, those allied animals, have

been reported from every ocean. Most of the reports, for his-
torical reasons it seems rather than ecological, come from the
populated shores of the British Isles and America, where in
some places these animals seem to be permanently established.
In the Pacific, off the coast of Vancouver Island, we have the
haunt of the Cadborosaurus – Caddy for short – a journalist's
nickname invented in the monster-haunted months of 1934.
Further south off California is the territory of the so-called
Old Man of Monterey, the San Clemente monster. These
animals, as their pet names show, are now familiar and little
feared animals. A few words about them might not be out of
place as a conclusion.

Caddy was first reported in 1933, but a spate of reports confirmed its existence in earlier times. The Chinook Indians
knew it quite well and called it hiachuckaluck, a jawbreaker
few whites have used. Local people actually distinguish two
types of animal. Caddy is said to have a mate called Amy, who
is smaller, browny grey rather than dark green, with a horsey
head with no eyes, ears, whiskers or mane readily visible. The
pair were said to be "loveable and homely" with "warm and
kindly eyes". So much for monsters!

Heuvelmans makes light of these distinctions – yet in the
Hope On case one of the pair was smaller and shorter-necked.
And such differences of shape, size and features have been
reported at Loch Ness. The basic long-necked and humped
pattern is the same everywhere, only the features vary, as they
would between different sexes and ages.

During the last war a Japanese submarine was said to have
shelled Caddy, doubtless mistaking it for another submarine.
But the animals survived that and other perils, and are still
seen from time to time.

Down in California in 1947 a reporter was surprised to
discover, after a monster had been reported off Cape San
Martin, that it had been seen for nearly a decade and was
known as "Bobo". In Monterey Bay fishermen have also long
been familiar with an animal called the Old Man of Monterey. But the doyen of these monsters is the San Clemente
monster. This first appeared around 1914, and since then it –
or perhaps they – has – or have – been seen regularly enough
by sportsmen from the Tuna Club, a famous game fishing club.

It haunts the waters between San Clemente and the Santa Catalina islands.

Instead of putting money into the already well-supported Loch Ness investigation, perhaps those Americans interested in monster hunting should pursue their hobby in the waters and lakes of their own countries.

18

The Perennial Monster

The old-fashioned horror would inevitably raise its
dinosaurian head above the slime of his consciousness.
George MacDonald: *Mary Marston*

THE LOCH NESS MONSTER has turned out to be not much of a
monster after all. It is not a great dragon in the depths, it is
not a prehistoric reptile, nor what one writer called "Nature's
ultimate horror", but merely a half-blind, unaggressive relation
of the common seals. How is it then that this shy and self-
effacing animal should have been turned into the grotesque
Monster that haunts some modern imaginations as a creature
of dark and evil terror. This perhaps is the real mystery about
the Loch Ness monster to which an answer is needed.

Haunt is indeed the *mot juste*. Both Sir Richard Owen in
1848, and Sir Arthur Keither in 1934, classed the sea-serpent
and the Loch Ness monster with ghosts and ghouls rather than
any animals of flesh and blood. Sir Arthur was quite emphatic
on this point:

The only kind of being whose existence is testified to by
scores of witnesses and which never reaches the dissecting
table, belongs to the world of spirits . . . I have come to the
conclusion that the existence or non-existence of the Loch
Ness Monster is a problem not for zoologists but for
psychologists.

The only writer who seems seriously to have considered the idea
that monsters might be psychic penomena was the late T. C.
Lethbridge, and as Mr Lethbridge believed in many strange and
unlikely things, his conclusion that they are indeed animals
ought to be encouraging.

Nevertheless, apparitions undoubtedly take the shape of animals as was the case in another sensation of the 1930's, which is perhaps worth a short digression. Contemporary with the Loch Ness monster was the then very celebrated Talking Mongoose of Cashen's Gap, a remote farmstead on the Isle of Man. The family there claimed their house was "haunted" by a rather friendly "mongoose" named Jeff, which called out from its hiding places behind the walls, and carried on long conversations with its friends, gossiping about the neighbours and its own jaunts around the island on the public buses. At first the creature was reported in the local papers as a curiosity, like the equally famous ghost then haunting the chimney of a house in Saragossa, Spain. The case was looked into by Harry Price and R. S. Lambert, who came away doubting whether the "mongoose" had any existence outside the minds of the family. They had been shown physical evidence, photographs in which the "mongoose" was indistinguishable from the background, tracks and hair which turned out to be those of the family dog. So it seems that in those pre-television days, one family at least had found a more unusual way of entertaining itself on dark winter nights.

Jeff has a long ancestry, for a feature of several notable poltergeist affairs has been a "hare" or "rabbit" called Jeffery. It is possible – as Richard Owen and Sir Arthur suggest – to claim that the Loch Ness Monster is an apparition just like the Talking Mongoose. It is not a view I support – hence the existence of this book – yet the Loch Ness Monster and its relatives in their role as creatures of the imagination have a long history.

As Sir Arthur says, the Loch Ness Monster is indeed a problem for psychologists, but not in quite the sense he meant. After all the differing views of the zoologists, here, for relief, is the opinion of one psychologist:

We are often told [writes Dr Alan McGlashan] that if God did not exist it would be necessary to invent Him. But this is true of many other and lesser things. If, for example, so quaint a creature as the Loch Ness Monster did not exist already as a possibility, it would have to be invented. And if the Monster were fished out of the loch tomorrow and *proved* to exist, it would be urgently necessary to find a similar phenomenon somewhere else. For the mythic monster in the still waters of the Highland loch carries, however crudely, an intuition of something that is frighteningly real – the image of the destructive dragon powers within himself which man has always known to be there. It really seems as if man needs an image of this kind. The Loch Ness Monster is the latest of a long line of hair-raising creatures, half mocked at, half-believed in . . . In every age the more sophisticated have laughed at such things, but at the back of their laughter is often a faint frisson of unease. And even by the hard-headed standards of Fleet Street, claims, however unauthentic, of having glimpsed the monster in the loch are eagerly accepted as news.

The monster is part of what Dr McGlashan calls our daily paper pantheon, along with flying saucers and comic strip heroes. These are a poor man's poetry, the imaginative expression of the inarticulate. Such fantasies are the nearest thing to creativity, aside from sex and gardening, that most people ever come to.

A recent popular book on the supernatural takes such a psychological approach to sea-serpents and lake monsters, classing them with werewolves, vampires and the Yeti. "Such creatures", the authors suggest, "were first spawned not in the conscious imagination of ancient man (though certainly they were elaborated there) but in his inner world, his unconscious – they grew out of the symbolic monsters that people his dreams and fantasies".

The reality, I think, is slightly different. Certainly there is a symbolic significance about the Loch Ness monster that relates to the dragons of our mythologies, but both the dragon and the monster have a basis in reality. Real animals have been adapted to symbolic use, much as the Garter King at Arms adapts animals for heraldic use. Yet even so, the unconscious adaption of the Loch Ness monster and the others, and their imaginative elaborations, are astonishing.

Mrs Whyte, in her book, quotes Jung to the effect that the enlightenment that stripped nature and human institutions of the old gods "overlooked the god of fear who dwells in the psyche". She wonders whether the "idea of a monster in Loch Ness opens a door on that frightful region of the mind where terrifying creatures can appear, dragons, serpents and monsters of the deep, and these but the shades and images of horrors quite unspeakable".

Certainly it is very curious how often in reports of both lake monsters and sea-serpents, we are given far more than a mere objective description by some witnesses. Many people seem almost stunned by the sudden appearance of the animal, by a strangeness that has nothing to do with its size or appearance. For some of us, the monsters really are Monsters.

Here are some examples, culled from several sources, ranging from surprise through amazement to fearful awe:

> I was so taken up with the strange appearance of the head and neck – It was a really huge creature and we were all thrilled beyond words – It was an amazing sight . . . it was something not normal – In his own words, he was 'petrified with astonishment' – I said 'Do you see that?' and she said she did and asked what it could be, and was rather scared – They had undergone a most unusual experience which had left a lasting and rather unpleasant impression – It looked not like anything. Well, perhaps a prehistoric animal in a schoolbook. A lot of them never existed: just fairy tales. That's what I used to think anyway – What I saw was something out of a nightmare. I couldn't believe my eyes. On the water I saw a dreadful looking creature – When you have once seen the monster, there is no mistaking it for anything else. It gives one a rather uncanny feeling.

Tim Dinsdale speaks of the sense of unreality that effects one, the bemusing effect of the existence of the impossible.

Myths suit their age. During the Middle Ages when the whole of Europe was covered with dense primaeval forest, there was a widespread belief in the Wild Man of the Woods – a sort of Medieval yeti. Many scientists now think that the yeti is some kind of large ape, and that there is some substance to these earlier legends. Folklorists, on the other hand, regard such creatures as symbolic personifications of the Spirit of the Wilderness, the inevitable myth of the primaeval forest.

Today, when cosmic space has been opened up as another primaeval world, we have filled the "eternal silence of these infinite spaces" with Martians and Flying Saucers. These inexplicable phenomenon, Jung claimed in one of the last books he wrote, are a grim product of man's unease in a now seemingly empty universe. God has been replaced – as in *2001: a Space Odyssey* – by a mysterious black pillar as the creative intelligence in the universe. Whether flying saucers really exist or not, is perhaps for us here an irrelevant question. Undoubtedly many people believe they do, and that in itself is an interesting fact. (In contrast to the lake monsters, which are a repeatable phenomenon and therefore open to scientific investigation, flying saucers are unique and unrepeatable, hence the difficulties of investigating them which faced the Condon Commission.)

In the same way, sea-serpents were once personifications of man's basic fears during the ages of sail, when sailors were at the feckless mercy of the oceans' whims. Those so highly decorative maps of the period, alive with dolphins, whales and magnificent monsters of all kinds: such were the wonders of the deep seen by those who went down to the sea in ships. The all too terrifying unexplored blanks on their maps were filled by cartographers with "elephants on uninhabitable downs", and the seas with monsters such as the Ancient Mariner saw:

> Yea, slimey things did crawl with legs
> upon the slimey sea . . .

the denizens of those

> green hells of the sea,
> Where fallen skies and evil hues and eyeless creatures be.

So also with lake monsters, they have become objects of fear, beasts of ill-omen. Typical of this fear is the reaction of the tinker woman on Loch Shiel when the laird raised his gun to shoot at a Sileag, "Don't shoot", she cried, "It has done you no harm". One may not, of course, shoot or even mention taboo creatures in many cultures. Which was why T. C.

Lethbridge was admonished at Loch na Beiste in Skye, not to mention the beast for fear it would appear: the Beast from the Sea being the most terrible of all terrors in many mythologies. (Lethbridge thought the Skye beast might well have been originally a wandering walrus which had drifted down from the Arctic.)

The very word monster is derived from the Latin *monstrum*, a showing forth, a revelation. And the appearances of many monsters were regarded as fateful and portentous. The sighting of Morag at Loch Morar meant death to one of the McDonnell clan, and the fate of the old Royal House of Sweden was believed to be bound up with the appearances, or rather non-appearances, of the Mjosa monster. More often than not, the sighting of a sea-serpent was not recorded in the log, as they were regarded as ominous creatures by old sailors. In 1916, Captain Dean of HMS *Hilary*, for instance, had an argument with one of his officers about recording their encounter with a sea-serpent off Iceland. The captain insisted on writing up the incident. A few days later, after the ship had been torpedoed by a German U-Boat, Captain Dean noticed that the officer was the only one to have saved anything, for he had packed his bag at once, so certain was he that the sighting of the sea-serpent meant the end of the ship.

Monsters being such terrible portents explains the superstitious awe with which the Loch Ness monster and all these others are often regarded. Recent witnesses, such as those quoted above, are reacting to what they see much as their ancestors did. For these monsters, in some places, are the very gods of their fathers

> Proud gods, humbled, sunk so low,
>   Living with ghosts and ghouls,
> And ghosts of ghosts and last year's snow
>   And dead toadstools.

Some writers claim that Loch Ness is named after an otherwise unknown Celtic goddess Nessa, and that the Monster an Niseag – a femine diminutive – is her personification. Unfortunately, for we all like colourful theories, there is no evidence to support this notion, or that of human sacrifice at Loch Ness.

Nevertheless, I think there may still be something to the theory. Throughout the Highlands most of the monsters are called by feminine diminutives, a common enough practice to assuage the feelings of local godlings. Certainly there is no doubt at all that the Celts worshipped lakes and springs, or that it is a universal practise to offer sacrifices to the spirits of such waters.

At La Tene the Celts are known to have practised human sacrifice in the lake there. Loch Ness lay partly in the territory of the more primitive Picts, among whom human sacrifice is also possible. Loch Ness is reputed not to give up its dead – an unfounded legend, by the way. I do not know whether, like the Dee, the Dart and many other rivers, it is said to claim a victim every year. The faded goddesses of some rivers, such as Peg O'Nell in the river Ribble in Yorkshire, and Peg Powler in the Tees, certainly do. These are thought to be memories of decayed local deities. Earlier I have suggested that the kelpie and the water horse legends suggest that they too received worship. In Ireland the piasts are said to be allowed to appear every seven years; can this be a memory of the interval between sacrifices to a water spirit in the shape of some monster?

Another widespread tradition connects such monsters and dragons with hidden treasure hoards. Some examples are: in Beowulf the dragon broods over a treasure in a tumulus; in Malayan folklore around the Tasek Bera the Nagas are said to have golden scales, and a man made himself rich with a few of them; Siegfied, in Teutonic myth, kills the dragon which watches over the gold of the Niebelugen; in Ireland it is believed that the piasts guard treasure under lakes, and a similar belief exists in China about the lung. These legends may all have arisen from another form of sacrifice.

Many discoveries of great archaeological interest have been made in river beds, lake bottoms and swamps. These objects were thrown in as votive offerings to the water spirits. Again some examples: Strabo, quoting a lost work by another writer, describes a treasure deposited in sanctuaries around the pools at Tolsa, the modern Toulouse. At the eastern end of lake Nauchalet at La Tene, iron weapons and accoutrements, woodwork and the remains of a jetty from which these were thrown off were discovered on the shore of a small bay, along with human skeletons; at Port in Switzerland the offerings were discovered in the bed of an old river at the north eastern end of Lake Diel – the weapons were of fine craftsmanship, and traces of a jetty were found here as well.

In Britain there are other instances. On Anglesey, the holy island of the Druids, a find was made at Lynn Bach Cerrig in 1943. The site was once a pool of standing water, under a shelf of rock from which the offerings were thrown. Besides weapons, slave chains, cauldrons and such, there were also found large quantities of animal bones: oxen, horses, sheep, pigs and dogs. There was no sign of domestic refuse, so this was not a dump. The objects dated from mid-second century B.C. to mid-first century A.D. The sacrifices were apparently ended by the Roman occupation of Angelsey by Claudian troops in 61 A.D. In Scotland itself, smaller finds have been made in similar circumstances at Carlingwork, Blackburn Hill and Eckford (the horse's ford, perhaps haunted by a kelpie?).

These sacrificial treasures are clearly the origin of the legendary hoards under water. The water monster would be thought of as guarding all the treasures offered to it, hence the powerful taboo.

The animals found at Lynn Bach Cerrig – cattle, sheep, horses, pigs, dogs – correspond with those believed to haunt Irish lakes, according to the list in Dr O'Sullivan's *Handbook of Irish Folklore*, for water-bulls, water-horses, even water-pigs are among these. One might well say that these lakes were haunted by memories of prehistoric sacrifices.

The Temple of Nodens at Lydney Park – mentioned earlier – where the mosaic showing the two long-necks was found, was connected with some sort of Severn River Cult. The god Nodens is a mysterious figure whose name is found nowhere else. He is thought by J. R. R. Tolkien to be Irish, a god of healing with some as yet vague connections with the sea. Both of his functions are evident at Lydney Park: the offerings of cured pilgrims, mainly women, and the mosaic itself which was paid for by the sailors of the Roman British Fleet, evidently to gain the god's protection. The long-necks portrayed on the mosaic were, clearly, his special creatures.

Unfortunately, as I say, there is no evidence of sacrifices of either slaves or treasure at Loch Ness, nor any indication of any special reverence payed to the god Noden's animals that lurked in it's depths. Yet in some places they are still gods.

The oriental dragon, as the Laotian story related in an earlier chapter shows, is a relative of our lake monsters, but yet a creature still revered for his powers of making rain. (Nodens, by the way, is thought to mean "Cloud-Maker", so evidently he was also a rain god of sorts.) There is, as yet, no adequate study of the dragon myth, for the difficulties of its origins and development are immensely complicated.

Not only are dragons and their legends widespread, but there is no agreement on their meaning. Primarily the dragon, as the rain-making suggests, is a nature myth. In Chinese legend the dragon controls the waters and the rains, so that when there was no rain in the summer the peasants would once have punished the image of the god. The basic shape of the dragon, it has been suggested, was provided by the Yellow River alligator, and the fiery breath by the bright flickering flame-like tongue of the Komodo monitor. Yet behind the myth of the long-necked dragon there seems to have been, at some remote time, an animal like the Loch Ness monster.

However, by the time the dragon myth reached Europe it had gathered around it on the way the Indian python, which accounts for its sinuosity, as well as some Middle Eastern myths from which the story of St George was derived. Yet the older origin of the dragon as a water-monster seems to have been vaguely remembered, along with the offerings to rivers and lakes. On another plane, of course, the hero's rescue of the maiden was not only of ritual origin, but, as Jung observed, of profound psychological significance. The preservation of virtuous integrity from the forces of evil lies at the heart of our reactions to the monster today. Not merely do we feel ourselves face to face with something primaeval, we feel a fear which is also in itself very ancient. Hence we find that those who reject the existence of the monster on *a priori* grounds are also those who will reject any recognition of the ancient and instinctive fears, hates and evils which lurk in man's soul. The whole involved question deserves wider study by archaeologists, zoologists and psychologists, for at the moment the ideas of the three are often contradictory. The dragon, however, carries us over into the folklore of fossils, a new source of imaginative monsters for modern man.

During the Middle Ages, when dragons were still believed in, their existence was proved to the sceptical by dragon relics. Sometimes these were straight fakes, now called Jenny Hanivers, made from doctored rays, or from the small Flying Dragon Bats of the Far East. Dragon remains were also found in caves or dug up by miners, and almost all of these strange objects were fossils of various kinds. In the Dragon's Cave at Mixnitz in Austria, the bones of between 30 and 50 thousand cave bears were found, and the cave's name was clearly derived from a once profitable trade in these bones. An even more interesting example also comes from Austria. In the main square of Klagenfurt there is a statue of a giant killing a dragon which was erected about 1500. The local sculptor modeled the dragon's head from a skull which had been found some years before and which was thought to be such a monster's skull. The skull itself was preserved until recently in the town hall, where a scientist was able to identify it as that of a woolly rhinoceros which had roamed the area in prehistoric times. So it was a sort of monster, after all, though not a dragon.

During the 18th century it was slowly realised that fossils were the petrified remains of ancient plants and animals. This discovery of the appalling antiquity of the world, till then thought to be not more than 6,000 years old, affected not only the whole basis of religious and scientific thought but had also some curious effects on popular beliefs. When Mantell, Cuvier, Cope, Marsh and other paleontologists revealed the fascinating horrors of the world of the dinosaurs, these creatures from the great age of the reptiles captured the popular imagination and have held some small corner of it ever since. Today, every museum director knows that nothing draws a good crowd so much as a reconstructed dinosaur. And that is also why the idea (though quite mistaken as we have seen) that Loch Ness harbours a plesiosaur from the same remote age excites so many people. A living dinosaur in Scotland, four hours drive from London! Fantastic indeed.

This passage into popularity can be followed through the *Oxford English Dictionary*, where we can see the words coming into common usage. The term dinosaur, which means Terrible was coined by Sir Richard Owen in 1841, and first used in his report that year to the British Association. By 1851 Darwin is using it quite casually, and by 1873 T. H. Huxley, Darwin's faithful bulldog in the bishop-baiting battles of the day, was able to use the term in his speeches, certain that his audience would well know what he meant.

Wider education has made the strange vistas of geology common knowledge. By 1880 we have the *Library of Universal Knowledge* saying that "the number of dinosaurian reptiles was very large", and so it was. More interestingly the next year George MacDonald uses the word metaphorically in his novel *Mary Marston*, in the passage used as the epigraph to this chapter. MacDonald was one of the more imaginative writers of the last century and his use of the word is peculiarly arresting.

So in 40 years the word dinosaur passes from being a scientific term to being a common metaphor; indeed, substitute *unconscious* in the quotation and MacDonald might be summing up the whole effect of dinosaurs on the imagination: old-fashioned horror. They appeal, with their frightening appearance, to the timid little child in all of us that loves nothing better than comforting horrors before bed. The Creataceous is where the wild things *really* are, *pace* Maurice Sendak.

The plesiosaur, which people continue to search for in Loch Ness, was discovered in 1821 under suitably romantic circumstances to appeal to Victorian sentimentalists. Lyme Regis, on the south coast of England, was one of the resorts made popular during the Regency when sea-bathing became all the fashion. Mr Anning, a carpenter by trade, supplemented his income by selling fossil ammonites from his wife's fishstall. After his death, his 11-year-old daughter Mary realised the value of this sideline when a lady one day gave her half a crown for a fossil. With her mother's help she made the small business soon support the family. And, in true Victorian fashion, her honest enterprise was shortly rewarded with several unique finds. In quick succession she found in the cliff face below Lyme the first complete specimen of the mososaurus, a sea-reptile rather like an armoured fish, the first examples of the bird-like pterodactyl, and lastly the plesiosaur. Geologists soon were flocking to Lyme to visit her, and before her death at 49 this self-made woman was the admired friend of Sir Richard Owen, Conybeare and other notable scientists of the day. In one hall

316 In Search of Lake Monsters

of the Kensington Science Museum the visitor can see Mary Anning's photograph displayed along with a whole range of the monsters she dug out of the Lyme cliffs.

The original plesiosaur skeleton, which has since been lost, was described by her friend Conybeare in 1821; the dictionary quotes him as using the word in 1825. Till 1854 it is found only in technical works, but by 1876 Lowell is using it figuratively in *Among My Books*. Though it was not his original idea, the plesiosaur was popularised as an explanation of the sea-serpent by Philip Gosse in 1860 in *The Romance of Natural History*, and as we have seen this remains a widely held view.

The effect of these great monsters on the contemporary imagination has been paralled in our own day by the strange story of the coelacanth. The discovery of this very primitive fish, known only from fossils, alive and well and living in large numbers in the shallow waters off the Comoro Islands in the Indian Ocean was astonishing. If those fish had managed to survive so long undetected, many people naturally thought, why not the plesiosaur? The hideous appearance of these creatures seems to have some peculiar attraction for us: we shudder while delighting in the thought of their survival.

The Victorians shuddered as well. When the French scientist Baron Cuvier reconstructed the pterodactyl from the remains discovered by Mary Anning, he wrote that the picture of it in its living form "will be so extraordinary that it seems the result of a diseased imagination rather than the forces of nature". And that is the scientist speaking, though the words might well have been written almost a century later by Conan Doyle in *The Lost World*, at the climax of which Professor Challenger releases before the Zoological Society in the Queen's Hall a living pterodactyl. "The face of the creature was like the wildest gargoyle that the imagination of a mad medieval builder could have conceived . . . It was the devil of our childhood". The trained medical man in Doyle had rejected the doctrine of Hell that terrified his Edinburgh childhood: for him the Devil was as much a product of the diseased imagination as the gargoyles or this creature from the lost world.

This fascination with monsters goes back almost to Mary Anning. Science had provided new imagination with new monsters and the public were soon being given more of what they wanted. One of the most popular attractions of the Great Exhibition of 1851 at the Crystal Palace were the fantastic prehistoric monsters made of cast concrete. These were the work of the artist Waterhouse Hawkins who struck them in romantic if inaccurate poses. Before the Exhibition was opened, Hawkins gave a dinner for the leading geologists of the day, sending out the invitation engraved on a pterodactyl wing. The savants sat down to dine in great style *inside* the iguanadon. These marvellous monsters are now the last sad relics of the Great Exhibition, and can be found lurking in the reeds and bushes around the park lake at Sydenham.

In America, meanwhile, the American geologists Marsh and Cope were starting a fierce academic feud in their search for dinosaurs in the western states. They were the discoverers of the immense Brontosaurus, the largest animal that ever lived. Their search parties, roaming the frontier lands of Wyoming and Dakota, were often embroiled in fights over claims to particular sites, as if they were gold or silver mines. It was all slightly ridiculous, but entertaining, and in the end the fossils were hunted out with greater zeal.

And it was in America that the fossils went into show business. In 1854 an American doctor named Kock exhibited in New York and Boston the fossil skeleton of what he claimed was a "sea-serpent". He named it in honour of the great scientist Bengamin Silliman, Hydrarcho Sillimani – quite an appropriate name as it turned out, for many silly people flocked off to look at it. The sea-serpent was soon seen for what it was by competent zoologists, the parts of several primitive whales, which Kock had dug up in Missouri and put together to make a much more interesting creature than nature had. Exposed in America, Kock took himself off to Europe, where he exhibited his monster in London and Germany. When he had done with the fossils, they were bought by a German Museum which restored them to their proper shapes.

America also produced one of the very few instances where a monster was a complete hoax. A hoax, because it must live up to public expectations, is always revealing of contemporary fantasies lurking in the imaginations of the day. In the summer of 1855, the year after the Kock affair, the small town of Perry on the shores of Silver Lake, 50 miles south of Buffalo in northern New York State, was the scene of a monster mania almost the equal of Loch Ness.

In July two parties of fishermen reported that they had seen a monster in different parts of the lake. Their stories were written up in the local paper and before the summer was out all the usual events had occurred. Tourists flocked in and the only hotel in the town, which belonged to the newspaper owner Mr A. B. Walker, did a roaring trade. An Indian named John-John was interviewed and duly provided confirmation that the Seneca Indians had always known of a monster in the lake and had never fished it. The monster was reportedly "as big as a flour barrell", he added. A Mr Fanning, in August, said he had seen the monster spouting water, but nearly everyone else agreed it had a snake-like body with a calf's head and was dark in colour. It all sounded very genuine. Local businessmen formed a company to capture the monster, and whalers with harpoons were brought in to hunt it down. (The Buffalo *Daily Record* went so far as to publish a glowing account, in vivid detail, of how the monster was actually harpooned and hauled ashore: alas, merely a hoax within a hoax.)

Towards the end of the year the number of sightings declined and the next year they tailed off completely. Then in 1857 there was a bad fire at Walker's hotel. In the attic the volunteer firemen were astonished to find a very odd object indeed: a huge polka-dotted serpent made of rubber and wire. The Silver Lake Sea Serpent had been found! Mutterings of fraud were heard around the town, and Mr Walker thought it best to take a long hoiday over the border in Canada. Some years later, however, the town relented and he returned. Now quite proud of the affair, the local people occasionally organise a Sea Serpent Festival in memory of Mr Walker's clever hoax.

For clever we must admit it had been. Perry was a small, out of the way place, with nothing much to offer people in the way of excitement save a little fishing. Walker, whose various businesses were declining, wanted to change this and canvassed a few of his close friends about the possibility of a hoax lake monster to stimulate the tourist trade. The actual monster was made of rubberised canvas stretched over a coiled wire frame. The body was painted dark green with bright yellow spots, the mouth and eyes in red to make it as hideous as possible. The monster was inflated from the shore by means of a bellows and a long piece of piping, and operated by two ropes so it could be moved around the lake. Everything having been set up, the conspirators waited to reveal their monster, and on July 13, 1855, the party of astonished fishermen became the victims of their scheme.

If the monster had not been found by accident the Silver Lake monster might still be quoted as a classic case. The actual reports turned out to be accurate, as everyone, except the Indian, seems to have tried to be true to their experiences. Curiously, though, no-one brought themselves to mention the polka dots! What a pity there were no social scientists around in those days to rush off to Perry to look into the mass delusions of the credulous public.

The discoveries of the geologists, however exciting and entertaining some of their results might be, were also very disturbing for the Victorians. Tennyson, in the so-called "geological stanzas" of *In Memoriam*, reflects some of the fear they felt at the vast epochs that had suddenly opened at their feet, an abyss of time filled with God (if He still existed) only knew what strange and horrid monsters. In an earlier poem, called *The Kraken*, Tennyson had written of this terror lurking in the placid surroundings of nature as a threat to man:

> Below the thunders of the upper deep;
> Far, far beneath in the abysmal sea,
> His ancient, dreamless, uninvaded sleep
> The Kraken sleepeth . . .
> There he hath lain for ages and will lie
> Battening on huge seaworms in his sleep,
> Until the latter fire shall heat the deep;
> The once by men and angles to be seen,
> In roaring he shall rise and on the surface die.

In the same Victorian temper are Lewis Carroll and Edward Lear, in whom the terror is resisted by whimsy. The romantic painter and the professor of mathematics at Christ Church, Oxford, have both been displaced from view. The products of their leisure hours – or, if we must, of their peculiar neuroses – are what interest us today, the *Nonsense Rhymes*, the *Alice* books, the hunting of the Snark. Like many of the other Victorians who interest us today, Carroll and Lear lived uneasily in their own period. In their books monsters reappear for the first time since Shakespeare's death.

There is the Snark itself. Henry Holiday, the artist who illustrated the poem, prepared a picture of the creature surprising the unfortunate Baker. But, as he explains in his autobiography, it was never used:

> Mr Dodgson wrote that it was a delightful monster, but it was inadmissable. All his descriptions of the Boojum were quite unimaginable, and he wanted the creature to remain so. I assented of course, though reluctant to dismiss what I am still confident is an accurate representation. I hope some future Darwin, in a new *Beagle*, will find the beast, or its remains; if he does, I know he will confirm my drawing.

Holiday is referring here to the famous description of the fossil beds found by Darwin in Patagonia, which he says in his journal "must once have swarmed with monsters". Holiday's version of the Snark, surely the epitome of all much sought but unattainable creatures, might have been found nearer home: his pop-eyed seal-like monster bears some family resemblance to our Nessie.

Another dreadful creation of Carroll's was the Jabberwock, which appears in *Through the Looking-Glass*, and lived on the same remote shore as the Snark.

> Beware the Jabberwock, my son!
> The jaws that bite, the claws that catch . . .
> The Jabberwock with eyes of flame . . .

It seems to have been drawn for the book by Sir John Tenniel from models of pterodactyls and other such monsters. Did Carroll intend the slaughter of the Jabberwock as a blow at the new fangled evolutionary ideas of the day? Was Alice – "that prime heroine of our nation" – trying to slay the newer dragon of agnostic science, as Tenniel's woodcut shows her doing?

We should not be surprised that in the imagination real and fabulous monsters became confused. One witness of the Loch

Ness monster, as we saw above, thought that prehistoric monsters never really existed, were merely fairy stories until he saw the monster itself. Kenneth Grahame, whose personable dragon was reluctant to fill his traditional role, had this to say about dragons and dinosaurs: vitality he thought was the test of a legend, not truth.

A dragon, for instance, is a more enduring animal than a pterodactyl; I have never yet met anyone who really believed in a pterodactyl; but every honest person believes in dragons – down in the back kitchen of his consciousness.

How right he is, for this explains why the arrival of the Monster quickens our excitement, whether in fiction or on film.

The first writer to make fictional use of the new discoveries was Jules Verne, the creator of science fiction. In one of his earliest romances, *Journey to the Centre of the Earth*, (1864) his three characters penetrate into a sea deep underground where they become the breathless witnesses of a savage duel between an icthyosaur and a plesiosaur. Something of the intense interest which scientific discoveries, and such mysteries as the great sea-serpent, could arouse in people, is evoked in the opening of *20,000 Leagues Under the Sea* (1874), one of Verne's finest creations. In a novel written a few years before his death, *The Great Sea Serpent* (1900), he describes the adventures of a Breton carpenter on a whaling voyage around the world. The novel is very poor – the drive had run down in the writer years before – and though it is well-informed and based on Oudeman's research, the encounters with the sea-serpent lack the dash and colour of the earlier works.

Verne was the pioneer of a genre of which Wells and Conan Doyle were the real explorers. *The Outline of History*, once issued in parts with the gaudiest pictures of dinosaurs I have ever seen, was a work which popularised the more advanced findings of science. Wells, however, was not above a little bit of sensation, as when he suggested that the brutish looking Neanderthal Man might well be the original of the Ogre of our fairy tales. This was an idea that appealed to Conan Doyle as well.

In *The Lost World* (1912) he introduced the wildest display imaginable of extinct creatures into the mountain paradise of Maple White Land, the ape-man, the pterodactyl, the iguanadon and the plesiosaur. We have already seen how the novel resulted from several converging interests of his at the time. Here he uses the dinosaurs to dramatic effect, as Edgar Wallace also did in his novel *King Kong*. These novels, based only tenuously on actual science, provided the germ for countless films on the same theme.

One of the earliest cartoon films ever made featured a prehistoric reptile: *Gertie the Dinosaur* made in 1906. Once into movies she has never retired. Everyone remembers the climax of *King Kong*, but the early scene where the hunters are pursued through the fog-shrouded marsh by the diplodocus was also very effective. (A scene that was recalled in conversation with Rupert Gould by Mr Spicer, when he was telling him about his land sighting of Nessie.) In 1922, the year that Onelli was searching for the Andean plesiosaur, Conan Doyle was involved in an action with the producers of a film called *The Mystery of Sleepy Valley*, which also featured, in all their lumbering glory, a pair of battling dinosaurs. Gertie was the original ancestor of *The Creature from the Black Lagoon*, *Kwangi*, *Godzilla* and all those other monster movies of which Japan, for some reason, seems to be the main producer. Sometimes the monsters were forced into more "highbrow" situations, as in Disney's *Fantasia*, where the dinosaurs in the dawn of time dance to Stravinsky's *Rite of Spring*!

Lake monsters seem to be rarer fictional creatures. The earliest story about a lake monster that I have been able to find is the one mentioned earlier, "The Monster of Lake La Metrie", which was published in 1899. This rather charming piece of fiction – I like the touch about the monster singing Anacreon to the popular tune of "Where did you get that hat" – is chiefly of interest because the setting in the Wyoming mountains suggests that there must have been rumours of lake monsters from there at the time, even though the earliest reports of, for instance, the Flathead monster are from the 1920's.

I have tried in this book to relate such popular ideas as those above with the actual context of the real reports. I have no firm theory about the significance of the connections and

parallels that can be made, except to say that just because
people choose to believe that the Loch Ness monster is a
prehistoric reptile is no case against the existence of it or its
relatives. Here, however, is a recent incident which throws
light on the curious way people react to the appearance of a
mysterious creature.

Early in March 1969, a rotting carcase was washed up on the
beach below a small fishing village at Tecoluta, Mexico. The
carcase, or what remained of it, was 30 feet long and 18 feet
wide. According to early sensational reports the serpent-like
body was covered in hard armour and there was a ten-foot long
tusk sticking out of the head. News of the strange stranding
soon brought crowds of sightseers to the village. A dispatch
through the United Press International agency claimed that
"some scientists at the scene said it may be the body of a sea
creature from the age of dinosaurs, preserved in the Arctic
Ice" which had been released when the glacier it was entombed
in reached the sea and melted. This most interesting theory was
later credited to a Dr Bernardo Villa at the National University
of Mexico.

Eventually other scientists from the Marine Biology Station
at Tampico, who actually went down to look at the carcase,
identified it as that of a very badly decomposed sperm whale;
the mysterious "horn" was one of its jaw bones. There is no
doubt that they were right.

Where then had the sea creature from the age of dinosaurs
preserved in the Arctic ice come from? Not it seems from Dr
Villa's imagination anyway, but from an American film. In
1953 the science-fictionist Ray Bradbury wrote the script for a
production called *The Beast from 20,000 Fathoms*, which is
now a regular feature of the late night movie shows on television in the United States. The plot? In the Arctic an American
atom bomb test releases from its tomb of ice a million-year-old
monster. After various vigorous horrors, the film ends with
the monsters burning to death in a blazing funfair. Mr Bradbury's exotic fiction may or may not be the source for the
curious theories of the Mexican fishermen, let alone academics,
but it is certainly an odd coincidence. When that queer carcase
turned up on the beach doubtless some local bright boy
remembered the Yanqui film, and provided the tourists with a

good story for their pesos. Perhaps Ray Bradbury should have asked for a share of the monies. It is a warning to the curious: yesterday's science fiction becomes today's press sensation. Whether the press sensation becomes tomorrow's scientific commonplace is another matter . . .

The Loch Ness monster has also featured in films and books. In 1934, to capture some of the topical interest, Wyndham Productions made a film written by Billie Breston and Charles Bennet called *The Secret of the Loch*, which starred the popular Seymour Hicks. This film has the odd distinction of being the first "talking picture" made in Scotland. The film was announced the week after Gould's article appeared in the *Times*, and the writers made themselves conspicuous around the loch for a couple of weeks gathering local colour and selecting locations. They intended to include actual footage of the real monster swimming in the loch and some of Irvine's film was finally used. Actually it turned out to be a pretty bad film, with such stock characters as the eccentric professor, the young journalist and the professor's pretty niece, who happen to meet . . . What *was* unusual about it was the fact that the Monster in it was modelled on Gould's theory of it being a sort of giant newt. The film was hardly noticed at all – in those days film reviews were not commonly published in the better papers – though the critics in *Picturegoer* thought that the underwater sequence, where the monster surprises the diver, was "neatly devised and forms the key for the last part of the picture". But Milton Rossmer's direction took an unconscionably long time to get to the brute and the whole point of the picture.

During the summer of 1969, while Dan Taylor was trying to film the monster in the flesh, the American director Billy Wilder was also at Loch Ness making *The Private Life of Sherlock Holmes*. This film was to feature a version of the monster made of PVC and metal, towed by the Vickers Pisces submarine. Unfortunately the creature was no sooner ready than it was lost under tow. Later it was actually reported to the Loch Ness Investigation as the real thing. In the plot of the Wilder-written script, the monster is merely a dummy used as the cover-up to develop a new submarine for the British Navy. This was not actually a new idea: an episode of the

American television series *Voyage to the Bottom of the Sea*
had once used it, though they didn't bother to use the real loch
and their Highlanders were straight from Central Casting. In
the Holmes film, however, it was interesting to learn from Dr
Watson that a "serious newspaper like the *Evening Standard*"
on April 17, 1888, was reporting the third sighting that month
of the Loch Ness monster. Clearly an animal ahead of it's time!
Holmes considered the monster was "a cross between an eel
and a camel" – a curious feat of genetics.

Tim Dinsdale's appearance with his film on *Panorama* in
1960 suggested to a pair of BBC scriptwriters a serial about a
monster in a Scottish loch. Another eccentric professor, another
pretty couple, and at the bottom of it all, yet another secret
submarine. My memory of the story line is now vague, but I
do recall that for some odd reason they made the monster a
ceratosaurus (that's the one with the small paws and the horn
on it's nose) and not a plesiosaurus. And as every schoolboy
knows . . .

Though there may well have been others, the only novel I
know in which the Loch Ness monster appears is in one of
Compton Mackenzie's humorous views of Highland life, *The
Rival Monster*, published in 1952. Nessie, to the consternation
of the laird Ben Nevis and his friends around Loch Ness, is
reported to have been killed by a low-flying saucer. But when
another monster is reported from Little Todday out in the
Hebrides, Ben Nevis leads an expedition to retrieve what he
firmly believes to be an amnesic Nessie. After all the complica-
tions and the love interests have been tidied up, the Todday
monster is revealed to be a wandering Arctic walrus, one of
which had actually turned up in the Hebrides in 1949. The
Loch Ness monster finally reappears alive and well, "eight
humps moving slowly towards the middle of the loch where it
submerged".

The Monster also leads a fugitive life in newspaper cartoons.
I am rather fond of these myself, even though they must be
regarded as not really worthy of scientific attention. Nevertheless one by Allan Dunn of the *New Yorker*, suggested the
obvious answer to a problem which has bothered many scientists; how have the monsters managed to survive the centuries?
The cartoon shows two wild life officers outside the Loch Ness

Hatchery emptying a bucket of baby monsters into a stream down to the loch. My other favourite is one by Gammidge which appeared in the *Sunday Mirror* in London, which managed to combine the two leading mysteries of the day. It showed a scaley Martian standing on the bank of Loch Ness waving to a friendly-looking monster and calling out "Greetings, earthman".

Yet the monster, harried and oppressed as she is these days by rival expeditions of Abominable Know-men, must feel just a little distressed. The English poet Ted Hughes has written a delightful poem for children about Nessie. As that unfortunate animal has had no opportunity to speak for herself, we can take leave of her with the last words the poet provides her with on her sorry plight:

It's me, me, me, the Monster of the Loch!
Would God I were a proper kind, a hippopot or croc!
Mislaid by the ages, I gloom here in the dark,
But I should be ruling Scotland from a throne in
                                                                        Regent's Park . . .
Because I am so ugly that it's incredible!
The biggest bag of Haggis Scotland cannot swallow or sell!
Me, me, me, the Monster of the Loch
Scotland's ugliest daughter, seven tons of poppycock!
Living here in my black mud bed the life of a snittery newty,
And never a zoologist a-swooning for my beauty.
O where's the bonny laddie, so bold and so free,
Who will drum me up to London and proclaim my
                                                                        pedigree?

Given this long and fantastic history of monsters, real and imaginary, we should not be surprised that scientists are wary about committing themselves to their actual existence – never mind about swooning over their long-lashed beauty. Scientists have no desire to appear foolish, a very human failing on their part. Yet monsters are a subject on which scientists are completely unscientific. As we have seen, those who have been most contemptuous about the monster have known very little about it. Only those who have examined the evidence should be entitled to an opinion, and those who have, with one or two exceptions, have in the end been convinced.

In this book I have tried to do something about establishing the Monster's pedigree. But I cannot say that I would like to see one installed in Regent's Park or the Smithsonian. Eventually, a living specimen will fall into our hands, but that should be enough. For the rest, the freedom of nature should remain. For while they are at large in our diminishing and disintegrating world, nature will retain something of her old mystery, and man will be reminded that he is not yet master of all knowledge.

Ann Arbor
London
Dublin

Appendix:

JARIC REPORT ON DINSDALE FILM

Joint Air Reconnaisance Intelligence Centre
(United Kingdom)

Photographic Interpretation Report Number 66/1:
January 24, 1966

LOCH Ness

References: A. Loch Ness Phenomena Film Report concerning
1960 (Dinsdale) sighting TD/LNPIB/2 dated
November 18, 1965.
B. CRE letter CRE/S388/Prog dated January 5,
1966.
C. MOD DI 26(Air) letter S208/E.99/MIN(RAF)
dated December 21, 1965.
D. JARIB(UK) Order No. A1/66.

1. Material examined has been the original 16 mm film. NO copies have been made. All examination has been by optical enlargement of the film thus obviating losses by photographic processes. The majority of the examination and mensuration has been made at 20 × enlargement.

2. This report deals firstly (paras 3 to 11) with mensuration and secondly with interpretation or deduction based on visual examination and analysis of the mensuration (para 12 et seq.).

3. In mensuration the basic data must first be considered and the following has been accepted:

a. That the Observation Post (OP) was at the point shown in the map in Ref. A.

b. That the height of the OP above the loch is 300 feet (Note: if the height is NOT 300 ft then all measures require adjustment, i.e. if the height is 290 ft all measures will be in error by +10 per cent).

c. That the line of sight shown on the map in Ref. A is correct for the first sighting. Note that the track shown on the map is badly out of proportion, i.e. assume the track parallel to the shore occurs between frames 700 and 1700 (or 42 secs of the film) and the speed of the object is 10 mph then the distance travelled in this time is 630 ft, or approximately 0.12 inches on the map. See paras 5 and 9.

d. That the focal length of the taking camera was 135 mm.

e. That the speed of the camera was 24 fps.

4. The camera was NOT fixed in either axis during exposure therefore there is NO fixed frame reference and mensuration must also be based on the distance from OP to far shore of loch (accepting angle of sight at 3c) to control the scale in Y (or depth of view) and on image detail on the far shore to control the scale on X (or across the field of view).

5. A point which must be appreciated in near horizontal photography of this sort is the immense difference between the scale in X (across the field of view) and the scale in Y (the depth of view). As an example, at first sighting, the X scale of the photography, at the object of interest, is approximately 1:187,000. It will be realised that only small errors in measurement in the Y direction will have large effects. Furthermore since the shore of the loch is NOT truly parallel to the plane of the photography and is, in any case, NOT a straight line the Y measures become complicated.

6. The frames have been arbitrarily numbered, the fourth frame after first sighting being numbered 1 and consecutively thereafter.

7. In the first instance mensuration was carried out on the known objects with the following results:

a. The speed of the boat was calculated at 6.5 mph (agreeing well with Dinsdale's assessment).

b. The length of the boat was calculated as 13.3 (proving that the scaling is sensibly correct).

c. The vehicle on the far shore road has a calculated length of 14 ft and a speed of 39 mph. This again agrees reasonably well with the assumption that the vehicle is possibly a family saloon or a small truck and the speed seems reasonable for that road at that time.

8. At first sighting the distance OP to object = 5,00 ft = 1,667 yards. Dinsdale reports 1,300 yards which merely demonstrates the difficulty of "depth" perception.

9. Between frame 1 and frame 384 (16 secs) the object has travelled some 240 ft in Y (depth of view) but only some 30 ft in X (across the field of view). This means that during this sequence the object has been travelling almost entirely AWAY from the OP at a speed of about 10 mph. The speed and direction of travel have been further confirmed by measures on frames 120 (5 secs), 192 (8 secs), 312 (13 secs). Even by frame 504 (21 secs), where curvature of the wake is already pronounced, movement across the field of view is still only about 75 ft, further confirming that during the first 16 secs movement was AWAY from OP. NOTE: Difficulties of Y measure are mentioned at para 5 and during this sequence almost all of the measure is Y measure. However since the object is travelling on a fixed bearing relative to the shore, the point of intersection on the shore becomes a fixed reference point and measures become more reliable. Moreover, the speed has been calculated from observation on 5 separate frames and the given speed is the sensibly LOWEST speed from these observations.

10. The object image has been measured on frames 1 and 6 and size confirmed on frame 120. What one has to measure is a solid, black, approximately triangular shape, with NO impression of perspective. If this shape is assumed to be a plane triangle, in the vertical plane (parallel to the negative plane) it is a triangle with a base 5.5 ft approx. and height 3.7 ft approx. If in the horizontal plane it would be a triangle with base 5.5 ft approx. and height (i.e. length) 92 ft approx. but see later discussion (para 16).

11. Between frames 816 (34 secs) and 1440 (60 secs) the object is travelling approx. parallel to the loch shore. At this time it is approx. 100 yards from the loch shore. Measures made several of the frames in this sequence suggest that the mean speed is at least 7 mph and, due to the difficulties mentioned in para 5, it seems likely the speed may be as high as 10 mph. A reasonable assumption would be that during the complete film sequence the object was travelling at or approaching 10 mph.

12. The interpretation is a more difficult problem, but first consider whether this may be a surface vessel of any kind. The object appears to submerge but it can readily be argued that under certain conditions of light, reflectivity and aspect angle etc. objects may NOT be visible on the photography. The boat was photographed on the same morning and light conditions were probably reasonably similar. When travelling parallel to the shore the boat is discernable as a boat shape and can be measured whereas with the object there is NO visible sign at all.

13. When travelling away from the OP the boat image is NOT identifiable as a boat but the image has an irregular "broken" shape which one would expect from an object NOT having a continuous surface. The triangular object however has a solid look about it, as if in fact it was an object with a continuous surface.

14. As mentioned in para 9 during the sequence in which the triangle is visible it is moving AWAY from the OP and if it were a surface vessel it would be a view from the stern and the measure of $5\frac{1}{2}$ ft would be a beam measurement. In small craft length and beam are closely related and it is doubtful if a hull with this beam would have a length in excess of 16 ft. With small craft with "non-planning" hulls, the maximum speed, regardless of propulsive power, is limited by the waterline length, e.g. the 14 ft boat with Seagull outboard at $6\frac{1}{2}$ to 7 mph is probably at or near its maximum possible speed. The object is travelling at 10 mph and it is doubtful if a "non-planning" hull of under 16 ft could achieve this speed. A power boat shell with planning hull could easily achieve and exceed this speed and the design is such that it could appear to have a continuous surface. However these craft are normally painted in such a way as to be photo visible at any time and in any case the existence of such a craft on the loch would scarcely be missed by an observer. The assumption is therefore that it is NOT a surface vessel.

15. One can presumably rule out the idea that it is any sort of submarine vessel for various reasons which leaves the conclusion that it is probably an animate object.

16. Considering the shape and size of the object, it can obviously NOT be a plane triangle as mentioned in para 10.

It is an object with some "body". The base of the triangle is blurred as one would expect with breaking water behind it and the base measurement is probably a true expression of the width or beam of the object at the waterline. The height of the solid object will be somewhat obscured because in this type of view, with NO impression of perspective, part of the measure on the photo is a Y measure due to the fore and aft length of the object (depth of view). It is impossible to define this part without knowing the fore and aft length. However if ALL of the measure were a Y measure the fore and aft length would be 92 ft (para 10). It seems reasonable that the fore and aft length of that portion above water is considerably less than this and therefore the part of the measure due to Y is a small part and it may seem reasonable to believe that the height of the object above the water line is about 3 ft.

17. If animate, the surface shape of the object will NOT be angular. As expected the apex of the triangle has a rounded shape. The slope of the sides of the triangle suggests that there will be some increase in width below the water line and even if slight means the width of the object is at least 6 ft. Even if the object is relatively flat bellied, the normal body "rounding" in nature would suggest that there is at least 2 ft under the water from which it may be deduced that a cross section through the object would not be less than 6 ft wide and 5 ft high. This would certainly mean that when submerged the object was disturbing more water than the underwater surface of a small boat and would therefore give a more pronounced wake.

18. Further discussion of wake and wash patterns should be left for those more familiar with fluid dynamics.

19. Dinsdale suggested comparing the apex angle with that on the Stuart photograph. If, in the Stuart photograph, the three humps are part of the same beast then the view is most likely a side view. As explained in para 9 the Dinsdale photography is a stern or tail-end view and the two can NOT be compared any more than a front elevation and a side elevation in an architectural plan. Some assumptions as to the shape might be made from an end view and a side view but they would only be assumptions and the first assumption would need to be that both views were of the same object.

R & D/TER

TABLE 1: SIGHTINGS OF THE LOCH NESS ANIMALS ASHORE

(1) 1870's – group of children – northern shore near grave-yard.

(2) 1880 – E. H. Bright and cousin – shore near Drumna-drochit.

(3) 1890's – gypsy woman – near Dores.

(4) 1912 – William Macgruer and others – Inchnacardoch Bay.

(5) 1919 (September) – Mrs Cameron and brothers – Inch-nacardoch Bay.

(6) 1923 (April) – Alfred Cruickshank – road near Abriachan.

(7) 1933 (no date) – Mrs Eleanor Price-Hughes – scrub near Drumnadrochit.

(8) 1933 (July) – Mr and Mrs Spicer – Dores–Inverfarigaig road.

(9) 1933 (August) – Mrs MacLennan – near Foyers opposite Urquhart Bay.

(10) 1933 (December) – Mrs Reid – near Inverfarigaig.

(11) 1934 (January) – Arthur Grant – road near Abriachan Hill.

(12) 1934 (February) – Jean MacDonald and Patricia Harvey – Inchnacardoch Bay.

(13) 1934 (June) – Margaret Munro – shore of Borlum Bay.

(14) 1930's – Alec Muir – road near Dores.

(15) 1930's – schoolchildren from Drumnadrochit – bushy swamp in Urquhart Bay.

(16) 1960 (February) – Torquil MacLeod – beach opposite Invermoriston.

(17) 1963 (June) – Loch Ness Investigation – beach near Foyers (filmed).

TABLE 2: PHOTOGRAPHS AND FILMS OF THE LOCH NESS ANIMALS
(*Photographs dubious in provenance or content are queried*)

(1)   1933 (November) – Hugh Gray – one 120 B/W.
(2)   1933 (December) – Malcolm Irvine – 16 mm B/W film (lost – only stills survive).
(3)   1934 (April) – Kenneth Wilson – two ¾-plate photographs.
(4)   1934 (June) – ? – see *Scottish Daily Express* June 11, 1934.
(5)   1934 (August) – F. C. Adams – see *Daily Mail* August 25, 1934.
(6)   1934 (July–August) – *Mountain Expedition* – five B/W photographs.
(7)   1934 (September) – James Frazer *Mountain Expedition* – 16 mm B/W film (lost – one still survives).
(8)   1936 (September) – Malcolm Irvine – 16 mm B/W film (lost – stills survive).
(9)   1938 (May) – G. E. Taylor – 16 mm Colour film.
(10?) 1930's – Dr MacRae – 16 mm B/W film (unpublished – whereabouts unknown).
(11) 1951 (July) – Lachlan Stuart – one 120 B/W photograph.
(12) 1955 (July) – P. A. MacNab – Exacta 127 with 6 inch lens at f8 1/100 sec.
(13) 1955 (August) – H. L. Cockerell – one 35 mm B/W photograph.
(14) 1960 (April) – Tim Dinsdale – 16 mm B/W film.
(15?) 1960 (May) – Peter O'Connor – one 120 B/W with Brownie Flash 20.
(16) 1960 (June) – Maurice and Robert Burton – two 35 mm B/W photographs.
(17) 1960 (August) – R. H. Lowerie – one 120 B/W photograph.
(18) 1962 (October) – John Luff *Loch Ness Investigation* – 35 mm B/W film.

(19)   1963 (June) – *Loch Ness Investigation* – 35 mm B/W film.

(20)   1963 (June) – *Loch Ness Investigation* – 35 mm B/W film (object ashore).

(21)   1964 (May) – Peter Hodge – two 35 mm B/W photographs.

(22)   1964 (May) – Pauline Hodge – 8 mm Colour film.

(23)   1966 (August) – *Loch Ness Investigation* – 35 mm B/W film (two objects).

(24?) 1969 (August) – Jessie Tait – one 35 mm Colour photograph.

(25)   1972 (July) – Frank Searle – one 35 mm B/W photograph.

(26)   1972 (8 August) – Robert Rines and Harold Edgerton – one 16 mm B/W photograph – "single rear flipper".

(27?) 1972 (October) – Frank Searle – six 35 mm photographs.

TABLE 3: CAPTURES AND STRANDINGS

(1) 1522 – Lake Mjosa, Norway – remains sold to German merchants.
(2) ? – Gresskardfossen, Rogoland, Norway – ?
(3) ? – Klype, Lake Rein, Rogoland – remains buried under still-standing cairn.
(4) 1674 (before) – Lough Mask, Ireland – remains found in underwater cave after drought.
(5) 1776 (before) – Lewis, Hebrides – like a large conger eel, carried into Stornoway.
(6) 1861 (before) – Lagarflot lake, Iceland – large carcase examined by Dr Hjaltalin.
(7) 1876 (July) – Fish Haven, Bear Lake, Utah – small animal captured alive, fate unknown.
(8) 1899 (before) – Corpach Lock, Fort William, Inverness – eel-like animal with mane.
(9) 1914 – Lake Okanagan, British Columbia – seal-like mammal.

Bibliography

Adamnan: *The Life of Saint Columba*. Translated by William Reeves. Dublin, 1856.

"Sjøormen og innsjøormen" *Aftenpost* (Oslo), December 22, 1933.

Ananikian, Mardiros: *Armenian Mythology – The Mythology of All Races*. Boston and London, 1922.

Andrews, Roy Chapman: *This Earth of Ours*. New York, 1939.

Argus: "The Loch Ness Monster" *Northern Chronicle* (Inverness), June 7, 1933.

Baker, Peter and Westwood, Mark: "Sounding out the Monster" *Observer* (London), August 26, 1962.

Baker, Peter; Westwood, Mark and others: "The Loch Ness Monster" *New Scientist* (London), November 24, 1960 and January 5, 1961.

Baring-Gould, Sabine: *Iceland – Its Scenes and Sagas*. London, 1868.

Beckles, Gordan: "The Truth about the Monster" *Daily Express* (London), December 22, 1933.

Beliaff, Juan: "Folklore of the Indians of the Gran Chaco" *Bulletin of the Bureau of American Ethnology* (Washington), 143, 1, p. 379.

Bentinck, Count Graaf: "Het Dier van Loch Ness" *Levende Natuur* (Amsterdam), August 10, 1934.

Blakeslee, Sandra: "Hunt for the Loch Ness Monster Takes Determined Turn" *New York Times*, January 27, 1969.

Boswell, James: *A Tour of the Highlands with Dr Samuel Johnson*. London, 1785.

Botkin, B. A.: *A Treasury of Western Folklore*. New York, 1959.

Boulenger, E. G.: "The Loch Ness Monster" *Observer* (London), October 29, 1933.

———: "Aquatic Monsters – Do They Exist?" *Listener* (London), March 10, 1937.

Boyer, Charles: "British Columbia – Life Begins at 100" *National Geographic Magazine* (Washington D.C.), August, 1958.

Braithwaite, Hugh: "Sonar picks up stirrings in Loch Ness" *New Scientist* (London), December 19, 1968.

Brier, Warren J.: "Montana Has a Loch Ness Monster All Its Own" *New York Times*, June 13, 1965.

Brink, F. H. van den: *A Field Guide to the Mammals of Britain and Europe*. London and Boston, 1962.

Brown, Charles Edward: *Sea Serpents – Wisconsin Occurrences of these Weird Watery Monsters*. Madison: Wisconsin Folklore Society, 1942.

Burr, Malcolm: "Sea Serpents and Monsters" *Nineteenth Century* (London), February 1934.

Burton, Maurice: in "The Monster May Be a Walrus" *Daily Express* (London), December 29, 1933.

———: "The Mystery of Loch Ness" *Illustrated London News*, December 8, 1951.

———: *Animal Legends*. New York, 1957.

———: "The Loch Ness Monster" *Illustrated London News*, February 20, 1960.

———: "The Problem of Loch Ness: a Scientific Investigation" *Illustrated London News*, July 11, 1960; July 23, 1960; July 30, 1960.

———: "Loch Ness Monster; a Reappraisal" *New Scientist* (London), September 22, 1960.

———: *The Elusive Monster*. London, 1961.

———: "Is This the Loch Ness Monster?" *Animals* (London), July 30, 1962.

———: "Verdict on Nessie" *New Scientist* (London), January 23, 1969.

———: Private communications.

Calman, W. T.: "The Loch Ness Monster" *Times* (London), December 11, 1933.

Cameron, Simon: (Report of Loch Oich monster) *Glasgow Herald*, September 26, 1936.

(Campbell, Alex): "A Monster? Remarkable Sight on Loch Ness" *Northern Chronicle* (Inverness), May 3, 1933.

Campbell, Elizabeth Montgomery: *The Search for Morag*. London, 1972.

Campbell, John Francis: *Popular Tales of the West Highlands.* Edinburgh, 1860–1862.

Campbell, John Lorne and Hall, Trevor: *Strange Things.* London, 1968.

Carrington, Richard: *A Guide to Earth History.* London, 1956.

————: *Mermaids and Mastodons.* London, 1957.

Carruth, J. A.: *Loch Ness and Its Monster.* Fort Augustus, 1963.

Cathcart, Colin: "Baby Monsters in Loch Ness" *Sunday Express* (London), June 27, 1937.

Cleasby, Richard: "Skrimsl" in *An Icelandic-English Dictionary.* Oxford, 1957.

Cohen, Daniel: "Looking for the Monster" *Science Digest* (New York), January 1967.

Colgan, Nathaniel: "Field Notes on the Folklore of Irish Plants and Animals" *Irish Naturalist* (Dublin), March 1914.

Condor, Hartwell: (Macquarie animal 1913) in Fort, Charles: *The Books of Charles Fort.* New York, 1941.

Conyngham, Kathleen: (Letter on Lake Chunzi monster) *Times* (London), December 21, 1933.

Crofton-Crocker, Thomas: *Researches in the South of Ireland.* London, 1843.

Curtis, Wardron Allan: "The Monster of Lake Le Metrie" *Pearson's Magazine* (New York), September 1899.

"Where the Monster Passed By – Or Didn't" *Daily Mirror* (London), December 30, 1933.

"Doomwatch – Even the Loch Ness Monster Is Threatened Claims Lecturer" *Daily Mirror* (London), July 27, 1970.

"Monster of the Deep (Macquarie animal)" *Daily Telegraph* (London), August 19, 1913.

"Prehistoric Monsters – Possible Survivors" *Daily Telegraph* (London), March 9, 1922.

"Is This the Famed Monster" *Daily Telegraph* (London), December 6, 1933.

"Police Seize $\frac{1}{2}$ Ton Creature 'Found at Loch Ness'" *Daily Telegraph* (London), April 1, 1972.

Davies, G. H.: "Our Special Artist Investigates the Loch Ness Monster" *Illustrated London News*, January 13, 1934.

Davis, Anthony: "Operation Nessie . . . The Hunt to Find that Elusive Monster" *TV Times* (London), July 31, 1969.

Davy, John and Brasher, Christopher: "Science out to solve the riddle of the Loch Ness Monster" *Observer* (London), June 3, 1962.

Dickinson, Barney: in "The Loch Ness Monster" *Illustrated London News*, February 20, 1960.

Dieckhoff, Cyril: diaries quoted in Whyte, 1957.

Dinsdale, Tim: *Loch Ness Monster*. London, 1961, 1972.

————: *The Leviathans*. London, 1966.

————: *Monster Hunt*. Washington D.C., 1972.

Doig, Desmond: "Bhutan" *National Geographic Magazine* (Washington D.C.), September 1961.

Donaldson, Mary: *Wanderings in the Western Highlands and Islands*. London, 1920.

Doyle, Arthur Conan: *The Lost World*. London, 1912.

Erskine-Murray, Alistair: (Letter on Loch Ness tracks) *Scotsman* (Edinburgh), January 23, 1933.

"Camera Shot of Lake Monster?" *Evening Herald* (Dublin), June 4, 1968.

"Archill Island Monster" *Evening Herald* (Dublin), June 6, 1968.

"Monster Hunted in Lake Manitoba" *Evening Standard* (London), September 9, 1957.

"100 Ft Nessie is larger than life" *Evening Standard* (London), September 2, 1971.

Ewing, R. Lechie: "Rod and Line in Canada" in *Canada*. London, 1934.

Fawcett, P. H.: *Exploration Fawcett*. London, 1953.

Fife, Austin E.: "The Bear Lake Monsters" *Utah Humanities Review* (Salt Lake City), June 1948.

Fonahn, A.: "'Sjøormen' i Farrisvannet" *Tidens Tegn* (Oslo), December 20, 1933.

Fuller, F. B.: "Is there Life in the Ocean Depths" *Evening Dispatch* (Glasgow), November 23, 1933.

Furer-Haimendorf, Christopher von: *The Api-Thanis and Their Neighbours*. London, 1962.

Gellatly, Dorothy W.: *A Bit of Okanagan History*. Kelowna, 1958.

Giedion, Sigfried: *The Eternal Present – The Beginnings of Art*. New York, 1962.

"Loch Morar Claims 'Monster' Too" *Glasgow Herald*, July 31, 1948.

"Anglers See Monster in Lewis Loch" *Glasgow Herald*, July 29, 1961.

"Local Man Lays Claim to Having Caught Sight of Gigantic Plesiosaur" *Globe* (Toronto), April 6, 1922.

Golder, F. A.: "Eskimo and Aleut Stories from Alaska" *Journal of American Folklore* (Boston), vol. 22, 1909.

Gosse, P. H.: *The Romance of Natural History*. London, 1860.

Gould, Rupert T.: *The Case for the Sea Serpent*. London, 1930.

————: "The Loch Ness Monster – A Survey of the Evidence" *Times* (London), December 9, 1933.

————: *The Loch Ness Monster*. London, 1934.

————: "Aquatic Monsters – Do They Exist?: A Reply" *Listener* (London), April 7, 1937.

————: *The Stargazer Talks*. London, 1943.

Grant, Arthur: (Report of the Loch Ness Monster ashore) *Aberdeen Press and Journal*, January 6, 1934.

Graves, Robert and Hodge, Alan: *The Long Weekend*. London, 1940.

Graves, Robert and Patai, Raphael: *Hebrew Myths – The Book of Genesis*. New York, 1964.

Gregory, Augusta Lady: *Visions and Beliefs in the West of Ireland*. London, 1922.

Hamilton, J. S.: "The Loch Ness Monster" *The Field* (London), November 4, 1933.

Harris, J. C.: *Otters*. London, 1968.

Haslefoot, F. E. B.: (Letter on sighting the Loch Ness monster) *Times* (London), July 16, 1934.

Hasler, H. G.: "Jester in Search of the Joker" *Observer* (London), August 19, 1962.

Hassall, Ian: "More About the Monster" *Times* (London), December 14, 1933.

(Hay, A. F.): "Loch Ness Mystery – Edinburgh Expedition's Clues – The Walrus Theory" *Scotsman* (Edinburgh), January 22, 1934.

Herries, J. W.: "The Loch Ness Mystery" *Scotland's Magazine* (Edinburgh), 40, 4, pp. 92–4.

Heuvelmans, Bernard: *On the Track of Unknown Animals*. London, 1958, 1962.

————: *In the Wake of the Sea Serpents*. London, 1969.

————: Private communications.

Hinton, Martin: "Summing up the Loch Ness Monster" *The Field* (London), January 27, 1934.

Holiday, F. W.: *The Great Orm of Loch Ness*. London, 1969.

———: "Does the Paystha still exist?" *Ireland of the Welcomes* (Dublin), July–August 1970.

———: "The possible polarisation of monster phenomena" *Flying Saucer Review* (London), November–December 1971.

Hook, H. S.: *Middle Eastern Mythology*. Harmondsworth, 1963.

Howell, Alfred Brazier: *Aquatic Mammals – Their Adaption to Life in the Water*. Springfield and Baltimore, 1930.

Hunter-Blair, Sir David: "The Elusive Monster of Loch Ness" *Commonweal* (New York), April 20, 1934.

Ibanez, Blasco V.: *The Temptress* [*La Terra de Todos*]. London, 1923.

"The Loch Ness Monster" *Illustrated London News*, January 6, 1934.

"Return of the Monster" *Illustrated London News*, April 28, 1934.

"A Possible Clue to the Loch Ness 'Monster' Provided by a Film" *Illustrated London News*, May 5, 1934.

"Loch Ness Monster Has £1000 On Its Head" *Irish Times* (Dublin), March 2, 1967.

Izzard, Ralph: *The Search for the Buru*. London, 1952.

James, David: "'We find there is some unidentified animate object in Loch Ness . . .'" *Observer* (London), May 19, 1964.

Joint Air Reconnaissance Intelligence Centre: "Photographic Interpretation Report No. 66/1. Loch Ness" January 24, 1966. London: Ministry of Defence.

Joyce, P. W.: *Irish Names of Places*. Dublin, n.d.

Jung, C. G.: *Flying Saucers*. London, 1959.

———: *Man and His Symbols*. London, 1964.

Keel, John: *Strange Creatures from Times and Space*. Greenwich, Conn., 1970.

Keith, Sir Arthur: in "Sir Arthur Keith, the famous Anthropologist, Discusses: Is there a Loch Ness Monster?" *Daily Mail* (London), January 3, 1934.

King, Judith: *Seals of the World*. London, 1964.

Lambert, R. S.: *Exploring the Supernatural – The Weird in Canadian Folklore.* London, 1954.

Lane, Frank: *Nature Parade.* London, 1938.

Leach, Maria (Editor): *Funk and Wagnall's Standard Dictionary of Folklore, Mythology and Legend.* New York, 1950.

Le Fanu, W. R.: *Seventy Years of Irish Life.* London, 1893.

Leroi-Gourhan, Andre: *The Art of Prehistoric Man in Western Europe.* London, 1968.

Lethbridge, T. C.: *Ghost and Divining Rod.* London, 1963.

Ley, Willy: *The Lungfish, the Dodo and the Unicorn.* New York, 1948.

Leyden, John: *A Tour of the Highlands in 1800.* Edinburgh, 1903.

Liddel, Guy: "The Monster" *Times* (London), June 7, 1938.

"Monstrous Behaviour" *The Listener* (London), August 1, 1968.

Lyon, Ron: "Could This be the Loch Ness Monster" *Sunday Express* (London), September 7, 1969.

MacArthur, Ian: in "Anglers See Monster in Lewis Loch" *Glasgow Herald*, July 29, 1961.

MacDonald, Jean and Harvey, Patricia: in "The Loch Ness Monster Seen Again" *Glasgow Herald*, March 3, 1934.

MacGruer, William: in "Loch Ness Monster – Theory That It Is an Amphibian – Appearances on Land" *Inverness Courier*, October 10, 1933.

Mackenzie, Osgood: *A Hundred Years in the Highlands.* London, 1949.

Mackintosh, Alistair: *No Alibi.* London, 1961.

McLintock, A. H.: "Animals, Mythical" in *An Encyclopedia of New Zealand.* Wellington, 1966.

MacManus, D. A.: *The Middle Kingdom.* London, 1962.

Malmesbury, Lord: *Memoirs of an Ex-Minister.* London, 1882.

Matters, Leonard: "The Patagonian Plesiosaurus – An Antidiluvian Monster" *Scientific American* (New York), July 1922.

———: "Lake Monsters" *The Star* (London), December 12, 1933.

Maurer, Konrad: *Islandische Volksagen der Gegenwart.* Leipzig, 1860.

Maxwell, Gavin: *Harpoon at a Venture.* London, 1952.

———: *Seals of the World.* London, 1967.

———: "I saw the secret of the Loch" *TV Times* (London), July 31, 1969.

Maxwell, Herbert: (Letter on Loch Arkaig monster) *The Field* (London), February 3, 1934.

Maxwell, William Hamilton: *Wild Sports of the West*. London, 1843.

"The Monster – His Mark – Zoological Detectives Call the Bluff" *Morning Post* (London), January 5, 1934.

Mountain, Sir Edward: "Solving the Mystery of Loch Ness" *The Field* (London), September 22, 1934.

Mulchrone, Vincent: "He's the greatest monster hunter of them all" *Daily Mail* (London), September 24, 1969.

———: "Och Aye, Nessie's just a monster myth" *Daily Mail* (London). September 27, 1969.

"Sees Monster of the Reptile Age Swimming in Patagonian Lake" *New York Herald*, March 7, 1922.

"Not Worried About Mezozoic Monsters – Tales of Andean Monster Fails to Impress Scientists Here" *New York Herald*, March 8, 1922.

"Protests Capture of Andean Monster" *New York Herald*, March 13, 1922.

"Argentines Start to Catch Monster" *New York Herald*, March 24, 1922.

"Loch Ness Gremlins Plague Yellow Submarine" *New York Times*, July 13, 1969.

(Report of Lake Ontario monster) *Notizen Gebiete Natur und Heilk* (Erfurt und Weimar), August 1835.

"Loch Ness Monster – London Visitor's Strange Experience – Is It a Variant of the Plesiosaur" *Northern Chronicle* (Inverness), August 9, 1933.

"Loch Ness Monster – Similar Beasts in Lochs Locky and Quoich" *Northern Chronicle* (Inverness), October 11, 1933.

"Criticism of Daily Mail Findings – Creatures Identity Unsolved" *Nothern Chronicle* (Inverness), January 31, 1934.

"Monster in Lake Maggiore – Loch Ness Starts a Fashion" *Observer* (London), January 14, 1934.

O'Connor, Peter: "Clearest Picture to Date of 'Nessie'" *Weekly Scotsman* (Glasgow), June 16, 1960.

O'Flaherty, Roderick: *A Description of West or H-Iar Connaught*. Dublin, 1866.

Olsson, Peter: *Storsjöodjuret – framsstallning af fakta och utredning*. Ostersund, 1899.

O'Sullivan, Sean: *Handbook of Irish Folklore*. Dublin, 1942.

Oudemans, A. C.: *The Great Sea Serpent*. Leyden and London, 1934.

———: *The Loch Ness Animal*. Leyden, 1934.

———: "Het Loch Ness Monster" *De Levende Natuur* (Amsterdam), November 12, 1934.

Palmer, Wilfred: "The Loch Ness Monster" *The Universe* (London), February 10, 1934.

Patmore, Eric: "Now Nessie Has a Sister in Scotland's Deepest Loch" *Sunday Post* (Glasgow), May 31, 1964.

Peach, B. W.: in "Not the Only Monster – Hidden Terrors of Loch Treig" *Aberdeen Weekly Journal*, October 19, 1933.

Pontoppidan, Erik: *Natural History of Norway*. London, 1755.

"Is There A Sea Serpent" *Popular Mechanics* (New York), September 1934.

Powell, T. G. E.: *The Celts*. London, 1958.

Praeger, Robert Lloyd: *The Way That I Went*. Dublin, 1937.

———: *Irish Landscape*. Dublin, 1960.

"En Busca de la Ejamplar vivo de la Epoca Secundaria – El Plesiosaurio" *La Prensa* (Buenos Aires), March 13, 1922.

Price, Harry and Lambert, R. S.: *The Haunting of Cashen's Gap*. London, 1934.

Pritchett, Oliver: "Monsters, mints and mouth organs" *Guardian* (London), October 1, 1970.

Pycraft, W. P.: "Loch Ness in Possession of a 'Sea-Serpent'" *Illustrated London News*, November 11, 1933.

Reid, Mrs: in "Loch Ness Monster – Seen Again on Dores–Foyers Road – Inverfarigaig Lady's Experience" *Inverness Courier*, December 20, 1933.

Rees, Alwyn and Brindley: *Celtic Heritage*. London, 1960.

Rice, Harry: *Thanks for the Memory*. Athlone, 1952.

Richards, A. J.: (Report of Loch Oich Monster) *Glasgow Herald*, August 14, 1936.

Ritchie, James: "The Loch Ness 'Monster'" *Nature* (London), December 16, 1933.

———: "The Loch Ness 'Mystery'" *Nature* (London), January 13, 1934.

————: "The Loch Ness 'Monster'" *Nature* (London), August 18, 1934.

"Dynamite and Starshells – Black Times Ahead for the Plesiosaurus" *River Plate Observer* (Buenos Aires), March 31, 1922.

"Traveller's Tales – Cordoba Scientist on the Plesiosaurus" *River Plate Observer* (Buenos Aires), April 7, 1922.

"The Plesiosaurus Ban" *River Plate Observer* (Buenos Aires), April 14, 1922.

"Roosevelt and Plesiosaurus – Ex-President Thought of Huntint It" *River Plate Observer*, May 12, 1922.

"The Plesiosaurus – Evidence from Canada" *River Plate Observer*, May 12, 1922.

"Was It a Hoax – End of Plesiosaurus Hunt" *River Plate Observer* (Buenos Aires), May 12, 1922.

Roberts, Frank D.: *History of the Town of Perry, New York*. Perry, 1915.

Robinson, Anne: "'I dumped Nessie in the Loch'" *Sunday Times* (London), April 2, 1972.

Robinson, Phil: "Saunterings in Utah" *Harper's New Monthly Magazine* (New York), October 1883.

Ross, Anne: *Pagan Celtic Britain*. London, 1966.

Rukosuyer, G.: "The Mystery of Lake Khaiyer" *Soviet Life* (Washington D.C.), June 1965; reprinted from *Komsomolskaya Pravda* (Moscow), November 21, 1964.

Rose, D. Murray: (letter on early sightings of Loch Ness animals) *Scotsman* (Edinburgh), October 20, 1933.

Sanderson, Ivan T.: "Don't Scoff at Sea-Monsters" *Saturday Evening Post* (Philadelphia), March 8, 1947.

————: *Follow the Whale*, London, 1956.

————: *Things*. New York, 1967.

Scheffer, Victor B.: *Seals, Sea Lions and Walruses: a Review of the Pinnepedia*. Stanford and London, 1958.

"Loch Ness Mystery – Edinburgh Expedition's Clues – The Walrus Theory" *Scotsman* (Edinburgh), January 22, 1934.

Scott, David: "New Evidence Spurs Hunt for Loch Ness Monster" *Popular Science* (New York), November 1966.

Scott, Peter: "The Loch Ness Monster – Fact or Fancy?" *Sunday Times* (London), August 14, 1960.

Serra I Pages, Rossend: "Zoologica fantastica – El serpenti mari" *Bulletti de la Societat de Ciencios Naturals de Barcelona*, vol. 2, 1923.

Sharpe, Richard: "Submarine Monster Hunt" *Observer* (London), July 1, 1969.

Simpson, Jacqueline: *Icelandic Folktales and Legends*. London, 1972.

Skjelsvik, Elizabeth: "Norwegian Lake and Sea Monsters" *Norveg folkelivsgransking*, vol. 7, Oslo, 1960.

Slorach, David: "How I met the Loch Ness Monster" *Harper's Magazine* (New York), February 1956.

Smalley, Donald: "The Logansport *Telegraph* and the Monster of the Indiana Lakes" *Indiana Magazine of History* (Bloomington), September 1946.

Smith, Charles: *Ancient and Present State of the County of Kerry*. Dublin, 1756.

Smith, J. B. L.: *Old Fourlegs – The Story of the Coelacanth*. London, 1956.

Smyth, R. B.: *The Aborigines of Victoria*. Melborne, 1878.

Somerville, Edith and Ross, Martin: *The Smile and the Tear*. London, 1933.

Stalker, Philip: "Loch Ness Monster – A Puzzled Highland Community – Evidence and Theories" *Scotsman* (Edinburgh), October 6, 1933.

————: "Loch Ness Monster – The Plesiosaurus Theory – Old Stories Recalled" *Scotsman* (Edinburgh), October 17, 1933.

————: "Loch Ness Mystery – Lump of Peat Theory – Evidence Against It" *Scotsman* (Edinburgh), October 18, 1933.

"The Tylondosaurus Hunt" *The Standard* (Buenos Aires), March 14, 1922.

Stevenson, Jim: "They Call Him the Loch Ness Nut" *The Sunday People* (London), February 20, 1972.

Svedjeland, Knutt: *Storsoodjuret*. Ostersund, 1959.

Synge, J. M.: *The Aran Islands and Other Writings*. New York, 1962.

Thesiger, Wilfred: *The Marsh Arabs*. New York, 1964.

"Kong Le and the Dragon" *Time Magazine* (New York), October 21, 1966.

"The Sea Serpent in the Highlands" *Times* (London), March 6, 1856.

"Plesiosaurus Lying Low" *Times* (London), April 20, 1922.

"The Loch Ness Monster – Evidence of the Film" *Times* (London), January 4, 1934.

"Another Loch Ness Film – Record of Commotion" *Times* (London), September 28, 1934.

"Loch Ness 'Monster' – Plan for Scientific Inquiry" *Times* (*London*), June 14, 1938.

Tucker, Denys: "The Loch Ness Monster" *New Scientist* (London), October 27, 1960; November 17, 1960.

Vandano, Brunello: "The Coldest Place on Earth" *Life Magazine* (New York), January 22, 1963.

Vibe, Palle: *Gaden 1 Loch Ness*. Copenhagen, 1970.

Turner, Ron: "The Achill Lough Monster" *Evening Herald* (Dublin), June 5, 1968.

Wavell, Stewart: "I Sought a Monster" *Wide World Magazine* (London), February 1958.

————: *The Lost World of the Orient*. London, 1958.

Wheeler, R. E. M.: *Report of the Excavations of the Prehistoric and Post-Roman Site at Lydney Park Gloucestershire*. London and Oxford, 1932.

Williams, Graham: "The Ghost Ship of St Columba Sails Loch Ness" *Irish Independent* (Dublin), May 23, 1963.

Williams, Pat and Hill, Douglas: *The Supernatural*. London, 1966.

Whyte, Constance: *The Loch Ness Monster*. Inverness, 1951.

————: *More Than a Legend*. London, 1957.

————: Private communications.

W.P.: (Letter on Lewis monster) *Inverness Courier*, March 12, 1856.

Yeats, W. B.: *The Celtic Twilight*. London, 1895.

Index